A Vivid Canvas

A Vivid Canvas

by
Margaret Collyer

compiled by
Susan Duke
and
Veronica Bellers

Librario

Published by

Librario Publishing Ltd.

ISBN 10: 1-90675-07-0
ISBN 13: 978-1-906775-07-0

Copies can be ordered via the Internet
www.librario.com

or from:

Brough House, Milton Brodie, Kinloss
Moray IV36 2UA
Tel/Fax No 00 44 (0)1343 850 617

Printed and bound in the UK

Typeset by 3btype.com

This book is dedicated to Margaret Collyer's niece, our mother, the late Mrs Joy Williams, whose providence has made publishing it possible; and to all those whose encouragement and unstinting assistance has been the wind in our sails.

Contents

List of Illustrations

Book Two

We (Margaret Collyer's heirs) have done our level best to seek permission where applicable to reproduce the pictures in this book but have failed to trace some owners of Margaret Collyer's work. Where there is evidence of copyright about which we have been unaware, we would be pleased to know about it.

Introduction

*"We need to look on our forefathers with gentleness
so we ourselves are not judged harshly"*.

Mark Tully in "Something Understood" on the BBC

This book is an autobiography but it has more than one voice. Margaret Collyer wrote her story during the early part of the 20th Century and it was published without illustrations in 1935. Now, we, her great nieces, have revised it and included as many of her paintings that we can trace – which was something she was unable to do on her farm in the Kenya Highlands in 1935.

Miss Collyer was both ordinary and extraordinary. She was a young girl at the end of Queen Victoria's reign, and she painted for a living as the clouds of war rolled towards Britain and the Empire in 1914. She mixed with many of the luminaries of the time and then in 1915 the contrast was, she felt, almost comical when she found herself a pioneer farmer in Africa.

She was a gifted painter but she had human frailties. She was outspoken but she also had resolute courage. She revelled in the excitement of testing herself hunting while also having great compassion for animals. Her contradictions may not have made her happy but to those of us who live in a vastly different era, her life was as historically fascinating as it was colourful.

Susan Duke and Veronica Bellers

September 2008

MARGARET COLLYER – A SELF PORTRAIT 1929

AIREDALES
With thanks to Mark Jenkins

Book One

A Vivid Canvas

Born A Painter

Chapter I

Up to the time when I left my home at the age of eighteen I had always lived in the country surrounded by every kind of domestic animal I could collect. Dogs and horses had been my chief companions, as well as cows and pigs, to say nothing of rabbits, guinea-pigs, white rats, bantams, and several ferrets. I usually smelt strongly of these pets and was constantly being sent out of the room to change my clothes.

All the really happy days of my life are entirely connected with animals. As soon as I could toddle I owned a dog and a pony, and these two treasures are what I can actually first remember. People seem to have left little impression on me, with the exception of old Mr Shepherd, Lord Leconfield's huntsman, who on Sunday afternoons would rescue me from the nursemaids and take me down to the Petworth Park Kennels to see the hounds fed and give the hunt horses their evening treat of sugar and carrots. As Mr Shepherd always carried me on his shoulder I could not have been more than three. I can well remember resenting him holding my hand flat in his as I endeavoured to push lumps of sugar between the horses' teeth with my small fingers.

My first fox-hunting was undertaken in a basket-saddle, the pony was led by a young groom, a really wonderful runner. I was duly blooded at this early age and presented with the brush by Lord Leconfield, when hounds ran into their fox at the foot of the park. The brush had a lovely white tag and I returned home in bloody triumph to show my trophy to my father, and yelled with fury when the nurses insisted on removing the gore from my face.

Loving animals as I did, it is not much wonder that I eventually became an animal painter; they were ever my friends and I knew no fear of them. My pony was anything but the ideal child's pony, a beautiful black-brown baby Exmoor, a vicious spoilt little brute who used his teeth as well as his heels, quite untrustworthy both in and out of the stable; but he never hurt me and as I grew bigger I taught him several tricks.

My dog, a cross-bred bull terrier, was older than I was and there was a limit to the liberties he permitted to be taken with him. He did not like to be hugged tight round his neck and have hard kisses imprinted on his face; he would suffer it once, but after that he would utter a low 'purr' of warning deep down in his throat, but that is as far as it ever went, for I belonged

A DRAWING
BY MARGARET
COLLYER FROM
HER BOOK:
*Incidents with The
Warnham Staghounds.*

to him and it was up to him to take care of me. 'Tommy' and 'Box' spent their whole lives with me until they died of old age. They taught me a lot of animal lore and gave me my first lessons in animal psychology, which has since become a great interest in my life.

The wish to make pictures of animals came at a very youthful age. Instead of doing the addition sums set by the governess on my slate, I spent my time drawing portraits of Tommy and Box all over it, wiping the figures as they interfered with my pictures. In consequence I was forever in trouble and never learnt to add two and two. A pencil and paper meant pictures. Everything I read or was told of became a scene and the best method of description was to draw it. Possessing this particularly strong wish to portray my thoughts, I have often wondered why I never became more than a mediocre artist. I put the fault down to an uncontrollable versatility of mind, for I was never lacking in concentration.

Up to the age of eighteen I received no serious tuition in art. I had for a while attended an Animal Painter's Studio in Gower Street[1] once or twice a week, where I learnt nothing. My parents were not artistic and held the old fashioned idea that if you worked at anything for a living you became a tradesman, and this, of course, was outrageous, very nearly a crime. At the studio I attended, we messed about with paint and live models. These were mostly old cab horses enjoying a day off the streets, who were brought in from a mews at the back of the studio. We plied these tired thin animals with food and dainties in the most unwholesome quantities. Very little work was done, for the teaching was bad and we were provided with no knowledge of how to work.

Later it was decided to send me to Düsseldorf[2] to study art; more waste of time as it proved, for I began at the wrong end. In this dear little

---

[1] We estimate that Margaret Collyer may have gone to Gower Street in 1890 when she was eighteen.

[2] The move to Dusseldorf would have been when Margaret was nineteen in 1891.

town I was put to live in the house of a Music Professor and his wife – German of Germans, who spoke no word of English and I knew not a single word of German. They were dirty and so were the apartments they lived in; a more cheerless and uncomfortable place I could not have imagined. I was wretchedly miserable and half starved, for I could not eat the greasy German food, and the table manners of the Herr Professor and his large Frau positively made me sick. Every dreary afternoon I was taken for a walk and we never got further than the nearest beer-garden; here we sat while the Professor quaffed beer by the bucketful. Later he discovered that I had rather a pretty voice and wished to teach me to sing, but the lessons were not a success. His method of teaching was to bellow at his pupils and of course I, not understanding a word he shouted, infuriated him. He always wore a filthy coat, down which he had spilt lots of food, which so disgusted me I very soon gave up the singing lessons, as well as my lodgings, and found for myself an extremely nice *pension* kept by a couple of German ladies who spoke English fluently.

It was a splendid move, for the house was most comfortable and almost next door to Herr Rochell, who was a painter of animals and battle pictures. He called himself 'Battle painter to the Kaiser'. What exactly it meant, or how true it was, I never discovered, but the title gave him such immense pleasure that I would not have disputed his right to it for the world.

Herr Rochell was a virile and clever little man and in every way violent. Even his method of painting could only be described as violent; I can think of no other word to describe him. He used a palette the size of a small door, on which he bashed out whole tubes of paint in one squeeze; his brushes resembled those used by a house painter and if he had no work on hand in his studio, he would attack one of the walls of his dining-room and, without any pre-arranged idea of what he was going to do, would plunge into a terrific blood-and-thunder battle scene. In less than a week his mute little Haus Frau would have to breakfast opposite a panorama of bloody carnage: life-sized realistic horses rolling in their death agony practically on the floor at her feet; men falling in grotesque attitudes with gaping wounds in either stomach or head; flashes of fire from rifle and cannon, dense smoke and every conceivable nightmare vividly depicted.

This astonishing work used to leave me gasping; it was done with incredible rapidity with a certainty and knowledge of drawing that was positively amazing. Whether these enormous scenic effects were good or not, I then had not sufficient knowledge to say, but they must have been very full of realism and movement, for they left an indelible mark on my memory.

Herr Rochell took me as a pupil but he was too impatient to make a good master and I was set to run long before I could walk. He dumped me down in the vast tram horse stable to paint from life at once. These stables were immense and most beautifully kept; all the horses of an excellent type and in beautiful condition. They were fed the best food, never overworked and most carefully watched for any ailment or lameness. The shoeing of them interested me very much. All the shoes were cast with a hollow groove into which was hammered a piece of thick rope; this entirely prevented them slipping on the stone cobbles when pulling the tram into motion. A clever idea that I wonder we did not imitate. The cast shoes lasted a long time, as the rope got all the wear and could easily be changed.

The Herr Stall Meister was a certificated veterinary surgeon and a most knowledgeable man where horses were concerned. Herr Rochell put me in his charge and he let me paint what horses I chose. The second morning I was in the stable I remember making a little slip in my German and asking the Stall Meister for a 'little kiss' instead of the 'little cushion' that I needed. The amusement of the grooms can be imagined.

What German I learnt I got from the stablemen, *platt Deutsch*, which

I believe was not pretty, and many expressions which I used to air at polite German tea parties positively raised the hair on the heads of my old *pension* ladies.

Herr Rochell and I soon became friends. We both loved horses and sometimes he would bring a horse to ride. This horse exercise suited his explosive soul. We began by hammering the animals over the paved streets at a butcher's trot. When we reached the *Exerciert Platz* we started to gallop; we never ceased to gallop and, to liven things up still more, Herr Rochell would let out an occasional yell as though he had just viewed a fox or was riding in a charge of cavalry. The poor horses were taken home dripping with sweat and blowing as though their hearts would break. Although Herr Rochell was by way of being fond of animals, he showed no regard for them at all. I met him one morning running after a horse ambulance in which was an animal that had fallen in the street and broken its leg. He had a sketch-book in his hand and he called to me to join him, which I did not feel inclined to do. Afterwards, he told me the injured horse was going to be shot and he wanted to see it fall and make a lot of sketches of it for his 'battle pictures'. This cold-blooded callousness for the suffering of animals was foreign to me, but I soon learnt that almost every German was the same where animals were concerned. A young man, Count Schönberg, who was quite a friend of mine, deliberately stamped on his dog's hind feet because it jumped up to greet him. I hated him for it and told him so, and that ended our short friendship.

Another form of exercise Herr Rochell enjoyed was walking; not just simple walking, but a heel and toe marathon. He would sometimes call for me on a Sunday morning and we would pelt off to the nearest railway station and take tickets for some country place. On arrival, out of the train he would drag me and start to walk as though he were an hour late for an appointment. About midday we would get to a beer-garden, drink lots of beer, swallow some lunch then dance to the band.

After this, foot it more miles to another station and train back to Düsseldorf in the evening. Why these expeditions in my company pleased him so much I am at a loss to imagine; he knew no English and I no German. We both carried dictionaries and when there was any breathing time we looked up a few words; but we never used the words we wanted because we invariably picked the wrong one out of the list. Sometimes when our choice of words had been rather more inappropriate than usual, we would both go into shouts of laughter. Our friendship, however, was usually a silent one.

Besides the tram stables, I sometimes worked in the Zoological Gardens, which at first were peaceful enough and a pleasant change from the noise and bustle of clattering horses and chattering grooms. However a gang of male students got to know that I was working there alone and every day the place was invaded by this objectionable crowd. They became such a nuisance that I eventually went to the British Consul who managed to stop them and I was left unmolested from then on. Not only had these students bothered me when I was painting, but they had taken to following me in the streets and making life a burden when I went to hear music at the *Ton-halle*.

I attended these beautiful orchestral concerts twice a week and loved them. I would take some knitting and sit at my own table in a corner of the big hall revelling in delicious music for a couple of hours. I was also able to hear many of the Wagner Operas, for a ticket in the stalls of the Opera House only cost about three marks, whereas tickets for Opera in London were prohibitive for all but the very rich.

The year I was in Düsseldorf, the Rhein Festival was held there and I enjoyed a feast of music during that week. The conductor was Herr Richter whom I met with a mutual English friend. It amused me to see this great musician conducting that enormous choir of voices, arrayed in an old straw hat and a smoking-coat that had seen better days. His face was one big beam of complete happiness, delighting in the music

FAMILY GROUP AT VILLA MONTCHELLO, MAY 1876

Margaret is the little girl on the right.

With thanks to John Doble

produced by his own countrymen, wearing what was comfortable and behaving as he liked – no London clothes and etiquette here; a Bohemian amongst Bohemians giving his best to an appreciative and knowledgeable audience who enjoyed the production of that wealth of melody as much as he enjoyed producing it.

Shortly after the Festival, much to my regret, I was summoned home and I had to obey the call. All my friends came to the Station to see me off and I left Düsseldorf snowed under in my carriage with wreaths and bouquets of lovely flowers.

MARGARET COLLYER'S GRANDMOTHER, ROSA CLARKE.
We believe this to be one of Miss Collyer's earliest paintings.

Lonely and Uncertain Youth

Chapter II

Home life was no longer possible for me. I bore it just as long as I could, until one evening my father and I agreed to part. No second bidding was required and, late though it was, I took a horse and rode to Godalming,[1] where my grandmother and an aunt lived in a little house just on the outskirts of the town – here, anyhow, I was sure of a welcome.

WILLIAM JAMES COLLYER

MARGARET COLLYER'S FATHER

But Grannie had no stable, so I first had to find comfortable accommodation for my horse. It was midnight by the time I reached my destination and having no clothes with me but what I stood up in, I could not go to an inn, but I bethought me of a friend I had known since babyhood and went and threw gravel at his bedroom window. When he heard my voice asking for help he came down in some alarm, wondering what could have happened to send me wandering by night over the countryside. However he had enough tact to ask no questions until he had fed me and my

---

[1] This may have been late 1891 or 1892.

horse in the nice warm stable, when I became less tired and rather less miserable. We then walked to my grandmother's house, and managed to rouse my aunt without disturbing Grannie, who was old and not over-strong. For a few weeks I stayed with these relations, a haven of rest, while I tried to collect my scattered senses sufficiently to consider what my next move should be.

The chief obstacle that confronted me was lack of funds. I had no intention of appealing to my father for money, and my own worldly wealth consisted of £50 which did not look like carrying me very far. How to make progress in any profession without sufficient money puzzled me considerably; yet I could not allow my Grannie to keep me longer than was absolutely necessary. Undoubtedly London was the place to get to, but London I did not know. I had hardly ever been there and had no friends in Town with the exception of Mr and Mrs Alexander Cooper, in whose Animal Studio I had done a little work. These good people lived in Gower Street. One end of London was very like the other to me in those days; anyhow, I knew how to get to Gower Street, so to Gower Street I went.

Mr and Mrs Cooper were old and very poor. Though he had painted some nice animal pictures and in his younger days had had his work well hung in the Royal Academy, ill health had prevented him ever getting his head very far above water, and I fancy all they had to exist on was the small amount of money he earned by teaching. Oh! What a dirty, dreary house it was, far too large for the old couple and their maid-of-all-work to manage.

The old man's one remaining joy was music; he played the violin and was a member of an amateur musical society called The Wandering Minstrels. His sight was failing and painting was out of the question, but he could still practise his instrument and this he did for several hours every day.

I lodged with these people for a short time and was given most excellent advice. I had brought with me two very ambitious studies for Mr. Cooper to look at; one was '*Lincoln Horse Fair*' and the other I called '*Deserters*', two cavalry horses broken loose and galloping out of the picture.

My old master was careful and very truthful in his criticism of this work. He considered I had ability, but lacked knowledge and, that if art was to be my profession, I must put in the usual five years of study at a good school.

Incidentally, some years later '*The Deserters*' was bought by Lord Breadalbane, and the '*Lincoln Horse Fair*' by a dealer in Bond Street at a sale at Christies.

Five years' tuition, only £50 to do it on, and no one to help me! After several sleepless nights I gave it up, got an introduction to a big horse-dealer in the Midlands and went and offered to ride for him for any salary he chose to give me. The few days I was there I was well tried out on all sorts of animals in the schooling field and taken on provisionally.

GRANNIE IN
GODALMING

This dealer and his wife were exceptionally nice people, but they wanted to know more about me than I wanted to tell them. They insisted that if I took on the job I should live with them, but they had an idea that I would dislike the work. Before I returned to London to get some smart riding kit, the man told me that if by chance I found any way of studying art, I was to wire him and he would tear up the contract. Two days later I was walking down Bond Street on my way to Scott's, who was then considered the best habit maker in London, when I literally ran into a man whom I had always vaguely known as Uncle George. He was no relation of mine really, he had married a cousin of my father's, was a doctor, and had a very large practice as a consulting

MARGARET COLLYER'S
MOTHER, EVELEEN
(NEE CLARKE).
With thanks to John Doble

physician in Hertford Street, Mayfair where he and his ultra-fashionable wife kept open house and did a vast amount of entertaining. I was taken back to lunch and my poor little story was told, after which the horse-dealer was written to, my few possessions fetched from Gower Street and I settled down for a week or two with this so called Uncle and Aunt, who were kindness personified, and I began to recover from the dreary feeling of loneliness and destitution.

I was a very unsophisticated youngster with no love for smart clothes, long dinner parties, stuffy rooms and crowds of people. My short life had been spent in the fresh air and masses of people have always caused me to panic. To have to go to a ball was next door to torture and I do not think I have faced more than half a dozen dances in the whole of my life.

I felt sadly conscious that I was not cut out to become the adopted daughter of this Mayfair couple. To me the atmosphere was entirely artificial; no sincerity, no purpose. A useless butterfly existence in which I wished to play no part. I wanted to work and sooner than I had reason to hope for, I got what I wanted, and the best years of my life began.

A FINE HEAD OF AN UNKNOWN MAN

Drawn in Pencil by Margaret Collyer in 1936.

Working for a Scholarship

(1893)

Chapter III

Just as arrangements for my art education were getting on quite nicely, a hapless remark nearly put a stop to any chance I had of obtaining an artistic training. Frank Dicksee (during the last three years of his life he was President of the Royal Academy) who was destined some years later to become a friend of mine, at forty years of age was an attractive and very handsome man. He was a great diner out and much sought after by 'lion hunters', an ornament to any drawing-room, and at that time his pictures were highly thought of and much in vogue amongst modern art collectors. He was also just becoming a fashionable portrait painter of Society women.

My aunt knew him fairly well, and he often dined at the Hertford Street house, so it was thought advisable to get his opinion on various schools, also to find out whether he considered me worth the expense of training or not.

It was a nervous moment for me when I had to meet him at a Sunday luncheon party and afterwards to produce some of my work for his inspection. So well can I recall his very words after studying some paintings of mine of horses in action.

'This young lady certainly has a remarkable

'LA BELLE DAME
SANS MERCI'
Sir Frank Dicksee 1893
The Bridgeman Art Library

facility for reproducing animals, but the work shows no training, and I am afraid she has gone too far to submit to learning the alphabet in a preparatory school.'

Better knowledge of Frank Dicksee showed this criticism to be completely characteristic of the man. He did not mean to be in the least unkind, but he lacked all sympathy for the young. When a piece of work was not done his way, he would not allow that it showed a particle of promise.

His own imagination was very restricted, and the amount he happened to possess was somewhat commonplace, as most of his subject pictures demonstrate. His draughtsmanship and marvellous brushwork were the envy of more original and creative brains but there was no originality in Frank Dicksee's paintings. They were mostly conscientious and truthful reproductions of whatever was stuck up in front of him. He did not paint *colour*, he merely blended and copied *colours*, and there is a vast difference between the two; one is subtle and the other is not. There was no subtlety in the man. He owned not a glimmer of humour and in all the years I knew him well, I never saw him laugh because he could not help it. He attained the position he held in the art world by dogged and conscientious perseverance, backed up by very hard work. He had an interest in psychic matter, which was kept severely under control and he seldom spoke of it. Nonetheless he became a true friend and ready helper, but outside his art he was a rather dull companion.

Although there was much to be learnt from his wondrous technique, his stiff, brick-wall manner frightened his students out of their wits. He could make a curt and sarcastic remark that just wiped a young artist out of existence with the flip of a paint-rag. This curtness of manner, I am sure, was caused by pure nervousness and an intense dislike of teaching, for a kinder hearted man than Frank Dicksee never lived.

Despite Frank Dicksee's condemnation, it was eventually decided that I should attend the Pelham Street School of Art for a year and work for a Scholarship for the Royal Academy. This excellent little school of seventy students, was run by Arthur Cope (later Sir Arthur Cope, RA) and Watson Nicol, who specialised in preparing students for the Royal Academy examinations, and they passed more students into the Academy than any other school in London.

One found very few amateur dabblers in Pelham Street; nearly all were trying for the Academy and work was serious, no frivolling was permitted. Watson Nicol was a born teacher of drawing and a beautiful draughtsman. He insisted on thoroughness and his patience was inexhaustible. All his students loved him. The brunt of the teaching fell on his shoulders and in his part of the school nothing but black and white work was done. The room was full of casts of every description, from that of a hand to life-sized whole figures. It was always crammed with students, to whom he gave long and careful lessons. His charmingly quiet voice inspired us with confidence. He treated all drawings with respect, no matter how poor they were, and corrected with kindly thought for our feelings, never considering it necessary, like many teachers, to smash about with a stick of black hard charcoal, leaving one's drawing and paper in a dirty mess. It was a pleasure to see Watson Nicol work on a chalk drawing and I learnt far more by watching him modelling up a muscle than by doing the work myself.

Most young students are apt to start with the idea that to make a highly finished drawing from the cast is a boring job and a grind. If one is taught in the right way, as I was taught, it is absorbing and delightful work; one learns to appreciate subtlety of line and modelling in the cast that at first the untrained eye would not be quick enough to catch in the living model. One learns beauty of form and the eye gradually becomes educated until it knows what to look for. The brain learns to draw accurately long before the hands can do the work; it is only by constant practice that our hands come under complete control. John Sargent RA told me that he painted with his mind as he wanted to paint ten years before he could induce his hands to do the work he required of them!

The preliminary examination for probationship in the Royal Academy Schools was in my day very stiff indeed and many beautiful drawings were sent in from the Pelham Street School. We owed our success to the patient training of the 'little man', as Mr Nicol was affectionately called by all his pupils.

For that preliminary drawing I chose for my subject '*The Dancing Fawn*'. It took six months, working three days a week, to complete it. It is still in existence, and the work is like the finest steel-plate engraving and all done with carbon point. I marvel now at the patience and perseverance spent on it; yet gazing on it I can recall nothing but hours of intense enjoyment as with the aid of my master I brought to entirely a thing of beauty.

In the Life School at Pelham Street, models sat for six days a week; for three days they sat for the head and the other three days the students worked from a nude. Arthur Cope took the life work and his method of instructing was a complete contrast to that of Mr Nicol. To begin with, he was always in a hurry and would come dashing into the quiet school like a stiff sea-breeze. The whole atmosphere instantly changed and became painfully electric, for he exuded energy and pace. The student whose work interested him most always came in for the roughest time; this took a little realizing and I remember one poor girl, whose work was full of strength and cleverness, failed to understand him and eventually left the school. No sooner was Mr Cope inside the door of the life room than his quick eyes would be caught at once by this girl's canvas and he would make straight for her easel and begin cutting her study to bits. We, who were possibly composed of tougher material, were all green with envy; for a gentle lesson from Mr Cope probably meant that he considered you a damn fool and not worth the bother of teaching. We all did our best to persuade this girl that Mr Cope thought her the most promising student in the room, but his most valuable criticism only reduced her to such a sobbing mass of pulp that nothing one could say would console her; so she departed, much to our, and probably his, regret. I often wondered what became of her, for she was really gifted and under a less brusque master would have done well; but I never saw her or any of her work again.

Our school was a very happy one and during the time I worked there I made some good friends, but I lost touch with them. So does old friendship often drift into thin air as one wends one's way along the stony path of Life!

Every year before the Academy drawings were sent in for Examination there was a great festival held in the Pelham Street School. This was known as medal night and we looked forward to it as children to a school feast. All our year's work was hung round the walls of the painting room, and one of the Royal Academicians was invited to judge it and award the silver and bronze medals provided by Messrs Cope and Nicol; and very beautiful these medals were.

On medal nights we saw Mr Cope in quite a different guise; no longer was he the severe master before whom we trembled, but a joyous merry friend and the first to congratulate the prize-winners with a clasp of the hand, a kindly pat on the back and a word of approval on the improvement in their year's work.

By the end of the first year I was at Pelham Street, I had done my probation work for the Academy and taken the school medal for the best charcoal drawing of a head from life. Mr Frank Dicksee was chosen to judge the work that year and it was he who handed me my medal!

HELEN SMITH
(THE ELDEST OF
THE COLLYER
SIBLINGS)

*With thanks to
Mrs Lindsay Smith's
descendants*

A Student's Haven

Chapter IV

During the time I was working in Pelham Street and later at the Royal Academy Schools I lived at Alexandra House, which adjoined the Old College of Music close to the Albert Hall. This is one of the best institutions that ever was started. The house was built by Sir Francis Cook and presented by him to Queen Alexandra – then Princess of Wales – as a home for women students of music and painting. It had been in existence for just ten years when I first became a lodger and it was always so full there was some difficulty in gaining admittance.

Room was provided for ninety-nine students. Half of these belonged to the College of Music and the other half attended various schools of Art. For the poor and homeless worker this institution was a haven of comfort. The cost of living at Alexandra House was exactly £60 a year with everything included. For this absurdly small sum of money a student was given a bedroom and shared a sitting-room with one other girl, or maybe she even had a bedroom and sitting-room to herself. All clothes were washed on the premises free of charge. There was a gymnasium class and a dancing class once a week. There was as much coal as she wanted and plenty of bathrooms and an unlimited supply of hot water. A house doctor visited every Sunday and a hospital nurse was always at hand.

There were lots of excellent pianos and sound-proof practising rooms, and a very fine concert hall. On the top floor were the kitchens, a large studio and a small hospital. There was always plenty of food, though in my day it was not over-good; but that was probably due to bad management; anyhow, there was no need to go hungry. Fixing the hours for regular meals must have been difficult owing to so many of the students attending classes and lectures at different times. The bane of our existence was a dreadful six o'clock dinner and if we were not there, our rations were labelled and put into a gas oven to keep hot, or dry up, until we wanted them. The food saved in this way tasted strongly of gas and I am sure was extremely unwholesome, if not actually poisonous. But grumbling was very seldom heard and indeed we had little to grumble about considering all the advantages we got for very little money. I lived in this pleasant home for the best part of five years and was desperately sorry when I had to leave it.

Naturally in a big college fairly strict rules were necessary, but if you were a worker the rules did not interfere in the least. They certainly never bothered me at all, in fact, I seldom thought about them. One of the rules of the House was that we had to be in every night by ten o'clock. We were allowed two late nights a week, when we might stay out till midnight. A very good-looking Welsh/Indian girl, who owned a really beautiful contralto voice was soon expelled for spending a merry week-end with a Cambridge undergraduate. When we went away for a weekend we had to leave our address and that was how she got into trouble; a cable arrived announcing her mother's death and she had written a spurious address in the book. Rather bad luck. I never heard what became of her afterwards.

During the whole time I was at Alexandra House there was only one outbreak of illness, and that was an influenza year, when more that half the girls went down with it. There was only one death and that was after an operation that had to be performed at almost a moment's notice. This speaks well for the healthy conditions under which we lived.

Except for the ex-Guardsman commissionaire who kept the door, it was an entirely female establishment. No men, not even relations, were permitted to visit girls in their rooms. When the house was first opened, brothers and fathers were not objected to, but as most of the inmates produced about ten brothers and some very youthful fathers, the Council put a stop to all male visitors.

One day in the week we were permitted to entertain 'gentleman friends' to tea in the large public drawing-room, and the only occasion on which I deliberately broke a rule was when I had my eldest sister and her husband[1] to tea there. My brother-in-law was most anxious to see my rooms, which happened to be on the first floor directly over the drawing-room, just outside of which was the servants' staircase. I hardly thought we could be caught if we bolted up for a second and hastened back again, anyhow it was rather exciting to have a try; but it was a fairly big risk, for if caught, or my sin found out, it would have meant probable expulsion.

We eventually decided that the game was worth the candle. I went up first to explore and make sure the coast was clear. The long gloomy corridor was like a city of the dead, so we made the venture. I was on thorns while my brother-in-law poked around the rooms and even stopped to sniff the nice horsey stable smell of the mews on to which my windows opened. The corridor was still deserted when we were about to attempt the return journey, but we had only got about ten paces from the door of my quarters and just opposite a coal cupboard, when to my horror the Lady Superintendent came out of a room a few doors away! Luckily the door of the coal cupboard was open, and my brother-in-law close to it, so before the good lady had time to see anything I had pushed him inside and shut the door. Miss Palmer stood outside and talked to me for about ten minutes. I knew that the

HELEN SMITH – SEEMINGLY LIKE ALL THE COLLYER SIBLINGS, WAS KEEN ON HORSES.

---

[1] Margaret's elder sister was Helen Collyer who married Lindsay Eric Smith. The Smith family were bankers.

coal cupboard had just been refilled and there would be scarcely room to stand; also it was pitch dark with the door closed, and I imagined every second I should hear an avalanche of coal as my prisoner stepped on a lump and lost his balance. For once the gods were kind to me and after watching the lady stroll down the mile of passage and turn the corner to the main staircase, I flung open the door and we fled for our lives back to the drawing-room. My spic-and-span relation was not so dirty as he might have been; a little polishing with a handkerchief put him fairly to rights and our exciting escapade ended satisfactorily.

The only other man who ever got a peep into my rooms was Uncle George. At the time the house went down with influenza I was one of the victims. With so many girls ill at the same time the staff was unable to cope, and we got little nursing and insufficient food. I was very thin and the house doctor had ordered me to be fed on good nourishing food. The first meal I received after this order was given was two fried sprats!

Uncle George responded to my cry for help by coming in his brougham to take me away. How he managed to get past that hefty commissionaire and find his way to my room I have no idea. Anyhow, much to my delight he arrived, rolled me up in a blanket, carried me down to his carriage and took me back to his house at Hertford Street, where I soon recovered the strength I had lost.

Our dining-hall was a very large room installed with many tables, each seating about a dozen girls. The older girls of the house were created heads of the tables and their duty was to keep order during meals and insist on decent table manners. It was not an enviable position, for the greatest talent seldom comes from very high-class families, and we were a pretty strange mixture on the whole. The batches of likely singers brought up from the Welsh villages and coalmines gave the heads of tables the most trouble. They were not elegant feeders and most difficult to handle, suffering badly from swollen heads and strongly resenting authority. I soon gave up my table, as I felt incapable of telling grown girls to wash their hands and clean their nails, that forks were safer to eat off than knives, and that cups rather than saucers were meant for drinking.

Amongst the notable students in Alexandra House destined to make their marks in the world of music, was Clara Butt[2]. Of the painter students I cannot recollect anyone who was successful. Most of them were dabblers who had no real intention of making art their profession. I was the only Royal Academy student in the place.

It was the custom before breakfast and the six o'clock dinner to sing grace. Someone would attack the piano and a crashing chord would bring us to our feet. The hall would vibrate, even the teacups rattled in their saucers, and Clara Butt would boom out the grace single-handed. It was useless competing against her best chest notes.

After I had passed into the Royal Academy Schools I had comparatively few meals in the House. Liking exercise, I walked across Hyde Park every morning and breakfasted with my Uncle and Aunt in Hertford Street. Here my nosebag was filled for lunch. On lecture nights, when I never got home until nine o'clock, I either ate food from the gas cupboard, or if too nasty even for one who was starving, cooked a supper of eggs and cocoa in my own room. Other than lecture nights I usually dined out.

Before breaking up for the Christmas vacation, the Head Girls in the House had to get up an entertainment in the Concert Hall, when vast numbers of officials, relations and friends were invited. Only one of these rather dreadful affairs remains in my memory and on that occasion the onus fell on Clara Butt and myself. After several meetings it was decided to produce W.S. Gilbert's clever play *The Palace of Truth* with Clara Butt playing the leading male part and me the woman's part. It was an absurdly ambitious and difficult play for the best of amateurs to attempt, and I very soon saw that unless we could get a good coach, it was going to be a failure. I told Clara Butt this and she took it

DAME CLARA BUTT

[2] Clara Butt (1872–1933) was the daughter of a sea captain and oyster dredger. She was six foot two inches tall, with a booming contralto voice. She had a huge personality and was acclaimed and loved by her countrymen.

in very bad part, believing, I suppose, that she was capable of carrying it off.

A night or two afterwards, at a dinner party, I happened to meet and sit next to the author of the play. He was particularly charming to me and after dinner, I told him that we wanted to produce his play at Alexandra House. I confided to him my fears with regard to the performance and he instantly offered to coach us himself. It was a wonderful opportunity to give an entertainment really worth looking at and naturally I jumped at his offer and gave him the date of the next rehearsal which he promised to attend. I was so delighted at my good fortune in meeting Mr Gilbert that the next morning I called a meeting of the cast and told them what I had arranged. All the girls, with the exception of Clara Butt, were overjoyed at the honour of being coached by the author of the play himself. For some reason, Miss Butt took offence and declined to attend the rehearsal. As she was playing the most important part we could not have a proper rehearsal without her. There was some fur flying about by the end of that meeting, as I had no intention of being made to look a fool.

But 'man proposes, God disposes'. Before the day of the great rehearsal the influenza epidemic began and any idea of an entertainment had to be given up. I was one of the first batch to take to my bed and was much touched by receiving a large bunch of purple grapes, with Clara Butt's love. A peace offering so kindly thought of and so nicely given. I have never forgotten it.

It did not follow that because the Council of the Royal Academy had passed the first consignment of work sent in from the preparatory school, that I would automatically be admitted as a probationer for longer than the allotted month. I had to produce yet another set of studies. These also had to be passed by the Council before I could obtain the coveted ivory disc which made me a full student and entitled me to work at the Royal Academy Schools, free of charge, for a three year course.

This second examination was mainly to prove that the students had done the initial work themselves and that it had not been re-touched by a master.

During the probation course students were forced to work entirely alone and without any help or criticism. Moreover, the work set was more advanced and more difficult. It is so long ago that now I have almost forgotten what we were given to do, but to the best of my recollection it was a painting in oils of an antique figure two feet high. A tracing from this had to be anatomised, all bones and muscles fitted in and named. There was also the painting of a head from life, a painting of a still life and a copy of an old master. I think that was the lot and enough too to get finished to the best of one's ability within just one month. We worked from 10 a.m. to 3 p.m. and woe betide us if we were a minute late, for the doors were closed on the stroke of ten.

The mere thought that the whole of my future existence depended on passing this examination did not help to produce good work. In fact it had the very opposite effect. I spent miserable sleepless nights, could scarcely look at food and started to shake all over the moment I was inside the school doors.

I do not believe I should ever have got my scholarship if it had not been for my friendship with Mr Watson Nicol, to whose studio I constantly went when the day's work was over. His gentle reassurance was like spring water to a thirsty soul. He had a wondrous way of making me believe in my own ability, when my self-belief was evaporating like vapour and my will weakening after each nerve-wracking day. He knew how important it was for me to pass this examination, for my benefactors were far removed from the struggling artistic world, and if I missed my first shot it would have taken a power of persuasion to convince them I was worthy of a second try.

All things come to an end and the last day of my probation arrived. At three o'clock, when I put down my palette and brushes, and had written my name on the back of my studies, I much doubted if even a council of imbeciles would ever pass such work as mine.

Leaden-hearted, I packed a suitcase and made a bolt to some friends in Surrey; a whole month had to pass before I could know my fate and to remain in London doing nothing was unendurable. I had to get away to

A MEET OF THE
WARNHAM STAG
HOUNDS

fresh air and open fields where I could sit on a horse and forget that there were any such places as art schools in the world.

At this pretty place in Surrey I was always welcome, and for a while I basked in a thoroughly congenial atmosphere of affluent country life, amongst hunting, shooting and cricketing friends, hounds and horses. What could a young and weary soul want more?

While waiting here I got a couple of commissions for horse portraits, hunters, both of which I knew well and had often ridden in great gallops with the old Warnham Staghounds. It was therefore an extra pleasure to me to paint them and the money for their pictures reinforced my sadly dwindling bank account. So with work and play the month passed quickly until the morning arrived when I got the official letter from Burlington House informing me that my work had been passed by the President and Council of the Royal Academy, and that I had been accepted as a Student of the Schools for a term of three years. After breakfast we let off a little steam galloping to the top of Leith Hill.

That evening I was back in London to report my success to Uncle George and Aunt Agnes, and last, but far from least, to Watson Nicol, who, beaming with delight, told me that two other students from the Pelham Street School had also been accepted. Quite a lot of other students had been sent down for a second try, so I considered myself very lucky and happily went off to buy Mr Nicol a present as a thank you offering.

A GREY HUNTER
With thanks to The British Sporting Art Trust

'HER FAVOURITE PETS'
The Bridgeman Art Library

'The Expression in these Lovely Eyes Was Not Quite Normal'

1894

Chapter V

Alexandra House was now rapidly emptying for the summer vacation. The lucky ones that had homes went back to them and those left in College with no money and no homes suffered accordingly – 'Les Miserables'. Stifling heat in an empty London was a grim outlook. A gap of two months had to be filled somehow before the winter term began.

There is a loneliness in London when all one's friends houses are shuttered and closed, unlike any other loneliness I have experienced. To wander aimlessly round familiar streets and see the dead flowers in the usually bright flower boxes, a smell of paint pervading the vitiated air, a friendly door one has long known as brown in colour now being turned to a virulent green by white coated workmen, window cleaners in their zenith and drab servants, usually out of sight, now haunting the area railings exchanging coarse-witted banalities with dustmen and decorators alike. London at the close of the gay season becomes a city of depression and renovation and should at all costs be left to itself for the time being.

All this and more circled continuously round my brain as I tramped the streets for exercise morning and evening. I longed for the country, a dog and a horse, and saw no way of even getting one of my three wishes.

But luck was standing by me still, for one morning I got a letter from a lady of whom I had never heard, who owned a pack of harriers[1] in the Midlands. She had been given my name as a horse and dog painter by some hunting friends of mine in Worcestershire, and now wrote to ask me to go up at once and paint a couple of hounds for her.

I lost no time in sending a wire telling her on what day and by what train I should arrive, then hurrying on from the post office to buy painting materials in Charles Robertson's shop in Piccadilly where I spent a lot of money, I then bought some clothes at Harvey & Nicholls and passed my evening carefully packing all I should require. I left London early the following morning bursting with high spirits for 'Fields unknown and distance far'.

One of my wishes had been granted me; the other two had now taken wings and flown away, for I was contented enough with what I had got. But it so happened that the train I was travelling on only took me as far as Coventry and here I had an hour to wait for the Branch line train. Putting my things in charge of a porter, I went for a stroll in the town.

I had not gone any great distance when I saw a man coming towards me leading four couples of Scottish deerhounds. I stopped to look at the dogs and seeing I was interested, he came and spoke to me. All the dogs were winners at the big shows with the exception of a brindled fawn youngster who, their owner said, was not good enough for the bench and whom he wanted to sell. This young dog, the only one not on a chain, was the fellow who most attracted me. He was a big dog with a beautiful long finely chiselled head, straight and sound in legs and feet; I could not see where he failed to please. My longing for a dog came back with a vengeance and completely got the better of me, and

---

[1] Harriers are a type of scent hound bred for hunting hares and foxes in large packs. They are one of the few truly medium-sized breeds of dogs. Harriers stand between 19 and 21 inches at the shoulder, and weigh 45–60 lbs. They have short hair, hanging ears and come in a variety of colour patterns.

in the waiting-room at Coventry Station that hound changed hands for £8, the owner having first demanded £10.

It was a crazy thing to have done. Here was I on my way to stay with, and work for, a complete stranger, arriving at her house with a large deerhound in tow. Well, I had now got my second wish and the dog travelled in the carriage with me. Before we got to the end of the journey we had made friends and he had been christened, with water from the lavatory basin, 'Chieftain the 4th' his father being 'Champion Chieftain 3rd'. He was just a great over-grown baby, and a romp at that; luckily we had the carriage to ourselves.

It took a little nice adjustment to get the whole of him into the very high dog-cart that met me at the station; but the good-tempered Chieftain took all our lifting and pushing as a huge joke and enjoyed the drive to the house.

It was a biggish place and I was shown into a large square lounge hall where my employer was waiting to receive me. I feel sure that I must have opened my mouth as well as my eyes as she shook hands with me, for I had never seen anyone the least like her before.

She was very tall, and very gaunt in body, with a perfectly round fat face quite puce in colour. Her hair, which was black and crinkly, was clipped close to her head, on which she wore at a rakish angle, a wide-brimmed sailor hat of variegated plaited straw. From the back of the hat hung a black hat-guard which was fastened to a button on her chest. Round her neck was a hunting stock. Her dress consisted of a very grubby kennel coat which reached to her knees, below this appeared a couple of stick-like legs clad in thin cotton stockings, while on her feet she sported a pair of low shoes with straps round the ankles such as small children used to wear.

The one redeeming point of this wonderful lady was her eyes, beautiful deep-blue violet, mysterious eyes, wide set and fringed with thick black lashes. The expression in these lovely eyes was not quite normal, but very soft and kindly as she pointed a finger at my hound and remarked:

'I see, your familiar, and an exceptionally fine specimen of his breed'.

My hostess's appearance and unique personality certainly caused me a slight shock, but I was destined to receive several more really acute ones before I went to bed that night.

After tea, which we had by the fire in the hall, four children appeared dressed exactly alike in kilt, sporran, dirk and all correct. Every child had its hair clipped as short as possible and they looked so exactly alike it was impossible to distinguish the boys from the girls, though I gathered from their names there were two of either sex present; they were much the same size too, ranging from about eight to twelve. I was told that they were all great riders and rode astride, hunting regularly with their mother's pack. That was as far as I ever got with them, for they never came to meals in the dining-room, and when not riding their ponies were herded by an oldish lady, whom I supposed to be the governess.

We remained chatting in the hall until half past seven, when a young man like a rather superior footman entered the room from the back premises and said:

'Madame, I've prepared your bath, and it's time for me to dress you for dinner.'

On our way upstairs, Mrs B. casually remarked:

'That's my valet. I prefer a valet to a maid, and when I travel up to Scotland, I use his knees as a pillow.'

Was I dreaming, or was it really true that this lady was bathed and dressed by a man-servant?

I began to wonder to what sort of house I had come and was glad I had bought the big dog; I had got him in my bedroom and had now every intention of keeping him there for the night. No objection had been raised about having him with me, though apparently dogs were not usually kept in the house.

Having no valet with knees on which to rest my head, I bathed and dressed quickly. Finding my way back to the hall I was now surprised to discover a bevy of young men there, very much at their ease, who said they had come to dine and promised me some rare fun after dinner if only I could play dance tunes on the piano.

A few minutes later, Mrs B. entered. She waved a circular welcome to the young men and offering no introductions whatsoever led the way into the dining-room.

Her valet this time had excelled himself in clothing her. She was arrayed in a short green velvet skirt, a white silk stock and watered silk waistcoat, a green velvet coat with scarlet collar and cuffs and gold buttons of the hunt. There was a whisper on either side of me where I sat at the foot of the long table: 'Mrs B's hunt livery. *Watch her eat.* She only feeds once a day, like her hounds.'

I then glanced at the menu and calculated that, providing the going was good, we might reach the last obstacle in slightly under the hour. My reckoning proved wrong. We sat at the table, mostly watching Mrs B. eat, for the best part of two hours.

Never would I have believed it possible for a woman to eat so much if I had not witnessed the performance. The food was excellent, and so was the wine, but where we had one small helping from innumerable dishes, Mrs B. always had two and sometimes three large ones. She chatted away gaily all the time about her hounds and hunting, relating stories of extra good runs and the pretty work shown by certain hounds in her pack, until she arrived at the last morsel of the savoury, when she jumped up from the table, seized the decanter of port and disappeared through a small door at the end of the room. Dessert evidently did not interest her; like her hounds, I suppose she did not care for fruit.

I have mentioned already how struck I was with the beauty of this lady's eyes. All through dinner I had been gazing at a full-length life-sized portrait of a beautiful young woman in habit, scarlet coat and hunting cap, surrounded by a pack of harriers; the same lovely violet eyes identified the portrait as that of my hostess painted many years ago. The portrait face was full of animation, the joy of living and love of her hounds; no mystery or abnormality existed then in the facial expression of what must have been one of the handsomest women of her day. It was difficult to connect the girl with the red-faced middle-aged woman who had just left the room.

Dessert over, the men conducted me back to the hall, where about half an hour later Mrs B. reappeared, this time in the full dress of a Highlander, kilt, bare knees, dirk, sporran, plaid fastened on the shoulder and a bonnet on the side of her head. She asked me whether I was able to play Scottish reels and, if so, to come into the drawing-room where there was a piano. She led the way and we followed in her wake.

The drawing-room was a fine room completely bare of furniture except for a few straight-backed chairs standing against the walls: no carpet, no rugs, a polished floor and a cottage piano at the far end. I was given the music of the reels preferred and then a bell was rung. Almost immediately a man I recognized as the butler, came in, also dressed as a Highlander, and Mrs B. and the butler proceeded to dance together, or rather opposite each other. I was kept at the piano thumping out reels for exactly an hour by the clock. The dances were fast and furious, accompanied by whoops from the butler and unearthly screeches from Mrs B. As the hour struck, the audience, who had meanwhile sat on hard chairs by the wall, shouted 'Time!' and the Highlanders came to an abrupt standstill.

I was thanked for my valuable assistance and was told I should be expected to do this every evening, as the lady danced for one hour each night after dinner for the sake of the exercise.

At the close of this extraordinary performance the still giggling lot of young men were dismissed and we went up to bed. My night was peaceful enough and I was overjoyed at having a dog alongside me once more. Chieftain's life up to the time he became mine had been spent in a kennel, but being bred a great gentleman, he took kindly to luxury and gave me no trouble at all.

Next morning I began work on the portraits of the hounds and everything was done for my help and comfort. I had a first-rate place with a good light to paint in and a man to hold the dogs, no one being permitted to come near to bother me.

That first day, before returning to the house for lunch, I wandered through the stables to take a look at the horses, of which there were a good many, but not the high-class animals I had expected to see. The stables were somewhat rambling and, in trying to find a way out at the opposite end of the block, I opened a door into a saddle-room. My surprise can be imagined when I discovered, seated at a table playing a game of cards, Mrs B., the stud groom, a kennel-huntsman and a helper. By the side of the card table was another laid out with dishes of sandwiches, a decanter of whisky, and bottles of soda water. I uttered humble apologies for intruding, but the lady showed no embarrassment at being discovered gambling with her menservants; she merely told me to go and have a good lunch and not to wait for her, as she only ate sandwiches at midday.

'COMPANIONS' 1906
[It is possible that this
is *Old Friends, Old Times*
– see Chapter 21]

During the whole of my stay in this remarkable establishment Mrs B. was most considerate and nice to me. I really saw very little of her except in the evenings, when there were always some young men to dinner and the dancing performance afterwards. What became of her all day I have no idea unless she spent her time playing cards.

No callers ever came to the house and the only women I saw were the governess and the housekeeper. I was at work most of the day. Occasionally Mrs B. would come and look at the pictures for a few minutes and make very helpful remarks, showing me points in her hounds that she wished emphasized and always apologetic for in any way interrupting or interfering with what I was doing. Eventually the portraits of the

41

'WAITING FOR
THE MISTRESS'

hounds pleased her very much and she asked me if I would come again and paint some more animals for her.

Odd in every way though she was, I could not but help liking her, for she was kindness personified, not only to me but to all with whom she came in contact; and her servants, although they might well have treated her with disrespect, did nothing of the sort, and I believe would have done anything for her.

On one or two occasions she talked to me about her husband and as he was not visible I took it for granted that she was a widow, until about a year later, when I met him at a dinner-party in London. There was a very distinct twinkle in his eyes when I told him I had stayed with and worked for his wife.

CHILD WITH
ST BERNARD

It Just Wasn't Cricket

Chapter VI

While still with Mrs B. I was lucky enough to get another commission from a man in Derbyshire to paint a horse for him. He had also heard of me through some hunting people. As I had just about finished the hounds, I decided I would have time to paint the horse before returning to London for the beginning of term. His letter was not a very nice one, I thought. It was just an order to paint his horse, the sort of letter that might have been written to a plumber to come and mend the tap; but beggars and students cannot be choosers, so I accepted the commission and fixed a near date on which I said I would arrive to begin the work for him.

It was a very cross-country journey to reach the wayside station I was destined for in Derbyshire, and it was late evening before I arrived. A carriage and pair awaited my coming, and a footman superintended while my belongings were loaded into a luggage cart.

About two miles from the station the carriage turned into some lodge gates and we drove up an avenue of elms to a new and pretentious looking house. A pompous butler and a couple of powdered-haired and knee-breeched flunkeys opened the door, and I stepped into a marble floored hall with walls elaborately picked out with a great deal of gilt moulding. Through this I was ushered to a baize door at the back and shown into what appeared to be the head-servants' sitting-room, and here I was asked to take a seat while the master was informed of my arrival. After keeping me waiting for about twenty minutes the gentleman arrived. He was a big florid man with thin colourless fair hair and prominent light blue eyes. Although he did not condescend to shake hands with me, I noticed a heavy signet ring on the third finger of his right hand. He greeted me with a formal bow and polite enquiries as to my journey, after which he called a manservant to take 'Chief' to the kennels and a maidservant to show me to my room. Then, saying he would make all arrangements for the painting of the horse on the morrow, he opened the door and, with another nod of his head, dismissed me from his presence.

My room, which was at the top of the house, was very little removed from an attic. Mr C. evidently saw no difference between a horse painter and a house painter; neither did the house porter, who brought my things up and dumped them in the middle of the room, with no offer to unstrap my box or put it in a more convenient place for unpacking. A tweeny brought in a small can of hot water and, as it was time to dress for dinner, I changed into an evening gown and awaited events. These proved to be rather laughable, for after hearing a jingle of bells which announced that dinner was ready there came a knock at my door, and a footman entered with a tray of food and a note from my employer saying that they had guests dining that evening, and that he would see me in his study after breakfast the next morning.

A reception such as this I had never experienced before and I spent the rest of the evening planning a delightful revenge, writing to my friends who had given this man my name and asking them to see that he was treated accordingly at the opening meet of the season. One of the family, Douglas Everett, was a particular pal of mine, and a gallant man to hounds: I knew he would take a special delight in doing some rough jostling on my behalf.

The following morning I breakfasted alone in the servants' sitting-room. During the meal a footman brought me a verbal message from Mr C. to the effect that he would see me in the library as soon as I was ready. This time I retaliated and sent back word that I was about to take my dog for a run, and would be pleased to meet Mr C. in the stable-yard at ten o'clock, which was my usual hour for commencing work. One up to me, and I felt a bit better as I ran races with Chieftain in the park.

On the stroke of ten I had all my paraphernalia ready in the yard and was looking at some of the horses when Mr C. strolled up.

The stabling was pretentious, like the house, positively princely with lots of brass: brass chains and pipe-clay everywhere, wonderful straw plaits with intermingled coloured braid for the edging of the stalls and a long line of green buckets decorated with white initials standing in an exact line against the outside wall.

The chestnut horse whose portrait I was to paint lived in a spacious loose-box which was exceptionally well lighted: a rare thing to find in most stables. He was a nice model too, a fine big weight-carrying hunter, who, if as good as he looked, must have cost a mint of money. The sight of a good horse has always warmed my heart and I began to feel excited about painting this one. Surely a man who had the knowledge to pick out horses such as this could not be a very bad fellow after all. I knew I could get on with a sportsman and a horse-lover, even if he was a bounder. These thoughts were filtering through my mind when Mr C. came back to me, having spent the last ten minutes in deep conversation with the stud groom. He then opened the door of the next box, in which there was another handsome chestnut. Said he:

'I was told by the gentleman who gave me your name that you are a very fine horsewoman, and can handle young horses. I should therefore be obliged during the time you are here if you would train this horse for my wife to ride; you can take it out in the evenings when you have finished painting.' Then he added, 'Of course I shall pay you a bit extra for breaking the horse.'

Now, if this request had been made in a different way, I should have jumped at the pleasure of riding and handling so good an animal, but in the way it was put by Mr. C. it had the effect of making me see red. I had no intention whatever of being paid to break an unruly horse for a perfect stranger, neither did I intend any longer to be treated as a servant or an inferior being. Enough of his insolence – I had come as an artist to make a picture of his horse and I expected to be treated as a guest during the time I was doing it. My cheeks were burning with suppressed indignation as I deliberately re-packed my painting utensils and asked one of the strappers to take them back to the house. I then turned to Mr C. and very politely declined to accept his commission, asking that a carriage be ordered to take me to the station for the next train to Town. Now scarlet in the face, the gentleman began to stammer and splutter out apologies, and a most edifying scene it was for his grooms to witness; however, the bit was tight between my teeth, and I merely looked at him, and walking back to the house I went up to my room to pack.

Whilst kneeling down packing clothes with my back to the door of my room, I heard a gentle tap. Thinking it was one of the servants come to carry down my luggage I merely said 'Come in', and continued my occupation. I then felt a hand on my shoulder and, on looking up, was surprised to see the lady of the house standing over me, evidently very nervous and perturbed.

During the time I had been in this unpleasant place I had never even caught a glimpse of her who should have been my hostess. I now rose to my feet as I saw before me the very exact type of woman I should have imagined as mistress of such an establishment. A big woman in her early thirties, somewhat buxom, elaborately dressed, heavily be-brooched and be-ringed, and smelling of strong scent. Her position was not to be envied. She had been sent to repair the damage and to try to gloss over the execrable manners of her husband. She certainly did say her part well and apologized deeply for the mistake she and her husband had made.

She begged me to forget the unfortunate episode and oblige them by staying on and painting the horse as I had originally arranged to do. She was a good-natured creature and much distressed to think that my feelings should have been hurt. Naturally, and of course, I accepted the apology and returned to the stable to commence operations. It was, however, not a very satisfactory beginning to a picture; my feelings had been jarred and the power of concentration left me for the time being. But a lovely ride on my model after tea soon mended wounded spirits and when, on my return, I found my room had been changed to a nice one and my evening clothes laid out ready for me on the bed, all resentment quite vanished and I went happily down to the drawing-room with my young self-respect once more thoroughly restored.

The remainder of my visit passed pleasantly enough. I was quite one of the family, and duly broke and rode the young horse for Mrs C. but it was understood that I did this to amuse myself and not for any 'filthy lucre'. It gave me both exercise and enjoyment, as I told her.

In those days ladies' cricket matches were much in vogue and Mrs C. had been busy getting up an eleven to play a team from the next county. The match was to be played on the home ground and it was to be combined with a large garden party. I had arranged to leave the day before this entertainment took place; my work was done and there was nothing to keep me any longer. But on the morning of my departure a telegram arrived at breakfast time saying that one of Mrs. C's eleven was unable to play for her. There was no time in which to search for anyone else, so I was asked to stay and fill the gap.

The only game that I ever really cared to play was cricket. I had been born and reared in the midst of first-class cricketers. My father, considered one of the best bats of his day, had played for Surrey and for the Gentlemen *v.* Players[1]. I had in consequence been carefully schooled,

---

[1] Margaret Collyer's father, William James Collyer, captained the Surrey Cricket Team in 1867.

WILLIAM JAMES
COLLYER

and could stand up to pretty good bowling and could hit hard when I got hold of a ball; but having always played with men and boys I hesitated to accept this invitation for after witnessing Mrs. C's practice of pat-ball I was afraid I might damage someone. However, I was persuaded to join the team and, as I had not had a bat in my hand for ages, I got Mr C. to come and bowl to me that morning. I was glad to find that I was in quite good form, and could knock his sort of bowling about very easily, so they decided to put me in first wicket down.

It was an extremely funny cricket match and not the kind of hard game I had been accustomed to at all. We all had to wear coloured sashes over one shoulder and tied under the opposite arm, where the bow got horribly in the way of one's elbows. Mrs C.'s side indulged in pale blue, the other side sported pale pink. I did not understand the reason for the colour scheme, unless it was to prevent the batsmen and field in some way becoming mixed up but the game of cricket as played by these ladies was so bewildering that anything might have happened.

There is nothing much to relate about the actual match except that I disabled two players, one getting a knock on the shin and the other a crack in the tummy from a ball I swiped to leg. I noticed that both teams seemed to prefer body blows and instead of using their hands, invariably stopped a ball with some part of their person. The bowling was childish. I made as many runs as I liked and carried my bat, and in consequence we won the match anyhow. This was the first and last time I ever played in a ladies' cricket match.

Chieftain did not have such a nice time here, though he got plenty of horse exercise. It was strictly kennel for him; no dog ever entered the house. But he told me going back to London in the train that he had been very well fed and given a good bed of clean straw every night. He certainly looked very well, had put on weight, and his condition had improved immensely since I had bought him.

So it was back to London town again, Alexandra House and The Royal Academy Schools, with a large deerhound to house somewhere where I could exercise and feed him.

'THE OYSTER GATHERERS'
With Thanks To Andrew Pick Of Taylor-Pick Gallery

The Ups and Downs of Student Life

Chapter VII

I was quite glad to get back to Alexandra House again. It was the only place I could now call home, and youngsters who are forced by evil circumstances to break their leading reins early in life, like to feel that there is a haven to return to when required. Independence is all very nice when ready money is to hand, but when there is none it loses its glamour.

This term the House was full to overflowing. Everyone had employment of some kind and from early morning to dewy eve the house swarmed with busy girls and the wide corridors echoed with the sound of merry voices. A happier gang of labourers could not have been found in any college in the world.

When I arrived I found my stable-mate awaiting me in our old rooms, where she had already put our few belongings into apple-pie order. Tressie Wilde was a jolly Canadian girl and I was lucky to share rooms with someone so entirely congenial. She was small and round, with a pretty face beaming with love for her fellow beings, and ever anxious to do a thoughtful kindly turn for anyone who happened to cross her path. She and I got on splendidly together and we lived in peace and contentment for two and a half years, after which time she was obliged to return to Canada, and I, being by then a senior student, was promoted to one of the few single suites.

I don't think she took her studentship very seriously. She was always well provided with money and, strictly speaking, had no right to claim the benefits of an institution which was intended for those who had no means at all. The few finished studies I saw of hers were distinctly clever and individual in technique; but her brain, although acute enough, was on the volatile side and only functioned seriously in fits and starts – a pity, for she possessed a gift of portraiture which is not given to many, and I am sure that if she had concentrated on her work she would have achieved some purpose.

Tressie regarded me as a 'swot' of the most confirmed type and used all the influence she possessed to get me to be frivolous – without much success, I am afraid; for fond as I was of her, I did not like her friends or the girls in the House that collected around her. Moreover, she refused to realise that I had a dreary prospect before me if I failed to make good. But she was a dear unselfish soul, and many's the time she gave up an evening's amusement when she knew I would be late home from a lecture, staying in on purpose to cook me an appetising supper that she thought I would enjoy. I saw comparatively little of her; we had no mutual friends in London, and the only evenings we regularly spent together were at the weekly 'gym' nights. She was a very keen and excellent gymnast, and we passed many a jolly hour in the gymnasium practising feats of strength, stretching and refreshing tired bodies with strenuous exercise after standing at our easels in a hot stuffy atmosphere all day.

Change of occupation is the best rest in the world. Hard physical exercise after severe brain strain is a tonic all youthful workers should take regularly. I have crawled down to the gymnasium in Alexandra House so tired and brain weary I hardly cared whether I got there or not, and after half an hour's exercise, have been so entirely refreshed and resuscitated I could have done the day's work all over again.

I was now a full-blown Royal Academy student[1] and owing to the kindness of a little old lady, Miss Flora Smith, who had generously undertaken to pay the £60 a year for my maintenance at Alexandra House, I was safe so far as my work and keep were concerned for three whole years. I had earned a little money, I did not have extravagant tastes, I never went into a shop unless I was pushed in other than to buy artists' materials, because I have always had a dislike of shopping, shops and salesmen and invariably would get some friend to buy me anything I needed.

The Royal Academy School was part of the immense stone cellars which had their existence under Burlington House. On one side of the Burlington Arcade, running parallel with Bond Street, was a narrow lane entered through double iron gates. A few yards down this lane was a massive arched door in the side of the building; this was the entrance to the schools. From the doorway a flight of stone steps led down past the porter's lodge on the right into the main corridor. On the left of this wide stone passage were the doors opening into the various schools of drawing, modelling and painting. On the right was the male students' dressing-room, and at the far end on the same side, the female students' rooms.

There was one object in this cavern-like corridor of immense interest, especially to the few who intended making animal painting their speciality. It was a cast taken by Sir Edwin Landseer of a skinned lioness, one, I believe, that died in the Zoo and which was cleaned and prepared by him for casting. It is a unique and an exquisite thing, and a thousand pities for it to remain buried, seen by nobody except a few appreciative students, of which I was one; for no one other than the curators and academicians were permitted to enter the schools.[2]

The probation work had given me a slight introduction to the place,

---

[1] Margaret Collyer registered as a 'full-blown student' of the Royal Academy Schools on July 31st 1894.

[2] The Royal Academy Schools are still much as Margaret describes them here.

but not to the student part of it, and for most of that first term I felt very much the new girl. There is something rather alarming in having to work with a crowd of strangers who you know are criticizing your ability, your personality, and even your clothes. Art students on the whole are a rough lot and have little sympathy for shyness and diffidence in the newcomer; if nature so allows you, it is better far to take your place and hold your own from the start, or life can be made unpleasant for a short period.

The most important thing to do straight away was to make friends with Old Osborne, the Lodge Porter. He resembled Fagin and was a shrivelled elderly man with an iron-grey moustache and ragged pointed beard, the prominent piercing eyes of a hawk, a long thin hooked nose and a sinister cast of countenance. He had been in possession of the lodge for years and strongly resented the yearly invasion of new students. It was part of his duty to check their names and enter them in the book on first arrival and while doing this, he sat at a high desk staring at the innocent offender over the top of his spectacles and behaved as though he were President and Council rolled into one. He was indeed the Keeper at the Gate and stood on his dignity – no amount of ragging ever made him smile and no pleading would induce him to let you into the schools if you arrived a minute after the doors were closed. He expected and accepted tips at the beginning and end of term, but it was the donor who was made to feel grateful. These tips meant the loss of a good many lunches to us, but they were worth it, they bought a certain amount of civility. We could often get odds and ends that we had forgotten from Osborne such as drawing-pins, charcoal, bread, etc. For once in the school you could not go out again until one o'clock, when an hour was allowed for luncheon.

This stringent rule of shutting students out if a few minutes late was very hard and altogether wrong. As often as not it was through no fault of theirs. Many came from the suburbs, and trains were not always on time, blocks in the traffic stopped buses, and fog was often another cause of late arrival. If the President and Council had considered what might happen to their girl students who were obliged to spend hours loitering about the streets, I am sure that rule would have been rescinded, or any rate modified. On soaking wet mornings these late-comers had nowhere to shelter and spent their time until one o'clock standing in the Burlington Arcade, not a pleasant place for the best of us to idle in and, for the less good, a spot where mischief might be brewed. Later, when I had the honour of knowing Lord Leighton[3], the President of the Board of the Royal Academy, I pointed this fact out to him and the knowledge shocked him, but the Royal Academy was bound up in red tape and the alteration of rules was no easy matter, even if suggested by the President himself. The idea for not admitting late scholars was that they should not interrupt the rest of the class when the model was sitting. But there was no need to keep them waiting outside the building in the cold and wet. They could so easily have been allowed to go into the library, or dressing-rooms or the corridor – all a better harbour for them than the Arcade. But that iron rule bound in red by the gods could not be broken merely for the sake of protecting a few girls!

The rule never worried me for I always breakfasted with my uncle in Hertford Street at half-past eight, and it was no distance to walk from there to Burlington House; also my sense of punctuality almost amounted to a vice, I was far more likely to be half an hour too early than half a minute too late.

The school hours were not well arranged, being either too short or far too long. Four days a week we began at 10.00 am and stopped at 3.00 pm and on the other two days we had to attend lectures on perspective, chemistry or pictorial perspective until 8.00 pm. During the last lecture when we were allowed to sit on benches, most of us went to sleep. As

---

3 Lord Frederick Leighton 1830–1896. He became President of the Royal Academy 1878. His house and studio near Holland Park, London is now a museum.

long as one's name was written in the book at the door it mattered not at all where our brains were, and there were no examinations on these dreary lectures. The only lecture that kept me awake was one given by William Lionel Wyllie RA, the marine painter on pictorial perspective. He took the trouble to demonstrate this on a large blackboard with ships of all descriptions, most beautifully cut out in paper.[4]

It is rather amazing that a council of sane men should imagine that youth could possibly concentrate on work for ten hours, with only two short breaks! On the days when classes finished at three I spent the time modelling a half-sized thing of the Landseer lioness, which took me a year. I was then forbidden by the President and Council to have it cast, as the original was unique and belonged to the Academy so no permanent copy was allowed to be made!

During my first term at the Academy I formed one very great friendship with an older student who was just finishing her fifth year in the schools. Katherine Willis was one of the finest characters it has ever been my lot to meet. Tall, handsome and brilliantly clever, she would have made a great name for herself had she lived to fulfill all the promise she showed. At the end of her last term she took the big prize (which I think was £30 or £40) for the best cartoon, a life-sized figure in charcoal, the subject, 'An Orator'. It was such a fine piece of work that Mr Ouless, RA[5] eventually bought it and had it set under glass in the wall halfway up his staircase, so that it was beautifully seen from his hall. The purchase of this drawing was one of the greatest compliments ever paid to a student of the schools.

Katherine Willis was the eldest child of a family of three. She had been brought up in luxury, scarcely knowing the existence of poverty.

---

4 William Lionel Wyllie, 1851 to 1931.

5 Walter William Ouless, was born on 21st September, 1848 in St. Helier, Jersey, and died on 25th December, 1933. He was a notable portrait painter, and was elected RA on 5th May, 1881.

Her mother died when she was fifteen, and her father when she was just seventeen. Her younger sister was still at school and her brother on the *Britannia*. After her father's death it was found that he had gambled away every penny he had possessed, and the three children were left with a mere pittance. Katherine, who had always intended to become a painter, set to work and entered the Royal Academy Schools, and during the time of her studentship she managed by her portraiture to make enough money to keep her sister and brother at school and to support herself. In doing this she worked herself to a rag, and caught a cold which later developed into tuberculosis. When I knew her she was already very ill.

On leaving the Schools, Mr Ouless sent her to winter in the South of France with a friend to look after her, paying all expenses himself. On her return she was better; it was the first rest she had had for years. She then took a studio and rooms off Tedworth Square, and had her sister

'THE OPENING OF LONDON BRIDGE'
By William Lionel Wyllie RA 1851–1931
The Bridgeman Art Library

59

to live with her. Here she slaved at her work until her brother passed into the Navy, when she partially collapsed again, and I went to Mr Ouless to see if anything could be done for her. She was taken to the greatest lung specialists, who practically condemned her unless she could live in a warm climate. Mr Ouless and Mr Sargent[6] asked me to take her abroad for a while, but she would not leave her sister to fight alone, so there was nothing for it but to let her carry on and see that she had good food and enough of it.

And carry on she did, with the bravest heart in the world. She exhibited in the Academy for the three remaining years of her life and had four nearly finished pictures on her easels when she lay in the alcove of the studio on her deathbed, just a week before sending-in day for the coming Exhibition. She was so anxious that the pictures should be sent in that I went round to Tite Street and fetched Mr Sargent, who, to satisfy her, did some work on the portraits while she watched him from her bed. Mr Sargent promised her that he would get them hung, and as he was on the hanging committee that year it was a foregone conclusion.

Nearly all my spare moments were given up to looking after my friend. She held on to life until we got the official notice from the Royal Academy to say all was well. Then she suddenly let go, and died quite peacefully a few days later.

Katherine was twenty-nine when she died and the last ten years of her short life had been one long struggle of great self-sacrifice. I suffered the loss of a friendship I valued more than any other at that time. I must pay a tribute to these good kind men, William Ouless and John Singer Sargent. Without their help I do not know what I should have done, as I had no money to supply comfort in sickness. They not only saw to it that she had a good nurse, but also that she had everything else that saved her from unnecessary discomfort and pain.

---

[6] John Singer Sargent, 1856–1925 – son of a New England doctor, born in Florence.

'A Half Starved Hireling'

Chapter VIII

My big dog was residing in a stable of the mews on to which my windows opened and I was not happy about him. To exercise him I had to get up at six o'clock every morning and, after his run, brush and feed him before starting my day's work. It was the same routine at night; and many things I was obliged to do interfered with his welfare. This was not the proper life for any dog and for most of the time he lacked human companionship and he was so worthy of a better fate. He had fulfilled my expectations and grown into a magnificent hound.

One Sunday I took him round to see Mr A.J. Sewell, the great canine vet, and he was so taken with the dog that he persuaded me to show him at the Palace Show. I thought this would be rather fun, so I entered him in all the classes for which he was eligible and managed to find time to show him myself. Imagine my delight when he won first in Novice, first in Limit and second in Open, being only just beaten for premier honours and championship by 'Champion Swift' an older and very noted dog in his time. He competed against several of his Coventry kennel mates, and beat the lot of them, much to the amusement of his former owner, who wanted to

MARGARET OR
HER SISTER,
OLIVE COLLYER
c. 1895

buy him back at double the price! I refused the offer, because I thought I could get him a much nicer home.

Soon after the Show I gave 'Chief' to my benefactress, Miss Flora Smith, who loved the dog greatly. She owned a house in Cromwell Road just at the foot of Queen's Gate and kept a carriage and pair of horses; Chief slept with the horses and spent most of the day in the house with his new mistress, and had the gardens at the back to play in. Every day he got good exercise following her carriage to Wimbledon Common or Richmond Park, where the lady took the air. I was much happier about him and he was well contented.

Life was very full indeed, for during the season I had to spend most of my free evenings and all Sunday playing my part in Hertford Street with my Aunt. There was an endless circle of dinners, theatres, concerts, At-Homes and on Sundays the deadly business of Church Parade in the Park with long heavy luncheons to follow. It seemed to me I was for ever changing my clothes from one smart gown to another and, as these were provided by my Aunt and always kept in her wardrobes, they were in no way my possessions or part of myself. I used to feel like a half-starved hireling decked out with a borrowed saddle.

I certainly owed my aunt a great deal of gratitude and did my best to be of use to her, but this social business was a strenuous job on top of all my school work, and the late nights tired me severely. No. 4 Hertford Street was small and stuffy, and it was always crammed with people. My aunt was a pushing, superficial Society woman. At the age of forty-eight or so, she still possessed a remarkably fine figure and a certain amount of good looks; tall and thin, with a clean cut hard face, an aristo-cratic well-chiselled nose, a pair of fine blue eyes and a straight line of a mouth enclosing the most beautiful teeth I have ever seen. A curiously ungenuine person who inspired no love amongst her own sex, I doubt if she ever had a woman friend. Flattery was the sustenance of her life. She owned a remarkably retentive brain and was clever enough to make all possible use of it; from the intelligent and gifted people she continually mixed with, she managed to absorb a smattering of knowledge and originality which she could reproduce sufficiently fluently to give the impression of considerable intellect. It was an admirable piece of acting which I watched with appreciation. She was a first-rate hostess and housekeeper, her dinners were works of art and the wines of the highest quality. Her parties were always a success and owing to Uncle George who gave medical treatment to artistes free of charge, extra good music was heard in her drawing room.

I feel a little disloyal writing of my Aunt as I have done; but for a short time she played a big part in my life and I must tell of her as I saw her. If her affection for me had been genuine it would be a different matter; but it was not in the least sincere and I was never foolish enough to imagine it was. Youth and artistic success are attractive and useful in the house of two elderly people who wish to entertain and be entertained. They are something of a decoy and she liked taking me about with her and insisted on me being present at all her parties.

Notwithstanding the help she gave me, I regret to say I had very little regard for her; but Uncle George I loved dearly: a somewhat dull but delightful personality, with the kindest heart possible. He was music mad, quite untrained, and played second violin more badly and more out of tune than most amateurs. He attacked the stiffest music with the delightful nonchalance of the ignorant and got up quartets with up and coming musicians.

I am sure that Uncle George must have been tone deaf; at times he played so excruciatingly out of tune that it made my skin prickle and my teeth ache. If at the beginning of a song he jumped off wrong he remained off the note to the bitter end, and it *was* bitter for those in the audience who knew and liked him. However I often heard excellent music in the Hertford Street house, and also met painters, musicians and other men of note who had made or were destined to make, their mark in the world.

One man of interest I was constantly meeting was Dr Alfred

Williams Momerie, DD[1]. Some years before I knew him he had been requested to leave Cambridge University owing to his unorthodoxy. On his dismissal Gladstone is supposed to have written of him: 'Cambridge is making a vast mistake in so discarding the services of Dr Momerie whom I consider to be one of the greatest scholars of the century.' When I first met Dr Momerie he had just returned from his travels in Australia and America, where he had preached his own reading of the Gospels and written some of his many books on the Creeds. When parted from his clergyman's clothes, he appeared as a small, ordinary and somewhat common looking man but the moment he donned his surplice, his pale blue hood and his exquisitely embroidered stole, he became an entirely different being. His voice was so piercing and vibrant that in an ordinary room it grated on the ear. He was a master of elocution but elocuted too well in a dining room and invariably held the table with racy and not always very nice stories. I was introduced to him at a luncheon where several men and women of considerable calibre were present, but Momerie with his strangely ringing voice dominated the table with egotistical conversation. He told of his journey round the world and of the huge congregations that flocked to hear him preach. I remember clearly one thing he said, 'If any church, charity or society wanted funds I was invited to preach, for the collections made after one of my sermons filled their money bags!' He had no church of his own but was always to be heard at The Foundling Hospital or St James's Hall; he never spoke for more than twenty minutes, and I write the

---

[1] MOMERIE, ALFRED WILLIAMS: Church of England; b. in London Mar. 22, 1848; d. there Dec. 6, 1900. He was of Huguenot stock and restored his name from its phonetic form of Mummery. His father was a Congregational minister, who, after sending him to the City of London School, sent him to the University of Edinburgh and Cambridge. He was curate of Leigh in Lancashire from 1878 to 1880. In 1883 he became morning preacher at the Foundling Hospital in London. His sermons and his teaching attracted great attention, but their outspoken 'Broad Churchism' brought him into trouble, and he was forced to retire from his preachership and professorship in 1891. After that he preached at the Portman Rooms, London. In 1896 he married.

truth when I say that it was twenty minutes of pure bliss to listen to him. I disliked him, both his manner and his personality, yet I never heard my own language more beautifully spoken. I had walked with him and talked with him for hours, but except when he was actually preaching, I never believed in his sincerity, and all his arguments left me cold as stone.

The end came one Sunday when, after hearing him give a more than usually moving discourse on Charity I walked back to Hertford Street with him and remarked on his perfect performance. He said, 'Yes, you've hit the nail plumb on the head. That is just what it was, a very carefully rehearsed and artistic piece of acting. You don't suppose that I just climb into a pulpit and spout gems of speech without first studying my part thoroughly? Of course I don't. I first write my sermon, then learn it by heart until I am word perfect; then I act it in front of a large looking glass. I rehearse every intonation and every gesture, even facial expression is studied; then I get an actor friend under whom I have trained, to come and see the performance and correct deficiencies. Every twenty minute sermon means for me hours of hard work and that, my dear, is how I draw the crowds. It is not only the intellectual discourse that does it, it is the superb delivery.'

For some reason this blatant admission so shocked me I never went to hear Dr Momerie preach again. My faith was in rags, and never got properly repaired.

Two very true and dear friends were in my life at this period. One was Sir Frederick Haines, late Commander in Chief in India, and the other my benefactress Miss Flora Smith. She was a birdlike little lady with quite white hair and the clear blue eyes of a child; she was the sister of Valentine Smith, a millionaire and

DR ALFRED
WILLIAMS MOMERIE
With thanks to the
Cambridge University
Library

owner of that beautiful property Ardtornish[2] in the Morven Hills opposite the Isle of Mull.

Miss Smith was also wealthy and lived by herself in her house on the
Cromwell Road. For several years she had been a regular patient of
Uncle George, who had a standing engagement to visit her once or
twice a week. She was pretty and fragile to look at, but I seldom noticed
any fragility in her demeanour, for she seemed to be made of live wire
and steel springs. She liked to pose as a semi-invalid, mostly because,
like everyone else, she adored the doctor and besides the mysterious
ailments she was supposed to suffer from, they had music in common.
Miss Smith was highly trained both as a pianist and singer. She also
had a nice collection of watercolour drawings by eminent artists.

She was very particular and 'early Victorian' with no real sense of
humour; a joke had to be clearly perceptible to produce her shrill shriek
of laughter. She was fond of giving large, dull dinner parties and one
evening when I was attending one of these funereal affairs a complete lull
in the conversation enabled her to catch something I was saying about a
Mr Hoare. In her high penetrating voice, she asked which Mr Hoare I was
talking about, then added at a still higher pitch, 'You know Margaret,
there are Hoares and Hoares'. I did know and so did a few others at her
table but the joke was too subtle for her and she could not conceive why
many of her guests were wiping tears of laughter from their eyes.

She was such a kind lady, so good and generous to me, not only
while I was studying, but at the time when I most needed help on leaving
the schools. She, her uncouth butler William, her old Scottish maid, and
her coachman, were a continual source of amusement to me. Where on
earth she got her servants from I cannot imagine. The coachman had a
surly ill manner and he would bring her very handsome and expensive
landau round to the house with two fat old horses attached to it; never
a matched pair, sometimes one clipped, and the other less than half

---

[2] See Chapter XX

clipped. His livery just hung on him anyhow and in this extraordinary turnout she would drive in the Park in the height of the season, having noticed none of the defects. She hired her horses from one of the best stables in London and, when I knew her well enough, I suggested that as she paid heavily for the hire of horses, she ought, at least, to insist on getting a pair of good ones. After that I used to be sent to the livery stables to choose her horses for her. I always had the good-looking pairs I picked out put into a brake and drove them myself through thick traffic before having them sent to Miss Smith's stables; but my trouble was often for nothing, for if one of the horses showed the smallest joy in life, the coachman condemned him as vicious and unsafe. My carefully chosen pair would be separated and reduced to a mere 'couple'.

My other friend, Sir Frederick Haines[3] was an elderly and distinguished soldier who was a great patron of art and drama, and a consistent first nighter; he personally knew many of the leading actors and actresses of his time. The most thrilling first night I ever went to with Sir Frederick was Sir Henry Irving's production of *Macbeth*. I, who had never seen Irving on the stage before, was quite mystified by his extraordinary mannerisms which, at that time, had become almost grotesque. Having heard so much about him, I was expecting to witness the finished performance of a marvellous actor and to find myself carried away by his artistry, but instead of this, I am ashamed to confess, I felt the strongest inclination to laugh during the whole of the first scene. His walk was almost that of a buffoon, he dragged his left leg after him in such a way that I quite thought he had a stiff knee and was sorry, thinking of the pain he might be suffering. His elocution and weird articulation were suggestive of an imitation of noises made by wild animals at the Zoo.

Mr Bernard Shaw, whose witty criticisms were seldom kind though

---

[3] Field Marshall Sir Frederick Paul Haines, served in India in the 1870's and 1880's ending up Commander in Chief.

often to the point, writing of Irving's impersonation of Hamlet, said, 'Irving achieved the celebrated feat of performing Hamlet with the part of Hamlet left out, substituting in his stead the fascinating figure of Henry Irving which, for many years, did not pall on his audience and never palled on himself.' But Irving was Irving and must have been far more than just an ordinarily gifted man to have filled the Lyceum Theatre with a cultivated and intellectual audience every season for more than thirty years.

Most certainly he failed to impress me on that first night of *Macbeth*, and after the entry of Ellen Terry I neither saw nor heard anyone else. I can recall her tall, graceful figure clearly now as she stood at the foot of the turret stair, slowly endeavouring to rub the blood off her hand. Still more unclouded is my vision as she appeared arrayed in that wondrous beetle-wing robe in which Mr John Sargent painted his masterpiece of her.

A gracious, beautiful woman with those curious tragically formed brows and the soft, slightly husky voice that without effort carried each word distinctly to the furthest corners of the theatre; an unforgettable utterance of sound that found response and echo in the hearts of all hearers. It is small wonder to me that during her 'golden age' she had half London at her feet.

The same thing could possibly be said of her as was said of Irving. She seldom, if ever, got away from her own personality. I saw her in many parts, but I never lost her own individuality in one of them; delightful to watch, charming to listen to, but always Ellen Terry.

As to whether this costly production of *Macbeth* was a financial success I have no idea, but that it was enthusiastically received, being an eye-witness, I can vouch for. As the curtain fell after the last act there was a positive storm of applause. Ellen Terry and Irving received an ovation, and had to take call after call before the excited audience could be persuaded to leave the house.

Long before the last shouts had died away, Sir Frederick and I were being conducted on to the stage. Such a stage as it was too, quite enormous, and lightning-like changes had already taken place on it. Many tables a-glitter with silver, glass, and flowers had now appropriated the place of properties. The setting for these was still the grey-green stone walls of Macbeth's castle, the sombre tone of which was an effective background for the brilliant reception now being held by the Stars of Theatredom. In the centre, surrounded by a bank of bouquets and wreaths, and still wearing the beetle-wing robe, stood Ellen Terry receiving her guests.

It was indeed a wonderful assembly of wonderful people. The Arts were represented by their most noted exponents; Lord Leighton as President of the Royal Academy, symbolizing painting and sculpture; literature, by the cleverest writers of the day, amongst them I recognized Oscar Wilde and Sarah Grand, both of whom I knew slightly. Of musicians present I saw Joachim, Richter, Mr Bispham, and Madame Albani. Mr Bram Stoker, of course, as Irving's manager, was here, there and everywhere, except where I wanted him to be, which was close beside me, pointing out eminent people I could not recognize.

Ellen Terry I had already met at Mrs Lewis's, her sister's house. She welcomed me with a beetle-wing hug which was rather scratchy, then she introduced me to Sir Henry Irving, who said I was just like my mother, and taking me under his wing, sat me down next to him at the corner of the central table with Julia Neilson, looking lovely, on my right.

As the other theatres closed, still more actors and actresses arrived, till the stage was packed with people. Sir Charles Wyndham was nearly opposite me, and Mrs Patrick Campbell next to him. I remember noticing what enormous hands she owned; when I saw her as Ophelia, both her hands and feet struck me as being grotesquely large. People were then beginning to rave about her acting, and flocked to see her in *The Second Mrs Tanqueray,* a play that I was not allowed to see, for in the early nineties young girls were kept from knowledge of the seamy side of life as far as possible.

I still regret not seeing that play with Mrs Pat Campbell in the leading part, for I believe it was the best of her roles. I saw her as Ophelia, her reading of which I did not greatly care for, and I saw her in *Phèdre,* but as I had shortly before seen Sarah Bernhardt in this part, it was much like water after glowing wine.

Supper over, speeches were made, which rather bored me, till Mr Bram Stoker came and took me in hand, and showed me the back of the stage and how all the scenery was worked. Bram Stoker, author of that thrilling novel *Dracula* was a big, burly, red bearded Irishman who owned a strong brogue and a vast sense of humour. He was such an entertaining companion, just like a big boy and seemed to romp through life laughing so kindly with, and at, his fellow-beings; a party was never dull for me if he happened to be about.

London seasons in the early eighteen nineties were very gay and very strenuous for those who had the money and inclination to live the butterfly existence to the full. It was also the golden age of opera and even those who hated music considered it the right thing to hear as many performances as possible. Caruso, Melba, Calve, the De Reszkes and Alvarez were then singing at Covent Garden and the Opera House was always crowded to overflowing.

I found myself living in two worlds, the world of work and the world of the London Debutante. What a waste of time and money! What was it all for? Where was it leading? These women of society who could not exist without one excitement after another and nothing but a round of gaiety to keep them from boredom. Women with daughters to dispose of rented expensive houses in the most fashionable localities, presented their daughters at Court, and deliberately put them on the marriage market by lavishly entertaining, pulling every possible string to fill their ballrooms with eligible young men, hoping that at least one girl would be satisfactorily settled in life before the strain on the family purse proved more that it could bear.

I often used to go to a perfect palace of a place on the top of Camden Hill, owned by Mr George Bouchier. Mr Bouchier and his funny little scraggy wife were Americans, and how he ever got elected a Royal Academician I cannot think; he was a good and jovial friend, but a shockingly bad painter. They used to give very big At Homes, and Mrs Bouchier received her guests at the entrance to the drawing room, always wearing the dirtiest of dirty white kid gloves. Also the old dear painted her face heavily and did it very badly. She was many years older than her husband and pathetically tried to disguise the fact. I feel sure that the money must have been hers, for he could never have made it from the piffle he put on to canvas.

It was at this time that I made David Bispham's acquaintance and he became a dear friend of mine[4]. Bicycling was fast catching hold and becoming very much the fashion; after dinner rides through the empty streets of London were delightful and I enjoyed those evenings tremendously. I often used to slip off with Mr Bispham, who lived in Kensington Gore, on Sunday mornings and spend whole delightful days in the country. I could get into Mr Bispham's back garden from the mews where my bicycle was stabled and many's the hour I have sat in his music room while he practised for a concert or opera; hours of delight lazing in comfortable painting smock in a comfortable chair and listening to the voice of a great artiste.

David Bispham was not just a fine singer, he was a most dramatic singer, and if God had not given him a voice, he would have achieved

---

[4] David Scull Bispham was born in Philadelphia in 1857 to Jane Lippincott Scull and William Danforth Bispham. His mother came from a devout Quaker family, and while his father had left Quaker meetings some years earlier, the Bisphams lived and thought of themselves as Quakers. As might be expected, Bispham's earliest years were without significant musical influence. His mother did not permit a piano in the home and is said to have been 'shocked beyond expression' the one time she attended a ballet. Nevertheless, William Bispham played the flute and his brother, John Bispham, took David to his first opera in Philadelphia. Bispham made his opera debut in 1891 and went on to star at the Royal Opera, Covent Garden and at the Metropolitan Opera between 1892 and 1903. In addition to operatic roles, Bispham excelled at oratorio and German song. In his later years he was a devoted teacher and when his voice was no longer in its prime, he won acclaim for his acting and dramatic readings. He led a colourful life, making friends with the likes of Mark Twain, Robert Browning, and John Singer Sargent. His manager was Bram Stoker. Bispham's autobiography *A Quaker Singer's Recollection* was published in 1920, just a year before his death at age 64.

fame as an actor. Without exception he was the ugliest man I have ever known, typically American, wide faced and coarse in feature with an enormous mouth of which he was very proud: he deemed it a sounding box of the highest quality. His eyes, wide set, were surrounded by rugged brows under a well shaped forehead. But his ugliness was counter-balanced by a charming expression of humour and kindliness; he loved animals and he loved his friends; a sympathetic and an entirely delight-ful companion. Although his singing enchanted me the actual voice was not particularly sweet. There was a distinct grate in it; but his production was perfect and his knowledge of his art was so vast that the slight roughness became rather attractive. I liked him better in opera than on the concert platform except on one occasion when he sang at St James's Hall, introducing the five serious songs of Brahms. In these he surpassed himself and that curious timbre seemed to lend itself to the music. '*The living voice is that which sways the soul.*'

'A Sprig of Rosemary for the Suffragettes'

Chapter IX

"When you have finished milking my dear.

We'll . . . .

A RARE CARTOON BY
MARGARET COLLYER

Despite my social activities, I was putting in heavy work at the schools every day, for I was quite determined to pass from the lower school to the upper at the completion of my first year. To achieve this, another set of paintings had to be done and passed by the Council, and the women students were badly handicapped throughout.

Why the female of the species should never be given the same advantages as the male is difficult to understand. At the Royal Academy Schools we women had to compete against the men for all the prizes and medals that were given each year, and we were only allowed half the amount of tuition and less than half their opportunities for study.

No nude model was allowed for posing in the women's painting room at the Royal Academy Schools. It was strictly against the laws that the women students be permitted to study from the human form divine. In every other school in London figure models were posed, but the Academicians blushed at the very thought of anything so shocking. To learn how the human body is constructed one must dive below the skin; before painting drapery or clothes on a body the artist must be able to visualize what is under the clothes.

The male students not only worked from nude models, both male and female, during the day, but they were given an evening class as well, at which they could make studies from the figure with the visiting Royal Academician instructing.

This seemed to many of us very unfair indeed and I am afraid I soon became a leading firebrand and rebel. Unlike most of the students, I had plenty of opportunity to meet and know many of the Academicians and I never missed a chance of attacking them on the subject of their meanness and inconsideration to their girl scholars. Mr Frank Dicksee came in for the brunt of my righteous indignation for I saw him more often than his colleagues. He was not the least bit encouraging although professing to see our point of view. He put forth arguments against spending extra money on the girls' school because girls usually got married and then dropped their work, therefore the money was wasted.

I soon realised that we must put our grievances before the whole Council and to that end I asked for a meeting with the President, Lord Leighton, who kindly consented to see me in his studio. I tried to persuade one or two of my fellow students to come with me, but when it came to the actual moment of bearding the great lion in his den, they ignominiously slid out of it and I was left to make the venture by myself.

The few times I had visited Lord Leighton's studio before had been on formal occasions, when I had merely exchanged a few words with him. This was going to be such a different sort of interview, that, on arrival at his house, my heart took a seat in my boots, and to regain sufficient courage I walked up and down a time or two before venturing to ring the bell. I was just about to do this when a friend of mine who was also on the Council, George Bouchier, turned up, and when he learnt of my mission he said: 'Come along in with me and as soon as you are happier, I will leave you to talk with the President.'

George Bouchier was a valuable ally, so I begged him to stay and back me up in the proposition I was about to put forward. He agreed that the female students were not fairly treated and thought it could do no harm to try and get a very stupid rule corrected.

The President greeted us at the door. I had never been inside his working studio before, nor seen

LORD FREDERICK LEIGHTON
With thanks to the Leighton House Museum

LORD LEIGHTON'S
HOUSE IN HOLLAND
PARK, LONDON
AS IT IS TODAY.
NOW A DELIGHTFUL
LITTLE MUSEUM
OPEN TO THE PUBLIC.
*With thanks to the Leighton
House Museum*

Lord Leighton in his working clothes. In his old coat covered with patches of paint, he looked much more human and his usual stiff manner was evidently kept in the cupboard with his velveteen jacket and blue silk tie. Shortly all three of us were discussing the advisability of getting the offending rules altered, and eventually Lord Leighton promised that he would lay the matter before the Council at the next meeting, but he was doubtful if any amendment would be made. Then Mr Bouchier had a brain wave and said he would suggest that the question of posing a nude model should be left to the wish and discretion of the visiting instructor.

I had been fairly heard, and it was for us now patiently to await the decision of the Council at their next meeting. I had some hope, my fellow students had none; but it so turned out that Mr Bouchier's proposal was accepted, and if the instructor liked to pose a figure model, there would be nothing to prevent him doing so. This was the thin end of the wedge, and gradually we persuaded nearly all the members to give us what we had asked for.

Some years later I met Annie Louise Swynnerton and her experience underlined the prejudice against women making a success of their artistic lives. She was a little, fragile, elderly woman when I met her, and so shortsighted that she worked with her model as well as her canvas close under her nose. There must have been something remarkably interesting about her vision, for how she produced the broad free paint she did, so original and beautiful, puzzled me completely. And what a crying shame that such an artist was never elected to Membership of the Academy until she was over seventy. Why the Council of the Royal Academy should for years have closed its doors against all women painters I cannot imagine. Frank Dicksee himself told me that when new Royal Academicians and Associates of the Royal Academy were

LORD LEIGHTON'S
MUSIC ROOM IN 1896
*With thanks to the Leighton
House Museum*

about to be elected to fill the gaps caused by the death of members, and women's names appeared on the board with those of men considered worthy of being put up for election, before any voting took place, a chalk line was drawn through the names of the women! Comparisons are odious, I know; but take the work of one or two of the Royal Academicians who must have been about the same age as Mrs Swynnerton – George Bouchier, Marcus Stone, Alma Tadema (he would have been older, I think) Philip Calderon and many others I could mention; compare their best work with Mrs Swynnerton's last Academy pictures painted just before she died and tell me who had the better right to member-ship, the four men or the one woman? She was an artist, the rest were poor imitations. At one time I had some animosity towards the suffra-gettes, but now I place a sprig of rosemary in remembrance of them, for women artists too, have much for which to thank them.

'THE DREAMER'
Anne Louise Swynnerton
The Bridgeman Art Library

We never did succeed in obtaining the advantages of the night class for women students and to arrange for such a class outside the schools worried me a great deal. Most of us were nearly penniless. It would necessitate in hiring the use of a room for two hours every night and paying a model to stand for us. A few of the senior girls and I formed a committee and between us scraped together enough money to rent a photographer's studio in Baker Street four nights a week; each girl in turn taking charge for a month. Her duties were to engage and pose the model, see to the lighting, provide tea and biscuits, and leave the room tidy. Those who wanted to join and could not pay we squeezed in, whenever possible, and I am afraid made them do the slavery work. This studio stretched all our resources especially for several poor hard working girls and we all agreed to pool our lunch sandwiches so that everyone could get a snack at midday. From Monday to Saturday I was often hungry and every Sunday glutted with good food. I used to wish I could share it with some of my school acquaintances whom I felt pretty certain never got a full meal.

Poverty, hunger, to say nothing of cold, are all too horribly prevalent in the student world. One came in contact with many sad and hopeless cases that one could do so little to help. I have many times seen nice, cheery girls collapse and faint dead away as they stood at their easels and although they invariably accused the stuffy atmosphere of the life room, I knew that perhaps only a cup of tea had been their breakfast.

'One of the Loveliest Summers'

Chapter X

'LAZY DAYS'
The Bridgeman Art Library

The term had been long and trying; I was tired and dispirited when I had packed my examination studies together and left them in Osborne's charge at the lodge. Even watching him take my sovereign tip and drop it into his pocket like so much worthless dross could not bring the usual smile to my lips, and the slam of the school door on my departing heels was the most welcome sound I had heard for some time.

Two months of country, and freedom, were before me, and I arranged to spend part of the time with Miss Flora Smith at Thatcham, where she had rented a house for several months.

My Uncle and Aunt were also joining her, so we went down *en famille* a day or two after I had bidden good-bye to Burlington House. Little did I know the pleasure that awaited me on the banks of the Kennet River, as from the train I watched fields and hedges fly past. I was looking forward to a dull holiday cooped up with three elderly people with whom I had few tastes in common. I had brought plenty of sketching things with me and hoped to be able to use them without causing offence to my hostess; but with her beloved doctor quite willing to play piquet for hours on end when she felt disinclined to walk, I saw a chance of escaping on my bicycle to paint, read, or fish as the spirit moved me.

The house was new and ugly, with only the suggestion of a garden half made. There were stables and coach houses at the back, where I found the two fat horses and the heavy landau already comfortably housed. I made up my mind on sight of them that nothing would induce me to drive behind such dreadful animals, whose best pace might touch five miles an hour, walking up every hill and down the other side, with the brake on as far as it would go. My bicycle was my safeguard and I determined to be many miles away every morning before the rest of the party had risen from their beds.

It was heavenly weather and one of the loveliest summers I can remember. Having fixed canvas, paints, easel and umbrella on to the carrier of my bicycle, I gave out my intentions at dinner that night of doing a lot of outdoor work while I had the chance. Miss Smith agreed

that it was an excellent idea and ordered the butler to serve me breakfast at any hour I wanted it, also to make a packet of sandwiches for my lunch. Next morning I was well away by eight o'clock, pedalling through country new to me, and heading for the river I had heard so much about. Three miles from home I came to the village green, at the back of which was an old and homely public house; here I left my cycle and materials and, taking my lunch with me, I walked along the river bank in search of likely subjects.

I had only gone a short distance when I espied an artist at work on a very large canvas fixed with poles and stay-ropes to keep it steady. His umbrella too was of colossal size, and an extra piece of awning had been erected to keep sun or glare off painter and picture. He appeared to be an elderly man, short and stocky in figure, with curly iron-grey locks and moustache. He wore a knickerbocker suit of Harris tweed and was resting on a camp-stool, absently filling a briar pipe while his eyes devoured the beauty of the subject he had chosen. The path led me within a few yards of his easel, across which he had pegged one of his stay-ropes.

As soon as he noticed my approach he came up and apologised for obstructing the right of way. I said that I would give him a free pardon provided I was permitted to look at his picture; and that was the beginning of the long and delightful friendship between David Murray[1] and myself.

For the best part of eight weeks we painted together morning, noon and evening. We took an hour's spell at lunch-time, and half an hour at four o'clock, when David always had a delicious tea brought out from the inn. We only closed our palettes and packed our canvases when the

---

[1] David Murray was born in 1849 in Glasgow. He spent some years in commercial pursuits before he practised as an artist. He was elected an Associate of the Royal Academy in 1891 and academician in 1905; and also became an Associate of the Royal Scottish Academy and of the Royal Society of Painters in Water Colours, and a member of the Royal Scottish Water Colour Society. He was a landscape painter of distinction and two of his pictures, *My Love is Gone A-Sailing* (1884) and *In the Country of Constable* (1903) have been bought for the National Gallery of British Art. He died in 1933.

sun had sunk too low behind the hills for us to do another touch of work. All paraphernalia safely stowed in an empty room at the pub, we mounted our bicycles and rode home in the cool dusk of the evening. Very occasionally Miss Smith persuaded David to dine at her house, but he much preferred his own snug lodgings in a rose-covered cottage. He was very appreciative of Miss Smith but he frankly detested my Aunt and all she stood for. To him she represented the idle rich who had never done an honest day's work in their lives. He feared her influence would be detrimental to my work.

He was then a man of forty-five or so, an Associate of the Academy and rapidly rising to the position of fame which he was determined to reach. One day we were resting at midday, enjoying tea and sandwiches in the sunshine before moving on to our afternoon subjects. I had deftly turned the conversation from the everlasting line of colour or technique, and had got well away on some scientific trail I was intent on following, when I was pulled up short by a dour David and severely reprimanded for my lack of consecutive thought. I was duly instructed that 'Fame' lay at the extreme end of a long straight road that any diversion from the main track delayed achievement, and several diversions prohibited it entirely.

I was twenty-two when I sat on that sunny bank of the Kennet and Avon Canal and discussed the subject of 'Fame' with David Murray but I remember thinking what a deadly dull trek it would be. 'Fame' did not hold out for me the entrancing light that it evidently did for David. It was not the amount of work that scared me, for I was ever a glutton for work at anything I wanted to do; but with so many wonderful and beautiful things in the world I thought about all I should miss in life with only one solitary purpose.

Sir David Murray rose from being a Glaswegian coachbuilder's son to that of a respected and wealthy artist but he had no particle of mind left for anything else. He practised what he preached, no side-line ever entered into his life at all.

I saw much of him in London after that summer at Thatcham. We were devoted friends and in his studio would stand arm in arm before his row of pictures, criticizing a little, admiring much, for he had an in-born satisfaction in his own work which, on one occasion, led to me being momentarily very much disliked.

He was just back from his summer's work and had that year been painting at Shoreham; one of his four six-foot canvases was a seascape with the tide half out and right in the foreground he had put an important group of horses with men bathing them in the sea. Now David's weak point was that he had never been taught to draw; so long as he kept to small unimportant figures in his pictures, his lack of drawing did not matter, but on this occasion he had ventured too far, and the faulty drawing of this group of horses spoilt an otherwise very nice picture. I, unfortunately, when looking at it, asked if the animals in the foreground were sea-horses, as I had never seen their like before. I do not remember what he said, but I very nearly got put out of his studio for good and all. His ego was wounded to the quick and I had to crawl back with apologies before I was forgiven. The scene ended by me promising to bring him a cast of a group of horses I had modelled, so that from these he might correct the anatomy of his sea-equines. Peace was therefore restored, but I never again tried to be witty when looking at his work!

Dear David, he attained the fame he worked so hard to reach and well he deserved all he got for no man ever stuck closer to his guns than David to his art.

'That Awful Room'

Chapter XI

Those quiet weeks of outdoor work came to an end rather abruptly, for one morning I opened a letter from Mrs B. reminding me of my promise to paint for her again, and asking me to come before the end of my holiday and make a couple of portraits of prize-winning Shire stallions. Much as I wished to continue the landscape work with David Murray, I could not afford to refuse these commissions, so I replied to her letter and arranged to be with her in three days' time. Having no wish to stay in her house again, I suggested that I should lodge in the village, making an excuse that I worked better when alone with no distractions. By return post she wrote that the horses lived at one of her farms where there was an empty manor-house kept by a caretaker, and that I could stay there close to the stables. This arrangement suited me very well, but I begged Miss Smith for the loan of Chieftain to keep me company in the evenings and to sleep in my bedroom at night. My urgent request was granted, and a day or two later Chief and I arrived at the same little country station and this time we were met by a milk cart. A smart looking cob was between the shafts with a peal of bells attached to the pad of its harness. I had noticed, when staying with Mrs B. before, that all her carriage horses carried chimes of silver bells on their backs, a curious eccentricity, one of the many practised by this strange lady. She was waiting at the farm to greet me in the same costume as of yore and gave me a warm welcome in which Chief took part.

While my luggage was being taken out of the milk float, we visited the two Shire stallions: a dapple grey and a dark brown, both good specimens of the breed, and I was thankful to find them living in large light loose boxes excellent for painting in. Both horses were very quiet and turned their great heads with friendly whinnies when we offered them carrots and lumps of sugar. The grey was particularly fine, and Mrs B. had him bridled and told the groom to put me on his back. I had never been on a Shire horse stallion before, but it was well worth the trouble of getting there, for no one can have any conception of the immense size of these animals from looking at them from ground level. To realise their width and bulk you must get on top and look down; you will then marvel at the breadth of crest and back and understand why the men who take these sires to mares around the country, always sit sideways when riding them.

The stallion boxes formed part of a substantially built old fashioned farmyard in which many pedigree cattle also had homes; everything was beautifully kept and the stock was in excellent condition. It needed only one glance to see that the owner was a proper animal lover and spared no money in making their lives comfortable and happy.

The house, which dated from the sixteenth century, had come down in the world. Such a building had never begun life as a farmhouse with a cattle-yard twelve feet away from its back door. It was built in grey weather-beaten stone, gabled, with an intricate roof and majestic chimneystacks: a house that should have been surrounded by a park with an avenue of noble trees. Instead the tall wrought iron gates only helped to enclose a small front garden and keep out a flock of sheep feeding in a muddy turnip field. All the pretty stone mullioned and latticed windows were severely closed, and had accumulated dust on the leaded panes. They showed it was a long time since the bedrooms had known a breath of fresh air.

We entered the house by the back door, opening into a wide flagged passage, immediately on the right of which was the original kitchen of this mansion, now arranged as a bed-sitting room for the blowsy old caretaker who waddled out to meet us. Mrs B. explained that the woman and her daughter lived in the kitchen, and only one other room on the ground floor boasted any furniture, it being occasionally used for shooting luncheons. Upstairs too the rooms were all empty, with the exception of the first on the right at the top of the stairs. In this was a bed, a table and a chair, but she added, 'I have not been upstairs for so long I almost forget what it is like. The bedrooms are never used; you can sleep there if you choose, but I should advise you to have a bed made up on the couch in the luncheon room.'

Having given the caretaker orders for my meals and bidding her look after me properly, Mrs B. returned home, leaving me to make what other arrangements I liked.

The sitting room, though sparse of furniture, was comfortable enough, but the couch on which I had been recommended to sleep was not an inviting bed, being very narrow and extremely hard; so I decided to try the upstairs room and asked the woman to make up the bed for me. She hesitated a good deal before complying, then called for her daughter to come and help her. The girl, on hearing that the bedroom was to be got ready, looked scared to death and began explaining how much better it would be if I slept on the couch. Taking them for a lazy couple out to shirk any extra work, I insisted that the bed should be made and a bath prepared, so that I could wash and change before supper.

From the cupboard in the kitchen they collected sheets and blankets and led the way up the black oak staircase. After opening the door on the right of the landing they stumbled down two steep steps into a room that had the appearance of a square shallow well, which smelt stuffy and damp from long disuse. It was with some difficulty I moved the rusty steel latches of the windows and flung them wide, at the same time telling the girl to light a fire as the room needed airing.

The bed was an immense four poster, now dismantled of its canopy and curtains. It stood out into the room with the head against the wall immediately facing the door, and the foot reaching to within four or five feet of the two steps. There was little space left for a dressing table and chair.

There was no artificial lighting other than oil lamps and candles, so the house was black and gloomy, and much as I wished to examine the upper storey, the long bare corridor facing my bedroom looked so eerie and dismal that I preferred to leave the exploration for a daylight amusement.

At about half-past nine that evening I lit my candle, and Chieftain and I went up to bed. The fire that had been lit before supper had been left unattended and was now out, and the bath I had used had not been removed. It was quite evident that neither servant had entered the room since I had left it earlier in the evening.

Before getting into bed I thought it might be advisable to lock the door, and I took the candle over to see whether the key was too rusty to turn. Instead of an ordinary lock I found the door was provided with a long flat steel bolt which passed through a couple of hasps fixed on to the lintel. So strong was this fastening that it looked as if it might have been taken from the door of a prison. Having shot the bolt home and turned the neck down into its notch, I jumped into bed by the side of Chieftain, who had already made himself thoroughly comfortable with his head on the pillow, and I expect we were both fast asleep within ten minutes.

How long I had been sleeping I have no notion, when I was suddenly awakened by a tremendous bang and a vicious snarl and bark from Chief, who leaped off the bed. The room was flooded with moonlight when I found myself sitting bolt upright gazing through the now open door right into the dark tunnel of the passage opposite. Chief, with hackles straight on end, was standing in the doorway growling as though about to attack.

It was some seconds before I quite realized what had happened, then, lighting the candle, I got out of bed to quieten the dog and examine the door. The bang had been caused by the door being flung back against the panelling of the wall; but how could it have possibly come open? There was nothing broken; the bolt had been lifted out of the slot and drawn back, both hasps remained firmly embedded in the wood. The window was certainly hooked back, but the night was still and no gust of wind could have flung a firmly bolted door open in this way. The dog continued to growl and stare down the passage; he was trembling with either excitement or fear, I was not sure which. I pulled him back by his collar, closed the door and again fixed the bolt, this time with extra care. I also shut the window, trying to persuade myself that a wind had caused the trouble. Chief was worried and restless; it took a little time to quieten him down.

I had put out the light and we were settling to sleep once more when there came another crash, and the door flew open again. This time the dog leaped right over the foot of the bed, sprang through the doorway and bounded down the corridor, barking, snarling and snapping. As soon as I could light a candle I followed him; he was then coming towards me with his tail down, continually glancing back over his shoulder at something of which he was afraid. I could neither see nor hear anything at all. He cowered against my legs whimpering and shaking all over as I led him back to the room.

Again I refused to become alarmed, although the dog's condition troubled me. He was afraid, and I had never known him to show fear before. His idea now was to get under the bed and hide. This I could not allow. With one hand holding his collar I fixed the bolt with the other and when all was secure managed to half drag, half lift him on to the bed by my side. I consoled him and encouraged him for some time, and the intermittent fits of shivering became gradually less frequent and the expression in his eyes more normal. He was responding to human comfort, licking my face and hands, when, turning towards the bedside table to put the light out once more, to my horror I saw the door opening again, this time quite slowly, as though someone had hold of the handle. There was no sound but the noise of my own heart going like a sledgehammer. Chief, who had seen the door move at the same moment as I had, became as a rabid dog in a fit of frenzy. With a roar like a lion he flung himself off the bed and tore down the passage, uttering the muffled sounds of a dog in the thick of a fight. Following up as fast as I could, I found him at the far end of the corridor close to a door that was bolted on our side; the dog was insane with fury and fear. The floor was thick in dust and I looked for footmarks other than my own; there were none to be seen. I then tried all the doors along the passage every one was locked.

As it was useless to shut the door I now left it open, got a book out of my suitcase and read for the rest of the night. As soon as it was day-light I dressed and took Chief for a walk.

I was both shaken and distressed, for, during the night, I had been up against an inexplicable force, a phenomenon that could not be reasoned away. Little things I had heard and noticed the evening before now returned to my mind with new meaning. The strong recommendation to sleep downstairs both by Mrs B. and the caretakers; the unwilling-ness of the latter to make the bed or bring up a bath; the room left in disorder because they would not enter it after dark – too frightened to tell me anything – the whole atmosphere thick with fear.

The house was haunted; that was the reason it had fallen from the aristocratic position it should have held; that was why it had been denuded of park, avenue and pleasure grounds, and left to dust and decay. As I looked back on it from a distant meadow I felt sorry, for one always feels sorrow when some object of loveliness gets broken and degraded; I so wished it could be swept clean of the spirit of evil that held it in possession.

A long walk in the freshness of morning soon cleared away the horrors of the night; I came back fit and hungry for breakfast and ready to start on the day's work. I had decided to abandon any attempt to sleep upstairs again, for a few more nights like the one I had just experienced and painting would have been out of the question. I was being paid to paint, and not to exorcise evil spirits, so after breakfast I brought my things downstairs and told the servant I would in future sleep on the couch. On hearing this she asked no questions, but I heard an unmistakable sigh of relief.

I had asked Chieftain to come and help me move my clothes to the downstairs room, but he refused even to approach the foot of the stairs, and when I tried to lead him up he threw himself on his back with paws in the air, imploring me not to make him face that awful room again.

I sent this story to *The Tatler* some years ago, when that paper offered a prize for the best true 'Queer Story' consisting of so many words; it was necessarily curtailed in consequence. It was published and I received a cheque for three guineas. The names of writers were not printed. I write this note to indicate that this story is not a crib. It is perfectly true, and everything happened as described above.

HRH PRINCESS
ALEXANDRA,
PRINCESS OF
WALES

by Theobald Chartran

*The Bridgeman Art
Library*

The Lovely Princess Alexandra

Chapter XII

It doesn't matter what you paint; learn to paint
Riviere

By the time I had finished the portraits of Mrs B's Shire horses I was due back in London. My last term's studies had got me my promotion to the Upper School, so I was to work with the senior scholars. That term I cut some of the schoolwork to start on a large cartoon for competition, which I was able to do at the Alexandra House studio. The subject was 'A Roman Empress' and I could not find a model that in any way suggested the type of head I wanted. At last in desperation I went to Lord Leighton to see if he knew of any woman who would fit the part and he gave me the loan of two models he retained for his own pictures, one for the head and the other for the figure.

The head model was a strange little creature. Her head was twice the size it ought to have been set on a pair of thin narrow shoulders, hardly strong enough to support it, but it was a beautiful head, clearly cut and Grecian in type. The figure model was plain, even ugly, but tall and very statuesque, strong as a lion and could hold a standing pose for over two hours.

Lord Leighton used her for the thin drapery he was so fond of painting;

he used to put this on her wet, so that it stuck to her skin and the lines of the nude figure showed through it.

Similarly the under dress of my Empress was of very fine silk muslin. She was posed on top of a flight of marble stairs, and from her shoulders hung a long heavy robe of dark coloured brocade which cascaded down to the step below her feet. This necessitated posing the model four and a half feet off the ground, so that I could look up at her. Very few models could have stood at that height for half an hour without falling, and I was nervous of asking this one to do it. The thin under dress was the trouble; it kept slipping and the folds I wanted would not remain in place. The only thing to do was to soak it in water and put it on the model wet, but I felt it would be cruel to ask a woman to stand with a nasty damp rag clinging to her body and legs; also I was afraid she might die of pneumonia and that I would be held responsible for her death. However, she herself at last insisted on wringing the stuff out in warm water and clothing herself in it as she stood on the pedestal, and whenever she felt it getting dry and likely to slip, she told me to apply a spongeful of water. She assured me that she had sat in wet drapery for Lord Leighton for several years, and was well accustomed to it. She was a heroic person, but I believe I suffered for her a lot more than she suffered herself. I eventually completed an enormous work, the size of the cartoon being 10 ft x 5 ft. It was hung later in the Concert Hall at Alexandra House.

One morning when my model was standing, and I was working as rapidly as I could with big lumps of charcoal, with which I had smeared my face and blackened my smock, the hall porter came and called me out of the studio, saying that I was wanted at once in the Council room.

A summons to the Council room usually meant that you were going to be severely reprimanded for breaking rules and this was the first time I had ever been called down. My conscience was quite clear, I was much annoyed at the interruption in my work, for I was paying double money to very special models, and I grudged every moment of wasted time while they were sitting. I therefore thought I would give the Council a treat and appear before them black and dirty as I was, a really pretty sight with a fine sooty smudge right across my nose. Serve them jolly well right for disturbing me when I had done nothing wrong.

I was taken from the top of the house to the bottom, in the lift, a thing we were forbidden to use unless dead, maimed, or arrested for some crime. The hall porter, a tall, very smart ex-Guardsman, wore a most annoying smirk on his face during our voyage to the ground-floor and would give me no information as to who was attending the Council. I dearly hoped Sir Francis Cook, the Founder, would be in the chair.

I meekly knocked at the door of the Council Chamber and was told to come in. On entering, I was much surprised to find no meeting; Sir Francis and the Lady Superintendent were standing in very deferential attitudes in front of three ladies who were sitting with their backs towards the door. When they saw me their expressions underwent a sudden change from deference to horror. So marked was the contrast of a moment before that all three ladies simultaneously turned their heads in my direction, and to my utter amazement I recognized HRH The Princess of Wales and her two daughters. Instinctively, I performed my best Court curtsey. A smile of intense amusement spread over the lovely face of Her Royal Highness as she beckoned me to her chair and held out her hand in greeting. I was profuse in my apologies for entering her presence in such a dreadful condition, and added that I had thought I was in for a Council lecture about something that I knew I had not done, and as I had a model sitting I had not troubled to tidy up. She said she did not in the least mind the smut on my nose or my charcoaly hands, she had sent for me because she wanted to see the girl residing in her House who had painted such an admirable portrait of 'Duke', the old blind lion at the Zoo. I had quite forgotten that at the request of the Lady Superintendent, Miss Palmer, I had left this life-sized study of the lion's head on an easel in the Council room, intending later to send it to the Academy. (This study was accepted and hung at that year's exhibition, and it was sold on the opening day.) The Princess told me she knew the old lion very well, and often went to visit him. After a few more enquiries about my work, and whether I was happy and comfortable in her students' home, I was dismissed to show Princess Maud over the College, she insisted on seeing my rooms, and also the drawing I was doing in the Studio. Before escorting her back to the Council room she kindly allowed me to wash and put on a clean pinafore, so my farewell obeisance was rather more dignified.

The Princess of Wales took a great interest in Alexandra House and the students residing there. She often paid surprise visits and I had the honour of meeting her quite a number of times.

The Mouse and Jim Crow

Chapter XIII

yours very truly "Mouse".

THE MOUSE

Much as I loved my work, in winter I could not resist the temptation of an occasional day with hounds. I had been given an adored little mare – The Mouse – who lived in a friend's stable in Surrey, and it was the delight of my life to feel her stout body under me and the steel spring lift as she cleared her fences, as well as the stiffest five barred gates we could possibly find.

On this particular mare I seldom bothered to open a gate; she hopped over timber with the greatest ease. I never heard her rap a bar. She rushed her fences and went the same pace at stiff timber as she did at water, but I soon found that it was her way of jumping and never attempted to check her. She allowed for swampy ditches and rotten take-off; she seldom made a mistake and never once put me down.

The only time I can remember her coming on to her knees was near Three Bridges, when the stag crossed the railway embankment and, at the place he chose, it was high and steep. The huntsman and I were in front of the field, and he was riding his favourite horse, old 'Blarney'. It was a long way to the nearest gate, and hounds were running like smoke. I sang out to the huntsman, 'Let's have it, Spence,' and we went at the quickset gate, with posts and rails through it, neck and neck. Blarney was a clever, sober Sussex hunter, and steadied to almost a trot when he saw what was in front of him; The Mouse was more fitted for Leicestershire, and, putting on steam, attacked the fence and bank at racing speed. The bank on landing was so steep we had to throw ourselves forward on to our horses' necks to prevent them falling backwards. Crossing the railway line on the other side both animals skidded down the bank on their hocks. I can't think how they managed to take off at all, but they did it somehow, cleared the fence and landed on nose and knees the other side. The mare and I did not part company. Spence just slipped off over his horse's shoulder, but was up again in a second; no one tried to follow us, and we alone whipped hounds off two or three fields further on.

People who know nothing about it make a song of the cruelty of hunting a deer taken by cart to the hunt for the chase. If there had been

'A nasty fence at the bottom of the railway
embankment, the wiser members of the hunt
had time to go round.
met at Rusper.'

any cruelty attached to it I should have been one of the first to shout. I never witnessed anything approaching cruelty, nor a single stag hurt. Two of the best deer that ran for the Warnham Stag Hounds were 'The Belle of Newdigate' and 'Jim Crow'. They both did ten seasons and ended their days in luxury in a lovely park. These animals used by the hunt were kept all the hunting season in sheltered yards, and fed on corn and best hay, as much as they could eat. They were in splendid condition and lived in warmth and comfort when their brethren out at pasture were often searching under snow for a bite of frozen grass. The

THE RAILWAY
CUTTING
'A nasty fence at the
bottom of the railway
embankment, the wiser
members of the hunt
found time to go round.
Met at Rusper.'

99

two I have mentioned with many others whose names I have forgotten, enjoyed the runs as much as the hounds, horses and horsemen destined to follow them over any line of country they chose to take. They had no fear of hounds or humanity; when 'taken' at the end of the day, anyone who was first up would throw an arm over their necks and lead them into the nearest shed, where they were fed and cared for until their cart arrived to take them home.

When Jim Crow was un-carted at a meet, he would walk out with head in air and the dainty springy step of a racehorse. Fit and full of corn, he would stand for some minutes sniffing and testing the wind; when he had quite decided the direction in which to take us, he would break into a steady trot to the fence enclosing the field, and spring with

THE STAG BOX THAT THE WARNHAM HUNT USED TO TRANSPORT THEIR 'CARTED DEER'.

unhurried perfect ease over the topmost twigs and carry on at the same confident pace – no hustle, no rushing, no driving, no fear. He had his liberty for the day and he made the most of it. He never gave us less than a ten mile chase and often more, and if the wind was right he invariably made for the sea, and had a good swim before being captured from a boat and brought to shore.

On Jim's days a second horse was a necessity, for one hunter could never have survived the distance he accomplished.

I remember one great run he gave from Rusper Village, a few miles from Horsham, when he landed us on the sands near Worthing at very low tide and where it took ages to launch a boat. The huntsman and whips waded in to try and coax him ashore, but he paddled up and down just out of their reach until a boat was got out to round him up.

JIM CROW

On another cold wet morning I left London for Horsham and drove there in a stuffy four-wheel fly to the meet. I was riding a grey, four year old filly as my first horse. She had never been hunted before and she fell as regularly as clockwork over the lowest rail of timber, but she was a good enough ride over fences. Jim Crow went off with an unusual rattle of speed and, the weather being nasty, hounds were loosed after him fairly soon; there was a roaring scent up to the time of the first check, and by avoiding every stick of timber like the plague, I had kept the filly going with the best of them. She had a good turn of speed, but the pace and deep going were fast cooking her, so I was relieved when I heard the huntsman check the hounds in a narrow lane ahead. The only possible way of getting into that lane was over a gate with the top rail up, both of which were nailed in. The fence was unjumpable and there was nothing for it but to have a shot at the timber. I knew what was going to happen before I put the filly at it; she did not refuse, but she took the top rail somewhere above her knees and turned a complete somersault into the middle of horses and hounds standing in the lane, and solidly lay on top of me until she was dragged off. I was rather cut about the head and face, but she was apparently quite unhurt, for which I was thankful, as she did not belong to me.

For the remainder of the run I rode The Mouse, and got home to the stables so late and so tired I did not see the grey filly until the next morning, when at seven o'clock the stud groom sent up a message to say that he thought the filly had been badly injured by the fall and was likely to die. I jumped into a few clothes and ran down to the stables. There she was like a fixture standing with her hindquarters propped up against the wall of the box, forelegs pushed right out in front, neck and nose stretched out as well. I had never seen a horse stand in such an unnatural and extraordinary position and what was worse, she would make no attempt to move. She had evidently been standing like this all night, and had not lain down at all. She would look at neither food nor water. When we rubbed her she grunted and groaned in a dreadful way. She really looked as though she might drop down dead any minute. Yet I could not understand this condition, for the second horseman said she had jogged home freely and well and had taken her gruel as well as a small feed of oats. Well, there she was, as still and stiff as a wooden horse, with her eyes starting out of her head. Everyone said 'done for' and a telegram summoning the best horse vet in London was sent.

Some hours later when he arrived and saw her still in the same position he was amazed. He listened attentively to the history of the fall and all the rest I could tell him, sitting the while on a stable bucket and staring at the mare. Suddenly his expression changed, and to my relief a smile broke in his eyes, as he asked me her age and what hunting she had done before. On learning she was four and had never been hunted before, he jumped up from his seat and called for all hands, and slipping a rope round her neck she was pushed and pulled and dragged into the yard. There she was given a tremendous crack with a crop over her quarters and, after a stagger or two, she walked away as sound as a bell. The whole trouble had been just stiffness and terror, because she had never been stiff and sore before, she was afraid to move! Our relief on seeing her walk was so great that we began to laugh, including the vet, who chaffed us unmercifully about paying a ten guinea fee for a horse doctor to move a stiff horse from its stable.

I also had some grand hunting with the Blackford Vale pack near Dorchester and with the South and West Wilts hunt, often having to leave Alexandra house at three in the morning. I had some nice gallops over the Sparkford Vale country but one needed a fast horse to live with hounds over the flat grassland and fly fences in which the vale abounded. It was a 'go as you please' steeple chase course, nothing to stop a bold horse and nothing to stop hounds who fairly skither when scent is good. In those days we had to work for our sport. When hounds went back to the kennel we did not ride to the nearest telephone office and call up a chauffeur with well filled tea basket to whisk home in luxury ourselves, leaving a groom the drudgery of riding back dirty, weary horses. No fast cars, fur rugs and foot warmers for us; we often rode many miles to a meet and many more home at night. But a few days hunting each season was not a waste of time, for I got to know more and more wealthy people who employed me to paint their favourite animals. In consequence, during the autumn vacation I spent my time going from one country house to another, painting animal portraits and, incidentally, having a very good time. One of these commissions was at a country house in Wiltshire, and what happened there is worthy of a chapter to itself.

'TRUE FRIENDS'

'A Country House in Wiltshire'

Chapter XIV

While hunting with the South and West Wilts I was introduced to a young couple, Mr and Mrs X, with lots of money and a fine old place. Eventually, I was asked to stay and paint some hunters for them. The day I was due to arrive, the Xs had unexpectedly been summoned to London for a night. Instead of putting me off, and altering my arrangements, they left a letter with the butler telling me to make myself at home until they came back the following evening.

There were no other guests and after dining in solitary state the butler, who had served the family for many years, showed me into the drawing room. It was a big gloomy looking room, hung all round with full length ancestral portraits and a wood fire was burning on the hearth. I chose the best chair and settled down to finish an exciting thriller I had been reading on the journey from London.

I was entirely absorbed in my book when I became aware of someone or something approaching me from the French windows in the wall opposite the fireplace. There was no sound, but a feeling that I was no longer alone and instinctively I looked round to see who, or what, it was. There was nothing visible but all the same, whatever it was was slowly coming towards me and the impression thrust on my mind was that I was being enveloped in an atmosphere of intense evil. It so terrified me that I lost control and sprang for the bell. A minute afterwards, when the butler opened the door, I realized what a fool he would think me if

I told him the reason I had rung. I therefore made the excuse that the fire needed attention. The old man looked at me rather strangely before sweeping up the hearth and adding a small log to an already bright blaze, and he pottered about for a few minutes before leaving the room once more.

By the time he left I had more or less recovered composure and settled to my reading, resolved to keep off foolish fancies and enjoy the remainder of the story. But I had hardly got the length of a page before I was again seized with the knowledge that something very dreadful was coming near me. Putting all power of resistance into force I kept my eyes firmly fixed on my book, yet the cold sweat of fear was trickling from my forehead. Nearer and nearer came this invisible terror until it seemed to me it actually sat on the arm of my chair, when again my nerve failed me and I rang a peal on the bell that must have alarmed the house. The butler appeared so instantly that he undoubtedly had been standing outside the door.

This time I was past making excuses and, trembling, I told him what I had felt and begged him to sit down and stay by me. He showed no surprise at all and remarked that I was not the first lady who had asked him to sit with her rather than remain in the room by herself. Shortly afterwards he escorted me to my bedroom; to reach it we passed through two swing doors opposite the first flight of stairs, which led into a long passage with many rooms both right and left, the one allotted to me being on the right at the very end; here the old man bade me good night and took his departure.

Next evening my hosts came home, and after dinner we played billiards to close on midnight. The billiard room was underground, part of a vaulted cellar over which the front of the house was built. This cellar was like a rabbit warren with narrow passages and small rooms, and the stone work, floors, walls and ceilings were covered with bright red straw matting, lit throughout with numbers of electric bulbs; the effect was fascinating and rather weird. One of these underground rooms was fitted up as a carpenter's workshop, where every conceivable tool had its place on the shelves. Mr X. was a clever carpenter and a lot of his spare time was spent in this workshop.

After billiards we said good night at the swing doors and went our separate ways: the Xs' bedroom being at the front of the house.

My bedroom was a good sized room with a single bed, a big window on one side and a fireplace on the other. There was no extra night lamp on the table and the light had to be turned off near the mantelpiece. As usual I was asleep as soon as my head touched the pillow. How long I slept I have no idea before I was awakened by a cold draught on my body, then the bedclothes were stripped off me and thrown over the foot rail. I cannot say that this scared me at all, as I had seen enough of my host already to think he would not be above playing a practical joke on a guest. Having by now turned on the light, I took my time searching for the joke string; but search as I did, I discovered nothing that could have removed the blankets and sheets at all. Setting to work to remake the bed I wondered how the trick had been accomplished. Still pondering, I slept lightly. The second movement of the bedclothes brought me quickly to a sitting position to watch while they were *lifted* off me and *placed* over the end of the bed. I write the two words in italics because it was just as though invisible hands had stripped the bed – a couple of housemaids could not have done it more neatly.

I now began to get jumpy, but determined to have another look round. Finding nothing to account for the mystery, I left the light on and got back to bed. I was wide awake when a few minutes later a heavy weight seemed to plump down on the edge of the spring mattress, and get up again immediately, shaking me violently up and down as I lay. For the rest of the night I read, and nothing further happened.

Before breakfast next morning I met my host on the verandah outside the dining room windows, where two or three small rifles were arranged on stands. Laughingly he said: 'No one is allowed breakfast until they have hit the bull's eye; take which gun you like and try your luck.' At the end of the lawn was a small target about fifty or sixty yards distant, and being a fairly good shot, it did not look a very difficult task. But I soon found that my disturbed night had so affected my nerves that I not only failed to get a bull, but even failed to hit the target, and in consequence I was unmercifully chaffed until I retaliated by saying that I did not like ghosts.

No sooner were the words out of my mouth than I regretted them, because such an expression of trouble showed on the faces of Mr and Mrs X. My host stopped his teasing and solemnly asked me if I would write down my night's experience, suggesting that I should change my room to one nearer theirs.

I very soon forgot all about things uncanny when I was taken to the splendid stables and in one spacious building saw twenty chestnut horses in stalls on either side! Mr X was a keen coaching man and these animals composed his teams; he drove nothing but chestnuts and was lucky enough to have the wherewithal to indulge his whim. I had never seen a better kept nor finer lot of coach horses. Substantial looking wheelers on one side of the building and the lighter made leaders on the other. My work, however, was with the hunters, an equally valuable collection, and I was soon transferring a prize winning heavy weight on to a large clean canvas.

Mr X was a big game hunter and a traveller, and was shortly going on an expedition to Egypt. Every afternoon he would go to his workshop to make folding chairs and tables which would pack easily on to a camel. As soon as the light failed I used to help him. This camp furniture was cleverly and neatly designed and being fond of using tools myself I would help him and my tables were soon as well made as his.

One evening I was alone in the workshop finishing something we had begun the day before. I was sitting intently at a lathe, when I once more experienced the same sensation I had suffered the first night in the drawing room. The same evil presence was approaching me and the same uncontrollable fear seized me. I dropped everything, made a rush for the door and up the stairs into the hall, where I ran into the butler, to whom I confided the reason for my flight. He begged me not to mention the matter to his master, who, though not troubled by it himself, was perfectly aware that the uncanny horror existed. It seemed that no servant whose duty it was to clean and dust the cellars and drawing room ever stayed more than a month, and often left at a moment's notice, not even troubling to take their wages. He advised me never to go to the workshop by myself, and never to remain alone in the drawing room. There was also an old tea house in the garden where again the terror attacked me.

One night another strange thing occurred. I had dressed for dinner and was walking along the passage from my room when I heard a parrot talking in the most wonderful way. I was so interested in the bird that I stopped to listen and, locating the room in which it seemed to be, knocked at the door. There being no reply I turned the handle and found that the door was locked. On arriving in the drawing room I at once asked to be allowed to see the parrot who talked so fluently. There was dead silence for a second, then Mr X said: 'You must have been mistaken; there is not a parrot in the house.' I persisted that there was, and that perhaps it belonged to one of the maids. I was again assured that no such bird existed, and the subject was quickly changed.

I visited this house several times to paint various animals for the owners and much the same things always happened. Some years later I had a photograph of the house in my studio, and the mother of one of my pupils, noticing it, asked me if I had stayed there. I told her I had done a lot of painting there and thought the place very beautiful. 'Beautiful!' she exclaimed. 'I once spent a night in that house and nothing would induce me ever to cross its threshold again. It is haunted by an indescribably evil spirit and should be shut up or pulled down.'

Many years later still I happened to be painting for some other people in this district, and rode over to call on the Xs. I found them living in a smaller house near the park gates; the big house had been shut and empty for some time.

These unaccountable facts I cannot attempt to explain. That I am susceptible to atmosphere I have no doubt at all. The lifting of the bedclothes I give up on entirely; it is far beyond my very ordinary comprehension.

I again met the atmospheric effect in a house in North Wales. This place had been lent for a few months to some people for whom I was painting, but though they were handed the keys of the whole house, only a few bedrooms were being occupied. When I was expected another room was opened and chosen because it had a good north light. The moment I entered the room I exclaimed at the nastiness of it, and then had to apologize for being so rude. The room was ugly, and there was a bad copy of Murillo's Virgin over the mantelpiece, but neither the ugliness nor the picture caused the exclamation, it was the feel of the room that I instantly disliked. Every night that I slept in that room I awakened at exactly the same hour, and for twenty minutes lay paralyzed with terror, my eyes riveted on the bay window. At the end of the time the fear would leave me and again I slept.

On leaving North Wales I went to paint a group of springer spaniels for the late Charles Everett at Denne Park, Horsham. The first evening I was there he asked me whether I had enjoyed my visit to North Wales, saying that the owner of the house was an old friend of his and the best trainer of gun dogs in the world. After talking about the Butters and their dogs, I referred to the house and told him of the horrid nights I had experienced there. He knew the house well and had stayed in it years before the Butters had possession. On learning which room I had occupied, he told me that I had been put into the haunted room which was never used by the owner of the place and that under the carpet in the bay of the window was the stain of a large pool of blood, and splashes of blood in all directions. A horrible murder had been committed there about a hundred years ago and the room had remained haunted ever since.

At the Zoological Gardens

about 1897

Chapter XV

Student days do not last forever and mine were now fast drawing to a close. Dr Hamilton, a vice President of the Zoo had procured a pass in to the Gardens for me and I was able to go in as early as I liked in the morning and get a lot of work done before visitors began to arrive and interrupt.

The big cats drew me most and I was usually to be found any morning at seven o'clock going round the cages with old Sutton, who had looked after the lions so well for twenty years that he looked like them. His beard started at one ear and passed under his chin in a ragged fringe to reach the other ear closely resembling the immature mane of a young lion. His hair, that stood out from his head and grew to a point on his forehead, was an excellent imitation of the top part of the mane.

The pacing backwards and forwards of these caged animals troubled me, but many years later I was destined to see lion in the wild pace in exactly the same way when watching a mob of my cattle standing round a camp fire on moonlight nights. They marched backwards and forwards, just out of the firelight, to a point on either side, when crossing their forelegs they wheeled as though stopped by a wall.

While I was painting at the Zoo a couple of young male lions arrived from East Africa. They were about twelve months old, fully grown in height, but still undeveloped, with huge paws and light-looking bodies.

These youngsters were put into a cage away from the public view, where they showed their misery by moping and refusing to eat. Sutton was dreadfully worried about them and was afraid they would break their hearts and die. The only time they roused up at all was when I went and talked to them; then they would rub against the bars of their cage and they liked me to stroke them and scratch their ears. As they would not come near a man, I suggested that they had been reared and tamed by a woman, and probably fed from a dish. I therefore got leave to feed them myself from a large tin basin.

The very first night I gave them the food they ate ravenously; Sutton was delighted at the change in them and I continued to feed them for a fortnight. It needed a great deal of persuasion before I got Sutton to let me inside the cage with them, but I eventually managed it and every day I brushed them and romped with them, until they recovered their spirits and condition wonderfully. They had so evidently been hand reared from an early age, and had been petted and talked to. These babies showed no vice at all – soft paws and no needles put out to claw; but their play was rough, and they were heavy to stand up to when they barged against me. Old Sutton suffered tortures of fear every time I went into the cage and kept his eye glued to a peephole. I never had the smallest distrust of the animals.

One was more gentle and would kiss my hands and face with his rough tongue. One morning, when it was his turn to be brushed, I was leaning over him and brushing a leg on the opposite side when the other lion sprang off a shelf on to my back, knocking me and the lion that I was brushing, flat. I was lying on the top of one lion and the other was standing on top of me. It was a unique position to be in sandwiched between two lions, and for the onlooker a rather alarming spectacle. There was really nothing to be alarmed about; the fellow who had jumped on top of us had only done it for fun and the paws on my back were still quite soft. The lion I was lying on did not mind at all and continued his gentle murmur 'ow-o o ow' as I stroked his ears. I heard poor

Sutton's gasping whisper, 'For God's sake don't move.' I had not the smallest intention of struggling, for if I had used any force it was as likely as not I should have felt claws in my back; but remaining limp I knew exactly what the lion on top would do. He soon realized that his joke had failed, and that there was going to be no scrap or rough and tumble, so after sniffing my head and neck he got off and sauntered away, taking no further interest in either of us. As soon as I was off the other lion's ribs he got up and wandered away too, and both sat gazing into space, as lions do, as though nothing whatever had happened. What did grieve me was that I was never allowed inside the cage again.

Another animal that became a great friend of mine was the big African elephant. The way to his heart was down his throat all right and I made a special study of his preference in delicacies. Fresh lettuces and carrots that crunched crisply between his huge back grinders were a most welcome addition to his regular diet and I spent endless trouble in going round small greengrocers shops buying up basketfuls of two day old vegetables to please him. I became so favoured a visitor that his trunk would gently embrace my waist and I would be lifted and securely placed on top of his head, where I remained a prisoner until he chose to put me back on the ground. Sometimes neither the command of the keeper, nor my pleading, would induce him to release me, and I spent more time on top of that elephant's head than I really wanted to.

He resented being put to bed and when told to go to his house he would get into his tank and lie down at the bottom under the water with only the tip of his trunk visible. On being prodded to make him get up he blew avalanches of water over everyone. But the best fun came when he was safely inside his bedroom and the doors were being fastened, for he was not driven out of his tank without first filling his trunk full of water. His good night blessing was a drenching spray which soaked his keepers to the skin.

I cannot leave the story of my large friend without the final touch. For a whole year I had not visited the Gardens when one afternoon I went to spend an afternoon there with a friend who was a naturalist and animal lover. We were walking down the wide drive from the old lion house, when I saw my elephant approaching on the opposite side with a load of children on his back. As he came nearer I noticed he was making attempts to cross the drive and the keeper was trying to prevent him; but he came straight over to where I was standing and put his trunk around my shoulders.

The only other incident that rather thrilled me during a summer's work at the Zoo was when the twenty-three foot python swallowed his mate, who was twenty-four feet in length. That extra foot was the undoing of him and he succumbed to an over lengthy meal!

'Studio to Let'

1897/8

Chapter XVI

'MOTHERLESS'

So it was that my years as a student came to an end and I was destined to leave Alexandra House and make a home of my own. My entire fortune consisted of £60, which did not seem very much to start housekeeping on. I had little idea of what I was going to do, or what was to become of me, as I wandered down Queen's Gate into Gloucester Road. It was an unpleasant sensation suddenly to become homeless and adrift in the world. Youth being intensely brave, I found myself laughing as I spied 'Studio to Let' in a slummy street on my left. It was one of a row of studios, empty, dismal and dirty, with a black stove and chimney sticking out from the wall. The big window was grimed with dust and someone's discarded ragged blind was hanging half over it, practically shutting out what light there might have been. The rent asked for this enchanting palace was £80 a year and since I could not live there, it was necessary to find lodgings as well. I wended my way up Gloucester Road and found the very room I wanted in Victoria Grove. A sitting room and bedroom separated by double doors, and French windows from the sitting room to a tiny square garden: thirty-five shillings a week including breakfast and supper. Mrs Robinson, who owned the house, was a clean, motherly woman. I fell for her at once and took the rooms.

Now I was really in it up to the neck. £164 a year for housing and two meals a day! Painting materials and clothes extra: that £60 looked smaller than ever when another horrible thought struck me – I had no studio easel and not a stick of furniture.

The studio easel, which is a most costly possession, was presented to me within a week by Sir Frederick Haines. I was encouraged to choose the very best, and I did. It was a real beauty; two sided and made of polished oak. I was the proudest woman in London. Then came two Persian rugs from my Aunt and a small sofa from another friend.

I had no money except what I could earn. I gave up all form of recreation such as dining out and going out to plays, feeling I had no right to spend money on cabs and evening clothes. The only outside pleasure I enjoyed was an occasional opera, when the Duke of Bedford was kind enough to lend me his box and, with his usual thoughtfulness, sent a car to take me and bring me back.

It was time to get to work. Luckily for me I got a very good commission at once to paint a large portrait of a golden collie and the money received for this paid for the material and frame of my first Academy picture, a sketch for which I had already completed. I called it *'Nothing venture, nothing win'* and considered it an apt title for a preliminary effort. I painted a bull dog lying asleep outside his kennel, and a black and tan mongrel terrier creeping up to steal his bone.

An old, but very good, white bull dog was lent to me by some

friends in Norfolk; I had to buy the mongrel and found just what I wanted in the Dogs' Home at Battersea – five shillings' worth of mongrel puppy. And as at that time Walter Long MP had passed a law that all dogs had to wear a collar and muzzle, more money had to be expended on these.

This pup was a guttersnipe of the worst description and must have come from a long line of them, for he resented every kindness shown him, and disliked any of form of cleanliness. For the first week I exercised him on a lead until I thought he knew me well enough to follow. I then took him for a run in the Park. No sooner was the lead off him than he bolted into the blue and I lost him. This was a nuisance, for I had already used him for my picture, and required a good many more sittings. I was advised to wait a day or two and go back to the Dogs Home and sure enough I found him there, but of course without his muzzle or collar. Not wishing to buy him again I claimed him and then got run in by the

THIS PICTURE IS
NOT SIGNED
ALTHOUGH SAID
TO BE BY
MARGARET
COLLYER

police for letting a dog out without these accessories. I had to appear at the Police Court, and was duly fined and cautioned by the magistrate, who refused to listen to my explanation.

Another collar and muzzle had to be bought for the little beast and, by tying him up and never letting him off the chain, I managed to keep him until I had finished his portrait. After that I let him run, and the first time he made off again, and I worried no more about him and doubtless he died in the lethal chamber.

When I was about three parts through with this picture, and with the sending in day for the Royal Academy fast approaching, I took Saturday and Sunday off and bicycled down to Godalming to see my grandmother. Coming back on Sunday evening, free-wheeling down Kingston Hill, I came upon a piece of road covered with newly broken flints and, thinking of my tyres, I jumped off my bicycle, which must have been going faster than I had imagined, for I landed with a thud on my left leg and fell with the machine on top of me. I felt no pain at all, but when I tried to get up I found that my left leg was quite useless; below the knee it would not move at all, although the bones were not broken. Nobody happened to be in sight and I could not get up.

Presently a carriage and pair came along, in which were a lady and gentleman. On seeing me, the coachman pulled up and they got out to enquire what had happened. As they were willing to help, I asked them to drive me back to my studio and get a doctor. This they most kindly did. On examining my leg the doctor declared that the sheath of the Achilles tendon was snapped and it would mean weeks on a sofa before I would even be able to hobble. This was dreadful, for if I could not stand, I could not finish my picture for the Academy and there was no money with which to rest and pay doctors. My heart turned to water with anxiety. I implored the man to get me on my legs somehow and, seeing that I intended to try anyway, he suggested putting the injured ankle into plaster of Paris from the knee down.

I managed to send a message to my landlady, asking her to bring a blanket for I had to remain where I was until the doctor could come the next morning to fix me up. I spent a very unenviable night suffering from shock, pain and worry. The next day my leg was encased in plaster, and with the help of a stick I could stand at my easel and get on with the work – a painful process, but it had to be done. More painful still was the walk backwards and forwards to my lodgings, for cab fares were out of the question. I stuck to it and got through; my picture was hung on the line and sold for £100 on the opening day of the exhibition.

And here I tell the rest of the story of this picture as a warning to young artists. I knew nothing about copyright and had no agent. I did know that when I sold my picture I should have put 'Copyright Reserved' on it and registered it at Stationers' Hall. This way there could have been reprints of the picture and I would have benefited. As it was a firm of publishers offered me £50 for the copyright and being unable to get about, I wrote to the purchaser of my picture explaining matters and I asked him if he would be so kind as to come and see me. When he came, I told him of the offer I had had for the copyright and of my ignorance in not registering it, thereby losing £50 unless he would be generous enough to give the publishers access to the picture. This he definitely declined to do, although I offered to paint a portrait of his pet dog in exchange. He was a low-class American, a type of man it is best to avoid. As he would not accept my offer for the rights of reproduction I said no more and bade him good afternoon. I have no recollection of the man's name and never saw him again; I believe he took the picture back with him to America.

The future never occurs to the young. I was quite content with the present. I liked imagining pictures and painting them and I certainly possessed the gift of touching the public mind. When one picture was completed I passed on to another. I never cared what became of them, or whether I got a good price or a bad one. The work I most enjoyed was painting pet animals for people who could not afford to pay for pictures at all, and I think I put better work into these. Not having a spark of business capacity in me, I lost chance after chance of making considerable sums on royalties and copyrights.

I never seemed to learn, for many years later I suffered a bitter disappointment over my Royal Academy picture entitled '*The World Forgetting, by the World Forgot*'. A bad fit of depression attacked me. I felt so convinced that it would not be hung that I did not bother to register the copyright but put rather a higher price on it and let it go at that.

In my misery I had apparently underestimated the quality of the work, for it was not only accepted outright, but hung on the line in the first room. On varnishing day, Mr Riviere told me while there was yet time to double the price, but my mood being such I did not take his advice, fool that I was. The picture was snapped up the morning of the opening day, bought by a clergyman from Devonshire. The next day I had notice that His Majesty King Edward wanted to buy the picture and I was told to find out what the original purchaser would take for it. I did my best, but His Reverence had bought something he wanted and refused to part with it at any price. I then got a good offer for the copyright which did not exist, never having been registered. But I repainted a smaller edition for the publisher, from my sketches, using the same model.

I had not been able to finish in time for the exhibition one rather large picture on my easel. It was called '*Eyes to the Blind*' – a nice subject and showed promise. On its completion a dealer called on me, who was by way of taking pictures and selling on commission. I wanted £200 for '*Eyes to the Blind*' and being hard up would not let it go unless he paid part of the sum down. He therefore gave me a cheque for £60 and took another picture as well.

This stupid mistake ended with a case in the High Courts, the man being convicted of theft by the magistrate and sent for trial.

If I had had the money with which to pay a good Counsel the man would have 'done time'; for during my search for evidence I found he had taken several pictures from the Hon. John Collier, Mr Wyllie and Mr Joseph Farquharson. Mr Wyllie was the only one of the three who

'EYES TO THE
BLIND'
*With thanks to Candace
Lape*

backed me up at all. At the conclusion of the case, the Judge ordered all the pictures to be returned to the artists except for my picture, '*Eyes to the Blind*'. He said he could not force the return of this painting because I had accepted part payment for it. The dealer was severely cautioned and got off with that.

For some years no trace of the picture could be found but many years later when I was in Kenya, I saw an advertisement for Spillers' dog biscuits and on it a reproduction of my missing work!

RORY

Rory

Chapter XVII

After leaving Alexandra House I just could not live another month without a dog and this is the story of the finest dog I ever owned. I wrote to a dog-breeder in Birmingham to send down two Irish terrier puppies for me to choose from[1]. They were pedigree four month old pups; one was priced at £3 and the other at £5. It took me just two minutes to pick the one I was going to keep and of course it was the more expensive. A real red dog with a perfect 'hard jacket', he was compact and square, with a most intelligent head but what pleased me most about him was his self-confidence and fearlessness when let out of his travelling box. His tail never dropped a point, but his brother's was tucked tight down and he hid under the sofa. His price was far more than I could afford at the time, but never was a five pound note invested so well. Rory became the most intelligent and cleverest dog I have ever seen. He earned his cost and his living, for he soon learnt to keep a pose and he became an invaluable model. I had him with me always for sixteen years and when he died half of me was buried with him.

I think Rory in a former existence must have been a yachtsman. One summer[2] after months of gruelling work trying to assuage somewhat the black devil of poverty that ever haunted me, I started to cough, but carried on until one morning I had a hemorrhage from the lungs. It

---

[1] About 1897 or 1898.

[2] This might have been about 1903.

was alarming and became more so when my own doctor took me to see a lung specialist, who gave me six months to live unless I stopped all work and went into a sanatorium on the morrow. It happened that I had a pupil at that time, Helen Compton, of whom I was very fond and it was a good day for me when I became acquainted with her parents. Mr Compton had made a lot of money during the Boer War and was an enthusiastic yachtsman, owning a 20 ton racing cutter, as well as a large steam yacht. They were a charming homely family from whom I always received a warm welcome and I consider that I owe my life to Mr Compton's kindness. On hearing of my illness, Mrs Compton told me that her husband had offered to lend me his sailing yacht for the whole summer, so that I could live on the water and sleep on deck provided the lung specialist approved. She bundled me into her car to see the specialist and he gave me leave to try the experiment provided I played no part in sailing the boat, and was not sea sick. As I was never sea sick, the matter was settled and Mr Compton drove me to Plymouth the next day and saw me safely aboard with Rory for my companion.

Rory had not been on the *Grisette* a day before he knew every hole and corner of her, and where everything was kept. I was afraid the chicken-ladder that led to the tiny pit-like saloon would be one too many for him, and that in descending it at such a perpendicular angle he must needs turn heels over head; yet he managed to keep his balance perfectly. His oilskins were kept in one of the saloon lockers which he could open himself. On fetching his coat one chilly day he stepped on a corner of it as he was bringing the coat up on deck and he fell backwards down the steps, landing with a nasty crash on his back. Mercifully he was not much hurt, but in future his wearing apparel was tucked under the cushions of the cockpit, where it was more easily got at, and there was no further risk of disaster.

He learnt in no time that hauling on a rope brought the dinghy alongside and that the dinghy meant a run on shore. The yacht's boy delighted in him and always pitched him the end of a rope to haul on if any sail shifting had to be done. He also most unwisely showed Rory the locker on deck in which all the brushes and cleaning apparatus were kept; the lid shut with a spring, but not such a strong spring that the little Irish nose could not push it up and take everything out. There was a hue and cry next morning at deck-swabbing and cleaning time, for the boy found the locker empty; the whole contents had been brought to my bunk by Rory during the small hours while we were all asleep. It must have meant many journeys before he had collected everything.

This joke perpetrated on the boy even produced a smile on the grim face of the skipper, who was anything but a genial character – in fact, he was the most uncouth creature of his calling I have ever met. He hailed from the Norfolk Broads and was a strong Salvationist and when not on duty, read the Bible and swore at the boy. I found all the southern ports full of salvation, though you would never think it to look at them. Cleanliness played no part in their godliness, I am afraid.

I persuaded my youngest sister[3], a bad sailor but a courageous woman, to join me on the yacht. She braved it until we ran into a bad squall when rounding Start Point, and were obliged to heave to. Then she lay in the scuppers while heavy seas poured over the deck, which smashed the davits and washed the dinghy overboard. The fun then became fast and furious, for what the waves washed over one side they brought back on the other and smart fielding of valuable property had to be done. Although the boat was pitching furiously with hardly a rag of sail on her, my sister forgot about sickness and thoroughly enjoyed rescuing goods that had gone adrift. We got to Salcombe Harbour that evening with the dirtiest boat and wettest crew that could well be imagined, but we had not lost a single possession.

On my return to London after three months idleness, I collected some sketching things and went up to Skye. I had never been to Skye before, but had heard from Mr. MacWhirter, Watson Nicol and other

---

[3] Olive Collyer – See Appendix I

Scottish artists, of the wild peace and beauty of the island and I was in the mood for it. Early autumn is the time when Scotland is at its best: the bracken turning to gold, the heather dusted to purple rust by fading flowers, the light mists veiling details of the hills and lending ethereal opalescent mystery to the distant landscape. Until I had wandered through Skye with Rory, I had not begun to live.

I was travelling by the night train from St Pancras to Oban. Having registered a seat in the train a day or two before, I put my rugs and Rory's coat into the near corner of the carriage and strolled over to the bookstall to buy some papers, Rory at my heels. The platform was packed with people going North for the shooting and there was the usual rush and hurry that prevails at large stations before the departure of an express train. I bought papers and a book with difficulty and bending down to give Rory something to carry for me, I was horrified to discover the dog was not near me and nowhere to be seen. I leave my feelings to be imagined by those who have ever lost a favourite dog in a dense crowd in a strange place. My reason completely evaporated. I tore up and down that train like one possessed. It was due to start almost immediately and Rory was lost. I feel a shiver down my spine, even now, as I think of it. Having implored the guard to delay the train for a few minutes, I was making my way with him to the carriage, intending to take out my things, when one of the many porters I had told of my loss came bustling up to say there was a little red dog in a carriage further down the train and 'that he wouldn't let no one get into it'.

Oh, the relief when I saw my little dog standing in the doorway defying passengers to come anywhere near my property! He had sensed some danger, I am sure, for at the first sound of my voice he jumped into my arms, and smothered my face with kisses, not his usual behaviour at all. It was I who had lost my head and behaved like a fool. Rory, after missing me, had kept his and done the only sensible thing there was to do. He had gone back to our carriage and waited for me. If I had stopped to think for a minute, I should have known that he would do this and I would have saved myself agony of mind.

If anyone ever troubles to read these pages, he or she may smile since I write of Rory as though he were a human being; but he was better than human and owned a brain far excelling that of any other highly trained dog I have ever seen, before or since. He needed no training, as the word is used regarding Alsatians, for instance. I only had to show him what I wanted him to do and he did it directly. He is also the only dog I ever met who really tried to talk. He could say 'Oh no' and 'Oh dear no' quite distinctly, but the formation of a dog's mouth prohibits pronunciation of all but a very few words, perhaps luckily for us. But I prefer them to speak in their own language, which comes straight from the heart, and which is so easily understood by those who love dogs.

Rory will come into these pages many times, but I must tell of one other memorable incident. At the end of our visit to Skye, of which there will be more in another chapter, we were to return to smutty London and enclosed spaces. We boarded the boat at Kyleakin and I left Rory to watch my things on deck, while I went below. On my return I found an old Highland gentleman, in kilt and plaid, with his wife, making polite advances to my terrier, who was behaving prettily so long as my possessions were not touched. Seeing the dog was mine, the gentleman approached me and asked if I would be willing to sell him, as he and his wife had taken a great fancy to him and would like to have him. Price was of little importance, he said, and would I kindly name my own. Since the whole of the gentleman's vast estates (for later I learned from the skipper who the Laird was) would certainly not have bought a hair of Rory; it was somewhat difficult to fix any price. So, thinking it would please them to hear Rory answer for himself, I sat him up on a box and said: 'This gentleman wants to buy you. Would you like to leave me and live with him?' A well-timed poke in the ribs with my hidden thumb produced from Rory's mouth the most distinct 'Oh No!' I believe he had ever uttered.

This verbal refusal from the dog himself so astonished his would-be purchasers that they almost gasped. The lady being the first to recover, said: 'My dear! Can he really talk?' I had to allow that he was not exactly a chatterbox, but that he tried to imitate a few words.

During the remaining hour of the journey, we gave a one-man entertainment at which all the passengers and most of the crew formed the audience. On our taking leave of the boat, the old Laird held my hand in his, saying: 'I am sorry I ever suggested the possibility of buying Rory. Were he only mine, all the American dollars would never purchase such a friend.'

An Artist's Menagerie

Chapter XVIII

'NONPLUSSED'
The Bridgeman Art Library

Back in London from Skye[1] having made a little money from '*Nothing venture, nothing win*', notwithstanding the loss of the £50 for the copyright, I had some funds in hand. It was at about this time that my friend Katherine Willis died and I had promised Katherine on her death-bed that I would take the remainder of her three year lease for a tiny house and studio off her younger sister's hands.

Tedworth Studio, which was quite nice, had been built at the entrance to a horrible slum, Smith Street, just off Tedworth Square. It was a new square box of a house with a small entrance hall, dining room, two bedrooms and a kitchen on the ground floor and over all a good studio and bathroom.

The drawback for animal work was that the studio was upstairs; but it was good enough for the moment and had the makings of a snug little home. Furniture was again the difficulty. I did not want much, but I wanted it to be good. I went and consulted Miss Flora Smith as to the best place to buy it. She came to see the wee house and insisted on giving me a bed, all towels, blankets and linen; and a most beautiful set of linen it was, with my initials embroidered on everything. Then I had a great stroke of luck. A doctor I knew in one of the Guards Regiments had just furnished a small flat for himself and had then been ordered off to the Boer War. As his furniture was precious and old, he had no wish to store it, so he asked me if I would keep it for him until his return from South Africa. It fitted in beautifully and there was my home complete.

I engaged a young girl as a servant, who not only did the housework, but held and amused the animals while I painted them and my animal family rapidly began to increase. A vet gave me 'Douglas' a Manx cat of notable character. The Duchess of Bedford, having smuggled two pariah dogs out of Constantinople, found they were far more like wolves than dogs. She could not cope with both of them and she gave one to me called Galata. Although I took a lot of trouble with Galata,

---

[1] This was approximately the winter of 1903.

she never was a dog to be trusted and did strange things. Her way of greeting me was to walk across the room on her hind legs like a bear. If touched suddenly, she snapped. Later she took to running along the top of the walls that enclosed the cat runs of the slum houses in Smith Street. Believing her to be a wolf the people were terrified and complaints were made to the police. So Galata was eventually dispatched to Mr Alexander of the Scottish Academy, who painted wolf pictures. She was an excellent imitation of a wolf, both in colour and shape, but I never heard what became of her or how the inhabitants of Edinburgh liked her wall act.

The first subject picture I painted in this studio was '*The Exile from Erin*' which Rory stood for. I sold it for £100 before it left my easel and in this case I did preserve the copyright, which I sold to the Fine Art

EXILE FROM ERIN

Society in Bond Street for a similar sum and have met people who had seen the reproduction of this picture in Australia and America.

That summer Rory and I went up to Perthshire and we visited, amongst other places, Loch Rannoch. Here we met a couple of Scottish terrier puppies about three months old – such a delightful brace of tykes that I had to take them both back to London with me, and began two pictures of them at once before they had time to grow out of the tyke age, with ears half down and half cocked. One of these small pictures of both pups watching a Scottish porridge pot hanging over a peat fire, I called 'A Watched Pot'. The companion to it was a single puppy looking at a toad creeping from a hole under a stone, an expression of puzzlement on the dog's face. This was entitled 'Friend or Foe' and I had to get a toad model. Writing to my eldest sister, Helen in Sussex, I asked her to collect a good looking toad from one of her hot houses, pack him carefully and send him to Victoria Station in charge of the guard, where I would meet him and bicycle him home.

'Mr Jorrocks' duly arrived and the guard of the train was most anxious to see the rare animal he had been asked to take such care of. A circle quickly formed and all began to eye with immense interest the box, which I had put carefully on the ground. Jorrocks was taken from his box and exhibited to the crowd. When a common brown toad crawled slowly out, there was a burst of laughter from everyone present: Jorrocks had scored his first success.

He scored two more a bit later when one picture of him appeared in the Academy and another at the Institute of Painters in oil paints. In both pictures he was portrayed in the attitude of stalking and, to get him to perform really well, I detached the hook from a gaudy coloured trout fly and with a fine gut dragged it slowly across a table in front of his nose. This induced him to give me a perfect pose. There were times when the fly was too close and with a lightning flick of his long tongue he caught it and swallowed it. It then had to be pulled up from somewhere in the pit of his stomach. This serious operation did not seem to affect him at all; he would continue his stealthy stalk immediately afterwards, as though nothing of any importance had happened.

It may not be universally known that toads can be made into the most entertaining and interesting pets; Jorrocks became quite an important personage in the household. Douglas the cat played gently with him, Rory always carried him into lunch by one hind leg. An Australian piping crow I had a little later would tap his back with its beak to see how much pace a toad could make. Jorrocks could eat thirty fat meal worms at a sitting without turning a hair and I believe he could have managed fifty, but being afraid of an explosion I drew the line at thirty worms for breakfast and a few half-drowned flies for supper.

The picture of the puppy and toad, and its mate – the two pups and the porridge pot – were hung on the line in the Gem Room of the

MR JORROCKS
STALKING A FLY,

137

Academy and on varnishing day Mr Marcus Stone RA offered me a £100 a piece for them without copyright. It was such a compliment that an Academician should wish to buy work of mine that I was on the point of closing with him when Mr Briton Riviere strongly advised me not to accept the offer, assuring me that the pictures were so charming they would certainly be bought on the opening day by some big dealer who would want the copyright included and this meant double the price Marcus Stone was prepared to pay.

Mr Riviere was right – both pictures were purchased outright by the greatest picture dealer of his day, Sir William Agnew, within half an hour of the doors of the exhibition opening to the public. Neither of these pictures was ever published, instead they found a resting place in a private gallery.

Another picture that gave me some fun and added a fearsome addition to my ever increasing menagerie was '*A Friend in Need*'. It represented a dead black-faced Highland ewe, her lamb standing bleating by her side and a collie dog coming to the rescue.

For the material for this work, Rory and I trekked off to Glen Affric, which lies twenty miles beyond Beauly which had to be done by 'coach'. The rickety wagonette with a pair of rickety horses was not my idea of a coach, but the slowness and discomfort of the drive did not matter, for the scenery was so beautiful as entirely to absorb my mind. Time passed pleasantly enough until I was deposited at the door of a small inn, opposite a tiny store and Post Office, this being all the village Glen Affric boasted.

After making a number of studies of rock, heather, burns, etc., I then had to get my black-faced sheep and eventually managed to buy an old ewe, who I think must have already had 'so many children she didn't know what to do', and had refused to have any more. Her head was fine, the horns large and perfect; she was just the model I wanted. I could have done without her temper, but beggars cannot be choosers, so I bought her for six shillings and had to pay another six for a crate to travel her in. A live lamb proved too difficult, but I acquired a dead one and carefully skinned it, trusting that Mr Rowland Ward would be able to stuff it and set it up in the position I required.

Taking an old Highland ewe, who had never been off her own mountains, across London on the top of a cab was good fun. She owned a particularly raucous voice and used it to some purpose all the way. Piccadilly, in particular, enjoyed it quite a lot, for the cab got into several jams and I had time to note the varied expressions of pedestrians as they gazed at the crate and listened to her real old Scottish ballads.

DANDIE DINMONT
TERRIER
*With grateful thanks to
Mrs Iona Joseph*

I made Sheila – as she was christened – a shelter in the back yard, and naturally expected her to be wild and shy for a while. She was neither, unless extreme savagery was indicative of both. She attacked head down and at great speed, springing right off her hocks like a baited bull in an arena. On the second morning she smashed the kitchen door and came in and ate all the bread off the table. Rory, who helped to put her out, got a bash in the ribs that he remembered for some time. As to getting the sheep up the steep narrow stairs to the studio, it was impossible for the small servant and me to attempt it.

In the midst of one of our prolonged fights with the sheep, when we had got her into the hall and prevented her eating everything or knocking the house down, a beggar man came to the front door and lent his assistance. By the way in which he seized a hind leg on one side and a fore one on the other, and tipped the animal on to its back, I was convinced it was not the first time that he had handled live mutton. I was right, for he had spent part of his life on a sheep station in Australia; I instantly engaged him to control Sheila and to induce her to behave like a respectable model. This he did in a very short time and got her to climb the stairs to the studio and lie on her side on the throne while he scratched her ears and fed her with bread and carrots. So much did she enjoy this life of petting and good food which had not to be searched for that before I had finished my painting of her she would come up to the studio and lie down on the throne with no assistance at all. Later our difficulty was to make her get up, for she quickly realized that so long as she lay still she got plied with all the food she needed.

When she became amenable I used to take her for morning exercise with Rory into Burton's Court; but she took to chasing the children, and one morning charged and upset a perambulator, which got me into trouble, so I tried to find her a home in the country, but without success. Most of my friends had met Sheila and therefore refused to take her. However, I was not bothered with her for very long. The first batch of cold foggy weather she succumbed to pneumonia and died in a very few hours. I cannot say that I grieved very much and Rory was delighted, for they never got on together, and he was always receiving nasty bumps from her horns when least prepared for an attack.

While Sheila was yet with me I had an Australian piping crow, a hedgehog, a large black and white rat (whom Rory loved), Jorrocks the toad, a tame thrush, a bullfinch, a large aquarium of assorted fish, the Manx cat, the two Scottish terriers, and a Dandie Dinmont.

At about this time I wrote to a girlfriend of mine who knew my weakness for collecting animals round me and mentioned that I had just bought a very interesting old seal. She answered, '*I am so looking forward to seeing the old seal you have bought, but I am wondering where on earth you will keep it. I suppose in a pond in the back yard!*' I had neglected to tell her that the seal in question was engraved with my father's crest!

The piping crow was one of the nicest pets. One of my brothers[2] had brought him from Australia when only a fledgling. To teach him to pipe, I bought a good contralto toned penny whistle and after much

---

[2] This would have been her brother Charles who was an inveterate wanderer.

---

serious practice on it learned to play 'Drink to me only with thine eyes.' Every morning for about a week I shut the crow in the bathroom, sat outside the door and played the tune over and over again on the whistle. He piped the melody in no time and with great expression; there was a sob in his beautiful voice; but the last two bars worried him so much that he gave the original up and composed two of his own instead. Unfortunately his improvisation was in a different key and ended on a high note that was somewhere near A flat, and very flat it was too.

When his song was perfected he sang it to all the animals in turn, including the toad. Standing in front of them, legs wide apart, head thrown back making a Caruso chest, the great singer himself could not have surpassed the pathos that the crow put into that song.

He also rode on my shoulder to Burton's Court each morning and played in the branches of the trees, but would sing all the way there and all the way home, causing some obstruction to traffic on the pavement, for people turned to stop, look and listen.

My aquarium was very large and held about ten gallons of water. I had it made myself from a design I found in a magazine. It was most carefully made and the decoration was worthy of a marine artist. But there must have been a weak spot somewhere, for during one night it burst and my bed was immediately under it. I dreamt I was drowning and woke up to find an avalanche of water pouring through the ceiling on to my head. After that I gave up keeping fish.

When I went north to collect Sheila the ewe, a little tragedy occurred during my stay at the Inn at Glen Affric that I have never forgotten. During my many visits to my Uncle and Aunt's house in Hertford Street I often used to meet a noted 'consulting physician'. He was an elderly bachelor, small of body, large of head, with the cold blooded eyes of a lizard. I had heard lately that this man had married a very pretty girl young enough to be his daughter. Much to my surprise, on entering the inn the first person I saw was this 'consulting physician' and his young wife, evidently on their honeymoon.

The occupants of the Post Office consisted of an extremely fat old dame and her fourteen year old niece. One morning the child came running over to the inn to get help; her Aunt had fallen on a stone flagged path in the garden, broken her thigh bone and could not move. Hearing that a doctor was staying at the inn, she had come to fetch him at once.

The doctor's young wife and I were standing at the door when the child arrived and, on learning what had happened, I said I would go to the cottage if she would call her husband to help move the woman on to a bed.

Having put a cushion under the poor woman's head and straightened the limb as best I could, I waited for the doctor before attempting to move her. After a little time, as there was no sign of him, I ran across to hurry him up and found him and his wife in their sitting room. She was in tears and he was sitting comfortably in an armchair looking more like a reptile than ever. He declined to help or have anything to do with the case whatsoever. All he would say was that he was a consulting physician on holiday and that we must get a doctor from Beauly. A forty mile drive there and back and only a rough pony to do the journey with!

This humane doctor would not even tell us how best to lift the woman and she could not be left out all night on the stones, in the end we had to do our best without him. Eventually we managed to get a doctor, but the woman died a fortnight later from pneumonia.

That being my first acquaintance with man's inhumanity, I felt a great compassion for the physician's young wife.

'A Gentleman of France'

Chapter XIX

CHAMPION CACKLER OF NOTTS
Cackler was born in 1898, owned by The Duchess of Newcastle
and considered the ancestor of every show wire since.
With thanks to the The British Sporting Art Trust, Roy Heron and Nicholas Waters

Painting the Highland ewe showed me that an upstairs studio was not the studio for an animal painter and, as my lease was running out, I searched London for the kind of place I wanted. My old master, Mr Nicol, joined in the search and we spent evening after evening bicycling through mews and disused yards trying to find some cheap and suitable spot where I could live and keep my livestock. I discovered that London, large though it was, had no habitation in it which would do for me.

Miss Flora Smith, with whom I lunched every Sunday, was again called into consultation, after which she told Mr Nicol that if he could find a place in which to build an animal studio, she would buy the building and charge me the lowest rent possible for the use of it. At long last we found a small detached house near Parson's Green Station, with good-sized yards on three sides of it and a large outhouse – just the thing for kennels or stables. The house, for some reason, had not been let for a time and Miss Smith bought the property very cheaply. It was quite a nice little place, two sitting-rooms, three bedrooms, a bathroom, kitchen and scullery. There was plenty of room in the big yard to build a studio 30 ft. x 34 ft. and still leave room for animal accommodation. An architect of repute and a friend of Mr Nicol's, designed the studio with an open-beamed roof and a small gallery across one end. There were two big fireplaces and one corner of the floor was cemented and drained for horses to stand on.

When it was completed, no artist could have wished for a finer studio. The yards were enclosed by six foot walls with broken glass on top, the front and back gates were solid and finished with a row of iron spikes. From the outside it looked rather like a small lunatic asylum. Even then I tended to be a bit of a hermit by nature and so I liked the feeling of being shut away from the world. There was another reason for safe-guarding the yards; I often had with me dogs of great value to paint, and at that time there were many dog thieves about London.

Although the house was quite close to Hurlingham, it was not in a good street, because along one side of the yards ran a slum which was much frequented by whippet and homing pigeon owners. To make the dogs safer still I had the doors and windows of the kennel wired with electric bell wires that rang in a sort of box over the head of my bed. One night, when my housekeeper happened to be away, the wretched bells started to ring like blazes, and I had to run down to the kennel in my nightgown to tackle the thieves. Not a dog was barking, so I imagined they must have been drugged. Creeping up to the door nearest the studio I silently unlocked it and peeped in, only to discover my tame fox, who was always in mischief, caught by his hind leg in one of the wires, the dogs peacefully sleeping on the benches, since they could not hear the bells ringing in my bedroom.

I must return for a minute or two, while my new workshop is being built, to Tedworth Studio and tell the way I got the poodle model for my picture '*A Gentleman of France*'. I had had the sketch for this subject by me for some time and decided that it was publishable. But I needed a poodle.

It was winter time and bitterly cold, but it was my custom, winter and summer, to take my dogs for long walks at night as the traffic was less and there was little fear of them being run over.

One bright moonlight night, very frosty and dry, I started off with the pack to Wimbledon Common. About ten o'clock, on my return journey, I passed a detached house standing in its own grounds on the top of Putney Hill. Somewhere in this enclosed plot a dog was crying bitterly. It was a howl and shivering whimper, of utter misery. I stopped to listen and then slowly walked on wondering whether the animal was being ill-treated. Almost without knowing it I turned back and stood outside the house again. The crying continued. It so tore my heart that I rang the bell of the house.

A maidservant answered the door and I enquired if the crying dog belonged there. She said: 'Indeed the brute does, and I suppose you are another come to complain of the noise he makes every night, keeping the neighbours awake!' This reply gave me an idea and I asked if I could see her mistress for a moment.

I was shown into a cosy, snug room with a young woman sitting by the fire reading a book. She looked surprised until I mentioned the howling dog, then she hastily began apologizing for the noise it was making and said it had been given to her husband as a valuable present, and as she disliked dogs it was chained to a kennel in the garden every night. Asking if I might see the dog, she took me out to a stone yard and there was a clipped and shaved black poodle tied up to an open barrel, no bedding or blanket to lie on, sitting on its tail, half frozen by the cold. He was a very handsome dog, and just what I wanted, so I offered to buy him. She hummed and hawed and said she would ask her husband in the morning. I pointed out that it was cruelty to animals to shave a dog and then tie him out in the biting cold with no coat, bed or proper house to sleep in, and that unless he was handed over to me, or taken into the house at once, I would go to the nearest police station and report the case.

It ended in me buying the dog for £2 (he was probably worth £10) and taking him home with me. I have never seen a dog more pleased to leave his home. So 'Peter the Poodle' became another of my possessions and the rest of his life was happy. As the dog needed more exercise than I had time to give him I sent him to a friend of mine in the country who kept several hacks with whom he could run.

Peter did a very clever thing that is worth recording. I had him only a short time before moving to my new house at Parson's Green. Twice I had taken him to see the building. He had followed my bicycle and I had gone one way and come back another both times. On the morning of the move from Tedworth Studio, nowhere could he be found. After the furniture van had gone I locked up the place and hunted the streets round about for him; at last, leaving word at the King's Road Police Station, where most of the Bobbies knew me, I asked them to watch and see if the dog returned to the studio later.

It was a very busy day and I had no opportunity of returning to my new studio at Parson's Green until late evening. I then took my bicycle and, on opening the door of my stronghold, there was Peter lying outside. The police told me he had been back to Tedworth Square and they had tried to catch him, but he had fled. Finding the old home deserted he had come straight on to the new one. I wonder how Peter knew that I had gone to a place he had only seen twice? When he got there it was easy enough for him to be sure, for he could smell me and the other dogs. When I found him at the door, he was no more pleased to see me than usual, in no way flurried, but rather ashamed of having run off on his own in the morning.

While the new house was being cleaned and tidied I went to my married sister in Sussex for a week and had my first drive in a motor car. It was a Darracq belonging to a Captain 'Polly' Lambton. It was made like a phaeton and unless one was sitting in it, it smelt awful. On Sunday afternoon we were all taken for a drive and we may have averaged twelve miles per hour perhaps. All the villagers out for their Sunday walk in the lanes must have 'benefited' from the black and nauseous smoke blown out in clouds from the exhaust and the smother of dust we left behind. My small nephew in the back of the machine sparkled with pleasure as he remarked: 'Nobody is enjoying this but us.'[1]

Captain Lambton offered to drive me up to London in this wonderful self-propelling machine. I said I would go with him if he promised not to run over any dogs. The promise was given. He ran over two in Croydon and knocked down a horse in Wandsworth Bridge Road. From there I walked home!

---

[1] This was probably Algernon Lindsay Eric Smith MC 1892–1914. (Killed in action)

A BROWN STUDY
by Margaret Collyer 1897

Ardtornish

'Land of brown heath and shaggy wood;
Land of the mountain and the flood!'

1897

Chapter XX

These lines describe Ardtornish nicely with the exception of the 'shaggy wood', which I never discovered. Rory and I had come all the way up to the Morven Mountains to paint Highland cattle for Mr Valentine Smith. The old, old tower of Ardtornish, or what remains of it, stands on the edge of the coast opposite the Island of Mull. A bit further up the Sound is a tiny pier and the entrance to Loch Aline.

At the landing stage we were met by Ducan, in the full livery of a coachman, except that he was wearing an old pair of plaid breeks, which rather reduced the effect. He was driving a 'machine' of great antiquity rather resembling a country jingle or governess cart, far too small for the bay horse between the shafts. Had the horse kicked, I should have arrived at the house *sans* a face. Luckily it was the last thing he wanted to do; in fact he would have much preferred to do nothing. Ducan continually belted him with the end of the reins to make him move at all, and talked to him in a language perhaps it was as well I did not understand.

The road to the new Ardtornish house lay all along the side of the loch and very pretty it was, but the hideous modern stone mansion was a shock to my artistic senses. The blasé quadruped was driven under a big arch into a stable-yard of which he was quite unworthy.

Rory and I alighted and waited outside while Ducan exchanged his disguise of a coachman for one of butler: his clean-shaven mouth and pointed goatee beard were not appropriate to the costume of the major domo, but the part was played excellently and I was welcomed as the flowers in May and shown into an ugly, but very warm, hall.

There was nothing trivial or flimsy about this house. The carpets were thick Turkey, the chairs heavy mahogany, the doors of the same wood and three inches thick. But what it lacked in daintiness it gained in warmth and comfort. I have seldom lived in more thoroughly accommodating rooms, for although I was alone there for a couple of months, I felt no loneliness.

Never have I seen more magnificent cattle, before or since; they were superb in size, colour and coat. I was at Ardtornish in October and they were getting their full winter outfit, the fringes on forehead and legs were fully twenty inches in length, the latter having the effect of a long petticoat. The highland cattle we see in English parks with merely shaggy skins give no idea of what they really look like on their native mountains, where, owing to climatic conditions, they grow this wondrous wealth of hair to enable them to withstand the cold winters.

Considering the free wild life these animals lead, I found them remarkably quiet, especially the bulls. One, who had carried off championship honours, allowed himself to be dragged to the top of a high rock every morning so that I could paint him against a sky background. It certainly took six or seven men to get him there, but once posed, and frequently plied with salt with which I filled my pockets every morning, he was most peaceful and never once charged my canvas or umbrella, as I had quite expected him to do.

This bull was entirely black, with a marvellous spread of horns. I used my study of him for a picture I called *'The Lord of the Isles'*, which was not exhibited in London, but sold privately while still on my easel.

There was a big kennel of Old English setters there which gave me great pleasure and in making friends with the dogs I got to know two interesting characters in Old Ross and his nice son Johnnie, the head ghillies of the establishment. Johnnie was a good companion and showed me red deer on the hills and golden eagle, which we stalked and got quite close to before they spied us hiding in the heather, and rose on enormous wings, circling slowly up and up until lost to sight in the mist. He also initiated me into the art of salmon fishing and the very first evening on the river I hooked and landed a nice fresh-run fish.

Why that fish was ever caught I cannot think; it was entirely its own fault and nothing whatever to do with me. The heavy 16 ft. rod completely baffled me at first and I failed to get out a line at all. I hooked Johnnie quite badly, I hooked bushes, trees and grass and eventually the line hit the water in coils with a Jock Scott mixed up somewhere in the centre. I started to wind up furiously for yet another shot, when suddenly a thing like a young shark rushed at the fly, seized it, and made off at racing speed. There was a frantic yell from Johnnie of 'He's well hooked, let him run!'

Then we started to run, Johnnie gripping my arm to prevent me falling headlong over rocks, shouting orders into my ear. Rory became wildly excited: every time the fish jumped I gave a view holloa and he gave tongue; it was more like a hunt than catching a fish and I have seldom run so fast. Johnnie said that from find to kill was twenty-five minutes; to me it seemed a lifetime before the fish was gaffed and safe on the bank. A sixteen-pound silver fish. I have landed many bigger ones since, but never one that I so enjoyed catching as the beauty I proudly carried home that evening.

The salmon in the Aline do not run very large; a twenty-pounder was a big fish for this sporting little river. The sea-trout were splendid fun, running five and six pounds and very game. I caught quite a number of these on a light rod and they gave excellent sport. Rory took to fishing like a duck to water. The moment a fish was hooked he tore down the bank on a level with it, watching intently every jump and every manoeuvre it made. When played out and on its side he would spring into the water and retrieve it, bringing it well inland before trusting it on the ground.

Johnnie did not hold with a dog retrieving fish and said that Rory would one day break the line and lose me a good one. But he never did; he was a sportsman who rarely lost his head or did foolish things. The ghillies soon began to appreciate him and said: 'He's verra wise, puir-r-r brute.' Johnnie treated him with respect and often requested his assistance to hunt vermin.

One late evening, when strolling by the loch, I saw the two Ross's with guns, terriers and other men with bags and spades, descending the hill from the keeper's cottage. Johnnie called to me to come along with Rory, as they were off to the cairns to try and shoot two foxes. '*Foxes!*' I gasped. 'You mustn't shoot foxes. Adam and Eve shot foxes and got thrown out of the Garden of Eden.' Old Ross muttered into his beard: 'I expect they kept sheep.'

Tagging along with these murderers I learnt that foxes in the Highlands had to be shot, as there were no hounds to kill them and they were lamb-killers of the worst description.

Once over the shock, I entered into the game and, taking the terriers and Rory away up the hillside, started to draw the heather down towards the guns. Presently, twenty yards ahead of us, up jumped a big dog fox and streaked for the cairns where the keepers were concealed. He was instantly shot and I and the dogs were called to heel. Here we all lay flat in the bushes silently awaiting the return of the vixen to the den. It was nearly dark when we glimpsed her unsuspiciously trotting back to her cubs and it seemed such a shame to murder her that I made an effort to warn her; but just too late; *bang!* went the gun and she rolled over.

The terriers were then put into the rocks to find the cubs, which they failed to do and it was Rory that located them. The hole was netted and digging began. By the time it was quite dark, five little fox cubs had been caught alive and put into the bags, later to be sent to Leadenhall

Market. They were about five weeks old, too young to know much fear, and in a few days they were lapping milk and playing about in the shed in which they were kept. One dog cub was prettily marked with a white shirt-front and white tag to his little brush. I made a great pet of him and when I was leaving Ardtornish Johnnie put him into a basket and gave him to Rory, saying that as Rory had found them he was entitled to the best. So 'Foxey' came with us to London and was added to the ever-increasing managerie.

But before bidding goodbye to Loch Aline I must tell of a wonderful piece of sheep-dog work I witnessed at the pier the night I left.

The evening I was to catch the 'Swuft' steamer that crawled with cargo, mails and a few passengers from Skye to Oban, Ducan drove me to the pier with the blasé bay horse who really deserves a much worse adjective. The weather was wet and boisterous, with a biggish sea running in the Sound. On reaching the tiny wooden pier, Ducan hauled up the flag, the signal for the boat to stop and pick me up. It was over an hour late and, when it did come, merely hooted and passed on.

I was nearly tearing my hair out with rage, for I had an important appointment in London which it would have been disastrous to miss. I cursed all Scottish captains of vessels, till Ducan explained that the coast was too dangerous for the boat to put in in rough weather and added that at three in the morning a sheep-boat was due to take the animals to Oban Market, and that if I went by the sheep-boat I should catch the London train. I therefore decided to wait on the pier till it came and looked forward to a horrible eight hours. Both Rory and I were wearing oilskins; even so we shivered violently as we sat on my luggage in a small tin shelter open to the sea in front.

I was rapidly becoming a frozen statue when we heard the distant bleating of driven sheep, and the woof-woofing of many dogs. Sheep and more sheep kept arriving, and with each flock a man and a dog. The men rolled themselves in their plaids, gathered together round a fire, black bottles being handed round the group, from which the shepherds took long and continuous draughts. The air reeked with 'whuskey' and I was politely offered some just to keep the 'cauld awa'. But I was not wanting drink or company at that moment; all my attention was fixed on the dogs, who were busily engaged in keeping the various flocks apart, doing the work entirely on their own, quietly and dexterously. They were of no particular breed, but I noticed with surprise that there was very little collie blood in any of them. They seemed more distantly related to old English sheep-dogs. During the hours we waited for that boat not a single sheep was allowed to leave its own flock and mix with another; if the dog in charge could not stop it, another dog came and assisted; yet, as the sheep had come from many different hills, I doubt if the dogs were acquainted at all.

When at last the boat arrived and two narrow gangways were pushed across to the pier, the dogs worked most scientifically and in combination, putting the sheep over the gangways and on to the boat. Not a man roused himself to help them; they did it entirely without human aid. Each flock was brought up in turn and pushed across the planks; if a sheep turned broadside on, blocking the entrance to the gangway, one dog raced over the backs of the packed animals and put it straight and through. This happened time and again; sometimes one dog did it, sometimes another.

By the time the last flock was aboard the boat was absolutely packed with sheep; not until then did the shepherds leave the fire, pocket their bottles and push their way to the centre of the deck, where we stood or rested on sheep's rumps during the short journey to Oban. The dogs, after their exertions, lay full length on the warm woolly backs of their charges, taking a well-deserved rest before tackling more strenuous work in the market square.

I did not in the least regret cold and lack of sleep, for I would not have missed seeing those dogs work for anything.

Tallo Ho! Forrard Away!
Fox Hunt In The Fulham Road

Six months after I returned to London from Ardtornish, every city clerk opening his halfpenny paper on the way back from work was confronted with the above headline in large black letters. And so it was that the intense curiosity of the Reynard family very nearly caused the death of my Highland fox.

By this time he was beautifully grown, in fine condition, and as tame as any fox ever gets. This means that a fox, hand-reared from a few weeks old, treated as a house pet and never chained, will be dog-like with those he knows and sees every day of his life; but should a stranger enter the room and try to touch him, he will become full of instinctive fear directly, probably snap if handled, and then bolt under a sofa or out of the window or door.

My fox had his liberty. He went where he liked and did what he liked, and mostly spent his time romping with the dogs in the yard; for he loved them to chase him round until he went to ground in a kennel, then he would poke his head out, mouth wide open, and roar with laughter, while he kept the pack at bay. The house and yards being all the world he knew, I never thought of him wishing to venture further afield, though the dustman was cautioned to shut the yard door whenever he called for the bin. Our usual dustman was to be trusted, for he took the greatest interest in the fox and was always trying to make friends with him. But a morning arrived when a strange dustman came and left the door open and the fox sprang out into the street.

It was early and I was dressing when Mrs Seamark, my housekeeper, rushed white-faced into my room to say the fox had gone. In two minutes I had my bicycle out in the street. No need to ask which way the fox had gone, for people were all staring in one direction. As I turned into the Fulham Road most of the population were holloa-ing and running towards Putney Bridge; buses were stopping, people climbing down and joining in the chase. Bending over my handle-bars I rode all out, passing runner after runner. Shooting through the traffic and with hair-breadth shaves, I reached the bridge and, being now at the top of the hunt, I steadied to ask the policeman at the corner if the fox had crossed. He shouted, 'Yes!', and that two dogs were on his tail. Away I went again, cutting between more buses that were stopping and more people running, then I viewed him on the other side of the bridge and sent up a prayer that he would head for Wimbledon Common and safety.

Like most prayers for material things, mine was unanswered. A man with an open umbrella ran straight at Foxey and headed him. He then doubled back, jumping over the dogs that were pursuing him and raced back over the bridge all amongst the chasing crowd. By this time I was shouting at the top of my voice, 'He's mine! Leave him alone! Don't chase him!' then whinnying off into a sob, 'Oh *please* don't hurt him, he's my tame fox!' All to no purpose, of course, for a London mob gone mad with excitement is quite unstoppable. My heart was now bursting with fear as I raced back over the bridge; I imagined my poor little fox torn to bits by horrid mongrels, or clubbed to death by ignorant people.

I breathed a fervent 'Thank God!' when I saw him clear the crowd and get well away down Fulham Palace Road, for this, in comparison with what we had rushed through, was like open country and go as you please. I held my breath and made a supreme effort to get up with him until he could hear my voice calling, and I think he did hear me; for a second later he turned and dived through the iron railings of an area out of sight. I jumped off my bicycle and peeped down into the pit. There he was crouched under a wall panting as though his heart would break. I daren't go to him until I had stopped the runners who were fast coming up. How could I stop such a gang of roughs? But the greatest ruffian of all was leading by fifty yards. I threw myself on his mercy and begged him to help me. He rose most gallantly to the occasion and between us we checked the chase.

As soon as I could make myself heard, I stood on the pavement and explained what had happened, that the animal was a pet and must not be hurt. I also asked for silence while I went down into the sunken area and got hold of him. This was difficult, as the fox was so terrified that he tried to snap, so I requested the loan of a coat, which somebody peeled off and handed me. In this way I caught him and carried him home, the kind ruffian leading my bicycle and keeping the crowd back. Such a procession you never saw as accompanied me to my house; there were two or three hansom cabs in it with panting horses, which I hoped were old hunters reminded of better days.

I was then collared by reporters, who wanted the whole story, but I had had enough and no breakfast. So after a heartfelt thanks and a good tip to the man who helped me, I closed the doors of my sanctuary with a big sigh of relief. Thus ended the only fox-hunt ever seen in the streets of London.

JAKE

'BUY A DOG MA'AM'
By Richard Andsell, RA
Signed and dated 1860
*Reproduced with the kind
permission of the Kennel
Club Picture Library*

Dog Thieving

Chapter XXI

My second and last hunt in London was after a foxhound that I had borrowed for a model from Colonel Charles Godman, Master of the Crawley and Horsham Hunt.

This hound possessed a homing instinct of no mean capacity. The third morning after his arrival he succeeded in jumping the six-foot wall of the yard and getting half an hour's start before I knew he had gone. Being a valuable stud hound I was in a terrible state of mind about losing him and, mounting my trusty bike, proceeded to try and find him. My friend the policeman on Putney Bridge had noticed a big 'black and white dog' galloping past him a while ago. I picked up the line again on the other side from a man who had noticed a 'fox 'ound streaking up Putney 'ill'. I traced him, by enquiring of pedestrians at intervals, as far as Epsom. Here I was at fault for some time, until I came on a ragged little urchin sitting on the side of the road. Having told him the kind of dog I was looking for, he grinned up at me with his grimy little face and said: 'If it's a gurt big hugly black and white dawg youre looking for, he fell dead in this ditch an hour past. I'll show you were 'e is for a penny.' I gave him sixpence, and he showed me where the hound lay – fast asleep in the ditch under some brambles. The pace he had come on hard roads had worn the pads of his feet, and he was very lame, otherwise he was all right.

I had to find a conveyance and get him driven home, which cost a lot of money. He had been heading as straight as he could for his kennels and I expect he would have got there if I had not caught him. '*Old Friends, Old Times*', the picture I used him for, along with its companion, '*Erin go Bragh*', were bought by C. Greenfield for a useful price, so I did not grudge the hound his carriage drive back from Epsom.

The close study of animals, and animal painting, is an intensely interesting occupation, but borrowed models can cause one endless anxiety. So also can the responsibility of valuable dogs brought and left for their portraits to be painted. I had had dogs valued at many hundred of pounds brought to me to paint and I have not dared to let them off the chain or out of my sight for a minute.

On one occasion a noted Airedale breeder and judge[1] brought me a champion dog of his to paint, which he had just sold for a very large sum of money. Honoured though I was to be entrusted with this dog, the responsibility was such that I got private detectives to watch my kennel night and day during the time he was with me. I have taken this precaution on several other occasions when housing well-known dogs.

In those days dog thieves kept their eye on the best show dogs and they always knew where they were. Within twenty-four hours it would have been known that a noted champion Airedale was in my kennel and they would have laid up and got him at the first opportunity. My neighbourhood was noted for its dog thieves and presently I will tell you how, through my help, one of the biggest gangs in London was trapped and imprisoned.

One day I had been to tea at Fulham Vicarage and, crossing the road to walk home via the King's Road, I got into a crowd of people scrimmaging for buses at the corner of Putney Bridge. Amongst these people I noticed a stout and breathless lady, who had a lovely little Yorkshire terrier on a light lead. The dog caught my eye and I turned to get another look at it, when, at that moment, the lady's bus arrived. Dragging

---

[1] Mr Holland Buckley. He was the best known early Airedale breeder. The Airedale was a relatively new breed at that time and thought to be a cross between the Wire Haired Terrier and the Otterhound.

the small dog after her she made a dive for a seat. The crowd was thick and violent and the dog was hanging back, in danger of being trampled, when I saw a man in a heavy overcoat snatch it up, push it under his coat, jerk the line out of the lady's hand and walk slowly away. It was so quickly done that nobody else noticed it; I only saw it because I happened to be watching the dog.

The man was well dressed and in no way remarkable but he had stolen the dog all right and was now sauntering along towards the Fulham Road. Keeping my eye on him, I quickly told a policeman that I intended to follow the man and I asked him to give my name and address to the lady. As he knew the lady and her Yorkshire terrier, no time was wasted and I started off to shadow the thief.

As soon as he was round the corner and out of sight of the buses, the man doubled down Fulham Palace Road, walking so rapidly it took me all my time to keep him in sight. It was getting dusk and being mightily afraid of losing him, I closed up to within twenty yards of his heels. I passed another policeman I knew well, who saluted and was about to pass the time of day, but by pointing to the man in front and putting my finger to my lips, I prevented him speaking and hurried on. It was no use taking the policeman with me, for I wanted to see where the man was taking the dog. I was quite prepared to follow him across London if necessary and, luckily, I had left Rory at home for once. I was led through many streets and by-passes that I had never been in before and as it got darker I had to get nearer my prey.

I had lost my bearings when the man turned into a narrow slummy mews and a few yards down this he went into a house on the right and slammed the door. Making careful note of the house, I walked past the door and up the mews to see where it came out at the other end. I found myself at Walham Green within a stone's throw of the Police Station, into which I went and told my story.

That night the police surrounded and raided the house and they arrested a gang of dog thieves for which they had been searching for

POINTER

months. We found thirty or more dogs, some shut up in boxes, some chained to rings in the wall and nearly all had gags in their mouths to keep them from barking. Some were starved and in dreadful condition and on opening one box I found two beautiful black pugs emaciated and dead. Besides the dogs, there were upwards of a hundred collars and muzzles.

It was a big case and I had to give evidence and identify the man who stole the Yorkshire terrier. Luckily I was able to do this, for I don't forget faces. All these thieves got long terms of imprisonment and many people received their dogs back. The black pugs were recognized as two well-known show specimens which had been stolen when at exercise in the Park over six months before. Such a rumpus had been made over the loss of these dogs that the thieves had not dared to pass them on, so the poor things had been shut in a covered box and allowed to starve.

The scourge of dog thieving touched me personally when my deerhound, Chieftain, was stolen from Miss Flora Smith's stable early one morning. She came to me in great distress and offered a £20 reward to anyone who brought him back. There was no response to her advertisement and after a few days I visited a man called Ravenscroft, who kept a dog and

KING CHARLES
SPANIELS

animal shop in the Seven Dials. I had known this man for some time, and had already managed to get one or two stolen dogs back through him. He was well in with most of the dog thieves who were stealing valuable dogs, right and left.

I used to haunt animal shops and had made quite a friend of Ravenscroft, who was a great character and a source of much amusement to me. However, this time he could give me no news of Chief and had heard nothing about him but he said he would put through some enquiries in the most likely places. A night or two later he came to my studio and said he had done all he could, but could find no trace of Chieftain. He then told me that an Indian Rajah had lately sent an order to England for a batch of deerhounds and Ravenscroft had little doubt that Chief had been sold to the man commissioned to buy the hounds and that he had already been shipped to India. Poor Chieftain was never seen or heard of again.

I must, though, tell a rather amusing story of the only dog owner I ever met who would not trust his dog to my care.

Since the year 1902 when Colonel Malcolm of Poltalloch showed a brace of white Scottish terriers at Edinburgh, much interest began to be taken in the breed that is now called 'White West Highland'.

Colonel Malcolm was a fairly tough proposition to reckon with. He

163

loved his dogs, he hated dog shows and snapped his fingers at the English Kennel Club. The Poltalloch terriers caused rather a sensation when first seen in public and some clever person handled the old Colonel nicely and persuaded him to bring some of his dogs to London for the Crystal Palace Show. A class was given for the breed, and one of Colonel Malcolm's terriers took a champion certificate. So delighted was the old man about this that he decided he must have a portrait of the dog painted at once and my name was given to him as being one of leading dog painters of the day.

I shall never forget his arrival in my studio, bringing the dog and an old Highland ghillie, who had never been to London before, to look after the animal while I painted it. Colonel Malcolm, who was dressed as though he had just come off the moor, with a plaid around his shoulders, was afraid of losing the dog and equally afraid of losing the ghillie. I suggested that he should send the man home to Scotland and leave the dog with me, but this he would not hear of. The man must be with the dog and the dog with the man and, as I could not take them both in, a lodging must be found close by. I suggested my washer-woman just around the corner, who had a room to let for the ten days I should want the dog. All was arranged and the man was instructed to bring the dog to me every morning at ten o'clock and hold him for me until one o'clock.

The next morning I was all ready to begin, but no man or dog appeared. After waiting for an hour I went round to their lodging to see what had happened. The woman of the house said the man had not gone out and she had heard no sound. I knocked at his door. No answer, so I walked in – to find our friend in bed with an empty bottle of whisky and blind to the world.

I took the dog home with me and kept him for the ten days, during the whole of which time I saw nothing of his keeper. I then wrote to Colonel Malcolm, who was still in London, asking him to come and see the portrait. His first question was to ask where was the ghillie? I said I had seen nothing of him, but we could go to his room and enquire. I showed the Colonel the bedroom and in he went, to find his trusted dog-keeper still blind drunk and incapable of speech.

The Colonel said nothing, but got a cab, lugged the man into it, took the dog and drove away, and that was the last I saw of Malcolm of Poltalloch, but I did get a very charming letter from him when I sent him up the picture a little later on.

'SCOTTIE AND KHAKI'
This picture is the most reproduced of all her paintings

Sketching on Skye

(c 1903)

Chapter XXII

On another memorable Autumn and after sailing all summer, I collected some sketching things and Rory and I set off for Skye.

Oban, at seven o'clock in the morning, when alighting from the train, stiff, dirty, cold and very hungry, does not fill one with any particular pleasure or enthusiasm. I walked across to the pier from which the 'Swuft' boats start for the Hebrides and, finding one sitting there, put all my things on board. I was moving off for a bath and breakfast at the hotel when I heard one of the officers say: 'Hello, Rory, so you're back in Scotland again.' It was the same boat that had taken us to Loch Aline a year earlier, when Rory had fascinated the men on her by showing off his many tricks. They now begged that he might breakfast on board with them and promised him fresh herrings carefully boned if he would say grace and salute the King. He seemed perfectly happy with his friend, so I left him. Coming back an hour later I found all the ship's crew in the saloon and Rory sitting on the table singing to the accompaniment of a mouth organ.

That long slow journey through the Kyles to Kyleakin was very beautiful and I was tempted to continue the journey to the outer Hebrides. But on second thoughts walking across the island seemed more attractive and I knew Rory would like it better so I got off at the little pier at Kyleakin and went in search of lodgings. I soon discovered all I needed in the house of Mrs Campbell and her two daughters.

The Campbell family were typically Highland. Mrs Campbell was over eighty, a splendid old woman, who still wore the mutch; she had the head of a statesman and the manners of a duchess. She spoke no English, so we could only converse when her daughter acted as interpreter. She was nearly bedridden and I did what I could to make her last days brighter. The younger daughter, then into her thirties, was extremely well educated and had travelled quite a lot. At Glenelg lived the brother, Dr Campbell, who had married a Maclean and had two or three small children. He was a charmer – very tall and good-looking, most intelligent, and an able doctor. To see Dr Campbell and his old mother chatting together in the language of their country was very pleasing. The mother was so proud of her son and he equally proud of her – indeed, he had occasion to be, for much self-denial had been exercised to give him the education he had received.

Connected in some way to this family were Murdo Campbell and his wife Chirsty. Murdo was a fisherman and became, at Dr Campbell's request, my pilot during the time I was on the island. The doctor lent me a sailing boat and was so afraid I would instantly drown myself that he came up to Kyleakin and put me in Murdo's charge, as he said Murdo knew that dangerous coast like the fingers on his hand.

It was great sport sailing that boat. Taking the harbour bar was like jumping a big fence at times. Murdo was rather too cautious for my liking, but later on I found the poor man could not swim a stroke, so it was natural he should dislike the idea of being capsized. None of the men I talked to at Kyleakin could swim, which seemed to me very strange, since they were born almost in the sea; they were certainly all old, for the youth of Skye emigrate at the first opportunity. I started a swimming class and taught several of the little boys to swim before I left.

I had quite good fun otter hunting in the rocks along the coast with a man who made his living by selling the skins. He had a pack of tiny rough prickly-eared dogs, rather like toy Scotties, but much lighter in bone and more foxy in face. They were of various colours, from biscuit, blue, brindle, to almost black, and were the gamest little varmints that ever went to ground. Being so small they could follow an otter through the crevices of the rock, and they worked in and out of these tricky places like a bagful of ferrets.

It was from this breed of terriers, which is the oldest in Scotland, that the present-day Cairn Terrier evolved. The original Skye terrier, from which the White Poltalloch dogs were made, by breeding only from picked cream specimens, eventually became white, and bred true to type and colour. But Colonel Malcolm's terriers seemed to be larger than the dogs I hunted with; probably good food produced more size. My poor little friends lived a hard life; a small dish of porridge once a day was all the fare they ever got; they were always wet and very hard worked. But you could not have bought a good worker for love nor money from their owner, even though he had not a shilling in his pocket.

It is rather curious that these dogs, which bear the closest resemblance to the 'tap root' of the terriers of Scotland, and are referred to as far back as the fifteenth century, were the last of the Scottish terriers to be recognized by the Kennel Club.

One evening after a day's otter hunting, when I was walking with Murdo to the cottage from where we had secured the boat, I remarked on a tremendous wash that must have occurred at some time or other. It might have been caused by a battleship coming through the narrow Kyle at full-speed, or a tidal wave. Sand and stones had been driven up so as to form high banks some distance from the edge of the water.

I asked Murdo what had caused it. He calmly replied: 'It was just the sea-sarpint the time she came through the Kyle in ninety-two'. I replied: 'But, Murdo, sea serpents don't play about round the coast of Skye much; it must have been a big whale that came through.' 'It was no a whale, I'm telling you it was the sea-sarpint that came thro' whateffer,' and the old man was very indignant that I should have doubted his word.

I gave the matter no further thought, putting the story down to something that had been seen after a funeral or a wedding. But later I read Commander Gould's book, *The Case for the Sea Serpent* and in it he gives a detailed account, by eye-witnesses, of the sea-serpent that was seen at Glenelg several times, and in other places round the coast of Skye, the date corresponding with that of Murdo Campbell's story. On top of that comes the account of the Loch Ness monster. Murdo was too matter-of-fact to be a romancer and I firmly believe that he actually did see the sea-serpent rushing through the Kyle.

To be lost in a Scottish mist on the hills ten miles from the nearest habitation for the best part of a night is not in the least amusing. And it is worse if, as in my case, you have not taken a bite of food with you.

The tiny village of Kyleakin was not noted for producing sustenance. Meat had to be got from the mainland and, as I invariably forgot to order it, my provender was mostly porridge, eggs, an occasional fish, also old hens from the postman, provided they died a natural death. The only provisions' shop in the village was kept by Mrs Macdonald and she had expended her all on a six foot plate glass window on which appeared in fine enamel letters the words: 'Pork pies, made fresh daily.' I ventured in and asked for a pork pie and was met with: 'I'm sorry, there's nae pork pies the day.' Next day and the day after I tried again with no success. The answer was slightly varied on the third day: 'I'm sorry, there's nae pork pies the day, it's not worth while.' So sandwiches or portable food of any sort was difficult to come by. Rory caught himself a rabbit at intervals, which he guarded jealously until it was in the pot: but as he was more in need of meat that I was, I seldom liked to ask him for a part.

I was told that on top of a hill some miles distant I should probably find a golden eagle and one morning I started to explore. It was a warm stuffy day, so before attempting the steep climb up the shaley side of the mountain I deposited my coat on a rock at the foot. Halfway up Rory chopped a rabbit and asked me to carry it for him. Before I got to the clump of crags where the eagle lived, it was a hands and knees scramble, for the shale was so slippery I could not walk upright. I found the birds and, hiding behind a stone, watched them for a long time, making pencil drawings and notes of them in my sketchbook.

It was getting chilly and about time to start home, when I suddenly found myself buried in thick white mist. I usually possess a good homing instinct, but the birds had so absorbed me that I found I had quite forgotten from which direction I had come to their eyrie. I could not see a foot in front of me; the hill was nearly perpendicular and the fog was like cotton-wool below me. I panicked, feeling that every step I took was into space and would land me at the bottom of an abyss. It was getting late evening, and I had had no food since an early breakfast of porridge. Whether it was from emptiness, pure funk, or because I was standing on a rock with nothing solid to be seen below or around me, I suddenly realized I was deadly faint and had to sit down.

My head was swimming and coherent thought was getting further and further away, when Rory roused me by putting a rough paw and wet nose on my face. His teeth were chattering and I was still clinging to his rabbit. I began talking to myself reassuringly, like *Alice in Wonderland:* 'Scottish mists come down in a moment and rise in a moment: skin the rabbit and feed Rory. Murdo knows I am looking for eagles and will come and look for me.'

The comfort of my coat which was reposing on some rock below enticed me to make another effort to get down to it, for the cold was penetrating and the blackness of night was rapidly approaching. I tried a sitting slide, but finding my legs over a drop that might have been three feet, or possibly thirty, I decided I would rather die of cold than go any further. Rory had eaten the whole of his rabbit and was now cuddling up to me for warmth, so I tucked him bodily under my tweed skirt, where he certainly generated his own heat and I felt less chilled.

It must have been three o'clock in the morning before I heard a shot and knew a search party was out looking for me. Rory heard it too and

White West Highland

was anxious to be off. It was no use shouting, for sound ascends and I was already far above the searchers. Again I thought of my coat; if they found that they would fire the gun again and I would let Rory go, and he would guide the men up to me.

I took out my sketchbook and wrote in large letters on a sheet of the paper: 'Follow Rory, he will bring you to where I am sitting,' and tied it to his collar. At the next shot – it was a good deal nearer – I loosed the dog and, though it seemed an age, it really was not very long before

Rory appeared attached to a cord, at the other end of which was a man with a lantern.

They had brought a bottle of milk and some whisky, of which nectar Rory and I both partook and, as soon as a little feeling had returned to my legs and feet, I was lugged down from my pinnacle and led ignominiously back to home and bed.

Rory's yachting instinct came out very strongly these days. He loved the 'bata beg' (little boat). On less wet mornings I would say: 'Go and tell Murdo I want the boat.' Away he would run to the cottage half a mile away, bang and bark at the door or window until he got Murdo up, then go with him down to the beach and see the boat launched. After that, he would race back to my lodging. He had the same love of a boat that dogs nowadays have for cars. The gulls attracted him. He would stand on a rock like a statue, watching them circling round his head. From the sketches I made of him while watching the birds, I painted my picture '*The Sentinel*' which found a good place in the great room at the Academy.

I was also able to sketch an old woman who was a hundred years old living in a black house. Although she lived quite alone she was able to cut her own peat and repair the heather thatch of her house each winter. She had no English so I could not talk to her; but I was told, having given her 5s. for a sitting, that she had a pile of sovereigns buried under the floor of her house, money sent by her grandchildren who were out in the world doing well. They were mostly footmen and ladies' maids, one a sheep-farmer in Australia. The old lady spent nothing. She lived on oatmeal and milk from two or three goats. The soap she used didn't cost her much, for I have never seen anyone dirtier and her bothy was a picturesque pig-stye with the peat fire and porridge pot in the middle of the mud floor. There being no chimney, the peat smoke had given an ebony polish to everything she possessed.

I suppose all the 'black houses' will have disappeared by now; a pity, they were such happy hunting grounds for artists. Murdo and Chirsty did not live in one; he had cut his house out of solid rock, which formed the back and side walls, the façade being mud and stones. The rock walls were beautifully chiselled, and it must have taken endless time to get them so straight and smooth – a remnant of the cave-dweller's art.

I eventually moved on from Kyleakin with the one and only pony cart to Broadford, and from there did some tramping; through the Cuchullins, jagged like dogs' teeth at their summit, to Marsco and Glen Sligachan, where fairies and folklore take one into another world. Walking alone with Rory, I could at whiles dimly hear the Little Folk talking and felt myself an intruder to their exquisite sanctuary. Further still I went, until I gazed on the wave drenched and wind swept fortresses of Dunscaith, Duntulm and Dunvegan, the latter still inhabited by MacLeod of MacLeod. My pen is quite inadequate to describe the dream of beauty with which the Island fills the eye and senses.

And so home, back to smutty London and enclosed spaces.

Horses! Horses! Horses!

Chapter XXIII

'AN INDISCRETION'
With thanks to Richard Williams

The Reverend G. O. Pardoe, President of the Dandie Club became a friend of mine and always stayed with me for the Crystal Palace Show. He was one of the old type of sporting parsons, loved a horse as well as a dog, and bred Arabs at his vicarage near Christchurch. It was he who first encouraged me to get something to ride and asked me to come and look at a four year old Arab stallion he had bred himself that he thought would suit me. I paid a visit of a couple of days to his vicarage and tried the stallion, also a young mare, neither of which I liked at all. I am not fond of Arabs, except to look at, and have never been on one that I considered a good ride. The stallion and the mare had all the faults that Arabs possess and had been badly handled into the bargain. I decided I was no buyer, until I spotted a dark chestnut mare standing in the paddock some distance from the house. She looked more like it and I asked if I could see her closer. She proved to be a five year old brood mare who had never been broken. I was looking for some sort of shoulders and hers were placed fairly right. I eventually bought her for £30, borrowed a Cavesson head collar and long lead and took her back to London. As she had never been out of a paddock, and had never been led, I wondered how I was going to get her across London. I decided it would be best not to unbox her until night and to try and get her through the streets when traffic was at its lowest.

That was a bit of horse breaking I never want to try again. We think London is empty at night because it is so full during the day, but that night it was nothing like empty enough for me with a terrified unbroken filly at the other end of a line. I cannot think how I ever prevented her leaping through at least a dozen shop windows, and her crazy dashes whenever a bus passed to right and left on the greasy wooden paving, ended several times in a heavy fall.

I got her home somewhere about one o'clock in the morning and I do not know which of us was the more exhausted. I backed her in the kennel yards and afterwards trained her in a riding school. Pretty as paint, I used her for one of the heads in my picture, '*An Indiscretion*' bought and published by Messrs Fores of Piccadilly.

I called her 'Rab'. She was never a hack to my liking, but I took a lot of trouble with her and showed her in a Ladies hack class at Olympia, putting a child up to ride her. She was left in until the last five, then, getting out of hand, slipped at a corner on the tan and nearly sat down; this put her out of the money. The next day I sold her in the Show for eighty guineas to a lady who intended hunting with the Devon and Somerset. I should think that lady's days were numbered, for an Arab that trips at a sixpence is hardly a safe mount over the rough going of the moorland.

Although I do not like the feel of an Arab under me, I must give the breed its due. It is the only breed of horse that owns dog-like intelligence. I believe Arabs could be taught almost anything. Rab could very soon open all the doors, whether fastened with bolt or latch. She would let herself into the studio at teatime, stand quietly by my side and eat as much bread and butter and cake as I would give her. To gaze at herself in the large mirror fixed on the wall, she would make her dainty way in and out of standing easels and never knock a thing over.

In Richmond Park I used to let her loose while I sat under a tree to sketch. She would race about and amuse herself for an hour or so, but at my call would come trotting to my side for the return journey. I have never owned an English horse that would do this.

After Rab went I bought two small ponies: one at Tiverton Market and an exact match for him which I found amongst a mob of Exmoors at Barnet Fair. Both were unhandled and as wild as hawks. I broke them to harness, and drove them pair and tandem, and very pretty they were. But I was too late for the horse market; carriages and pairs in the Park were fast giving place to automobiles, and all those who could afford it sold their horses and invested in motor cars. I had to part with the pair and sold one very well as a child's park hack.

Nevertheless, I found myself bitten again by the horse bug and I could not keep out of the saddle. For a month or two before the Olympia Show I took on an evening job training American jumpers

ANOTHER DELIGHT

This horse won the Grand Military at Sandown in 1912 and 1913.

With thanks to the Wyndham family

over fences by artificial light. I got the nastiest fall I ever had in my life at this game. One evening I was riding a notable jumper who, like many another, owned a temper and got sick of jumping. He had been round twice and cleared everything, with the exception of the triple-bar. This he had just flipped with his hind-feet. I was asked to take him over the bars again, but was not told that this time the top one would be fixed. The horse showed temper, rearing round before he would face the obstacle. He then launched himself at it with back-flung ears, hit the top bar with his knees and turned completely over, crushing me against the wall of the school. We were both knocked out for a short time, and both cut about the head, but no permanent damage was done – no thanks to the riding master, to whom I gave a bit of my dishevelled mind.

Painting racehorses was a necessary work that I did not much like. The first animal that fell to my brush was General Byrne's noted stallion 'Amphion'; but as it is nearly half a century since I saw the animal I cannot remember more than that he was a dark chestnut, compact in build. Mr Edward Brassey's 'Bay Ronald'[1] is still fresh in my memory. He was a horse with a club-foot and was reckoned to be a man-eater in the stable. His lad always held him for me with a rearing bit in his mouth and I was forbidden to touch him. One morning, the boy having stood with his eyes fixed on some object for about an hour, suddenly fell flat on his face right in front of the horse's forelegs. The animal savaged him at once. I cast palette and brushes to the winds and rushed to his rescue, managing to grab the rein and jerk the horse's mouth so severely that he let go the lad and went straight up on end, striking at my head. I swung him round clear of the lad, meanwhile shouting for help, which arrived before any damage had been done.

I did a big portrait of 'Orme'[2] in John Porter's stables at Kingsclere, just after he had recovered from the poison he was given before the Derby. The mystery of how the horse had been 'got at' was still the talk of the village and nobody so far had been convicted of the crime. There was a good deal of 'hush-hush' in the stables about it, but the greyhound trainers who spent most evenings in the inn where I was staying voiced their suspicions pretty freely and I heard a lot of what might or might not have been true.

---

[1] Bay Ronald by Hampton out of Black Duchess by Galliard. He is assured of his place in racing history through his son Bayardo, sire of Gainsborough and grandsire of Solario and Hyperion.

[2] Orme by Ormonde out of Angelica sister of St. Simon. A few days before the 2,000 Guineas in 1892 'he was found to be suffering from acute poisoning and for a time he hovered precariously between life and death. There was a theory that the cause was a badly infected tooth; more probably it was an act of deliberate villainy and Porter suspected one of his own employees. He sired Flying Fox and Orby also Witch Elm and Tobiary. Champion sire in 1899. [Our thanks to the National Horseracing Museum, Newmarket]

'Orme' was no beauty, and not looking his best. He was just about to be put into training again for the Eclipse Stakes, and 'La Fleche', his opponent, was in the same stable a few boxes away, while that enormous horse 'Watercress' divided the pair. I believe 'Watercress' stood seventeen hands and at that time had already been sold to an overseas buyer. 'La Fleche' was small, low in front with terrific driving power behind, rather arched in loin and, I imagined, most uncomfortable to ride. She was woolly in coat and reminded me of a hare. It must have been a difficult position for Mr John Porter, having two such noted rivals in his stable at the same time and both being prepared for the same valuable race.

I was at Sandown when these two champions met in the Eclipse Stakes. The gallant little mare put up a great race, but at a mile the horse proved too good for her and she was just beaten. I was standing amongst a group of her admirers and saw tears in the eyes of several as 'Orme' passed the winning post first; not because of loss of money but pure sentiment; they wanted the little brown lady to win.

It is true without doubt that handsome is as handsome does and that they come in all shapes and sizes. It certainly does not follow that the handsomest horses are always the best. 'Manifesto'[3], whom I painted when he was in training for his third National, is a case in point. To look at him in the stable no one would have thought it possible for him to hump the weight and win over that gruelling course at Aintree. A great-shouldered horse, with plenty of heart room, he had a short back, was on the leggy side and light of bone below the knee, with a small fine head and generous eye. Yet Willie Moore, who trained him, seldom asked him to jump in private. He must have been a great horse, and a great hearted one to do what he did; which was to carry 12 stone 7 lbs top weight over the National fences without a mistake.

---

[3] Manifesto was a bay gelding by Man o' War out of Vae Victis. Irish Bred. Twice won the Grand National and raced 13 consecutive seasons.

'Jenkinstown'[4], who I also painted at the same time as I did 'Another Delight', winner of the Grand Military at Sandown, was much more my idea of a National horse. An Irish weight-carrier, he had a peculiar trick in the stable of actually sitting on top of his manger; it was difficult to make him stand on his hindlegs at all. Poor fellow, he was killed on the line at Paddington Station very shortly after I painted him. (1912)

'Verny' was the last racehorse I portrayed, after his victory in the City and Suburban. Mr Gilpin trained him at Newmarket and the picture was a gift to him from an old friend. 'Verny' was the tallest thoroughbred I have ever seen, a golden chestnut gelding, high on the leg, lovely forehand, small head with the nose of an Arab. I worked under difficulties, for he was too large for his house, and I could not get far enough away from him.

While at Newmarket I was lent an old racehorse belonging to Joe Cannon to ride. It was the duty of this old horse to lead the yearlings in their canter ever morning. He knew his job so thoroughly that he would have done it just as well with a dumb jockey on his back. He made a dumb jockey out of me the first time out, for I was riding in front of the string and was not warned what to expect. The moment he reached the track, he sprang off his hocks as though loosed out of a gun, streaking away as if the hounds of hell were after him. I quite thought he had bolted and made futile efforts to stop him when, on reaching the four furlong post, he stopped dead and shot me forward amongst his ears. When I got back to breakfast at my lodgings all I had to do was fix the reins and stirrups, give the old horse a smack on the rump and he jogged back to stables on his own. I never met Joe Cannon, but I should have liked to thank him for the loan of his horse, who showed me the historical heath at Newmarket in a way I should not otherwise have seen it.

The few racehorse models I have mentioned are those that made the

---

[4] Jenkinstown by Hackler out of Playmate. Irish bred. Won Grand National 1910 carrying 10 stone five, at 100 – 8. He fell at two subsequent Nationals and never won another race.

BLACK PRINCE
*The Bridgeman Art
Library*

deepest impression on me. I have had as many and more horses through my hands than most ordinary people, but only a few do I recollect, some good ones and some rank bad ones. The following story shows how the form of a horse, apart from his colour, can impress itself on one's memory.

Around this time I stayed a few days with Colonel and Mrs Birdwood at Woburn; he was then Master of Horse to the Duke of Bedford. Colonel Birdwood had been over to the Dublin Horse show and had bought two hunters for His Grace, both winners in their class and both owned and shown by the same man, whose name was never mentioned to me. Both horses were bright chestnuts, one called 'No Trumps', the other 'Grand Slam' and they cost a great deal of money.

The Colonel, wishing to see if 'No Trumps' would carry a lady, put me up for a day with The Oakley. We drove to the meet, and when I was mounted on this prize winning five hundred guinea touch my pleasure knew no bounds. To cut a long story short, he was the most disappointing animal I ever rode. Very sticky over fences, he had no spirit and was dead idle. A small Welsh cob would have jumped better that day.

But the sequel was interesting. I had been living in Kenya several years when, riding through someone's farm, I came on a little house with a man standing outside, wearing very smart riding breeches and boots. He looked so nice and horsey that we began to converse, and he took me into his sitting room for a cup of tea. On the mantelpiece was a row of horse photographs, which of course I looked at. Suddenly I picked one up and exclaimed: 'But this is a horse I rode called 'No Trumps'!' I was right. My new acquaintance proved to be the man from whom Colonel Birdwood had bought both horses at the Dublin Show.

* * *

Having lived for twenty years in London, I now began to pine for a cottage and garden in the country. Moreover, after sixteen years of inseparable devotion, Rory had received his call and the studio was no longer home without him.

I went to live at Epping during 1913 and remained there until the declaration of war, when all the world went mad. Directly afterwards I crossed to Boulogne and joined up with the Allied Hospital, working as a nurse until it practically closed down in the Spring of 1915.

I draw a blind over memory at this juncture, thankful that time has now partially obscured the mind-pictures of agony and horrors I witnessed during those few dreadful months in France. More than enough has already been written of such matters. I therefore will ring down the curtain on Act One, and re-set the stage for Act Two, with suitable background for an exile, pioneer and cowherd in a foreign land.

Book Two

Exile and Pioneer in a Foreign Land

'Little Did I Dream Of What Was Still Before Me'

Chapter I

NAIROBI STATION 1900

In May 1915 I had a letter from my youngest sister, Olive[1], who had been living in East Africa[2] for some years, asking me to come and stay with her for a while.

After considerable difficulty I managed to get a berth on a cargo boat which left the London docks on June 6th. I took a return ticket, for I had every intention of going back to France to continue hospital work. Man proposes, God disposes.

The journey was a nightmare that lasted for seven weeks. The boat was not intended for carrying passengers, having hardly any deck room and only one bathroom and lavatory for the officers and passengers alike. If clothes needed washing you did it yourself. The accommodation was vile and the food nasty.

On the fore part of the vessel was stacked a lot of petrol with a tarpaulin thrown over it and when we were shelled in the English Channel, one shot just missed the petrol dump by a few feet. A submarine fired a torpedo at us the second night out; that also went wide of the mark and the enemy was driven off by our destroyers.

We lay at Marseilles for days, right out in the harbour, and no one was allowed ashore. What we were waiting for I do not know; some said guns and ammunition, but all I saw loaded were several very nice mules and two Catalonian jackasses which are huge black donkeys with nine inches of bone below the knee. Having nothing to do, I measured their legs myself. These were going to South Africa. It is the Catalonian donkey that sires the magnificent mules one sees in South Africa.

At Port Said the boat was sandbagged before going through the Suez Canal, and ridiculous notices were stuck about stating that anyone going on deck went *at his own risk.*

The glory-hole was now full of Armenian refugees and a packet of Tommies[3] on their way to Port Sudan. The heat was becoming intense

---

[1] See Appendix 1
[2] At that time Kenya was known as the East African Protectorate.
[3] British Soldiers

and, of course 'at my own risk', I spent the night behind the sandbags on deck, watching through a chink in the barricade, as the sun rose over the desert which had been partially flooded for some reason. The reflections in wet sand and water were too lovely for words, the dawn picture being enhanced by graceful standing camels and praying Arabs. It was my first sight of the East, and it so enchanted me that for a while I forgot everything else.

At Port Sudan we coaled and never shall I forget the heat or the smell: a peculiar odour rather resembling that of the musk-rat with something added, and the hotter it became the more penetrating becomes the perfume. We were kept a night and day at this delightful place, and I could but think that if Mark Twain had swopped Texas for Port Sudan he would still have preferred hell.[4]

So far the journey had been on a sea like a millpond and it was not until we rounded Guardefui that there was any movement at all. Here we ran into the monsoon which was a blessed relief after the killing heat of the Red Sea through which we had crawled at four knots an hour owing to the fact that our scratch lot of firemen were unable to do their work. Hardly any of them had been in the tropics before and they were constantly being lugged up from the engine-rooms in a fainting condition.

We suffered badly enough, having only a single awning over the deck, but our suffering was nothing compared to those in Second Class. Here many poor creatures went down with heat stroke every day and so much ice was used to resuscitate them that we ran out of our only luxury before reaching Mombasa.

At Mombasa I was met by an agent and taken to the nice big airy house

---

[4] It appears that Miss Collyer may have mis-attributed the quotation. We thank Mrs Linda Snow, Head of Reference Services at the University of Texas who wrote the following: 'I'm not aware of any such quote by Mark Twain, but there is a similar quotation familiar to all Texans by General Philip Sheridan: '*If I owned Hell and Texas I would rent out Texas and live in Hell.*' These words are sometimes attributed to Mark Twain, but they originally seem to have come from General Sheridan.'

of Messrs Smith Mackenzie. Apparently our ship had been mislaid for several weeks. No news being received of her, my sister had become very anxious and had been telegraphing to Smith Mackenzie to find out what had happened to the ship. We therefore sent a wire at once, telling Olive of my safe arrival.

That night I boarded the train for Nairobi and decided that the Uganda Railway would not spoil you for any other. It took the best part of two nights and a day to reach Nairobi. The line at Voi had been blown up by the Germans the day before, and we had to wait hours for it to be sufficiently repaired to let us through. The Germans were constantly hovering around Voi, and on one occasion the Indian stationmaster got so alarmed that he sent a telegram to headquarters in Nairobi: 'Twenty Germans marching on Station; please send twenty rounds of ammunition.'

At three o'clock the following morning my sister and Mr Berkeley Cole[5] met me on Nairobi platform, and we spent the remainder of the night at the house of Dr and Mrs Milne[6].

From the top of the hill on which this house was built, the town of Nairobi looked to me like an indiscriminate dump of tin shanties. There seemed to be no layout or design about the capital at all. Government Road was in existence, but with few stone buildings of any importance.

The Stanley Hotel, which is still the centre of the town[7], existed, while the *Standard*[8] offices, a few banks, the Treasury and Post Office,

---

5 The Hon. Berkeley Cole was brother-in-law to Lord Delamere. During WWI he raised Cole's Scouts which consisted of several hundred Somalis. At first they performed admirable work along the German border, but after a while a number of the rank and file mutinied. The loyal remnant was later reformed with a mounted company of the Loyal North Lancashire Regiment, and served for some time under Cole's command. (The Permanent Way by M.F. Hill)

6 Dr Arthur Dawson Milne CMG, MB, CM (Aberdeen). Born in Kingston Jamaica, in 1877 initially a medical officer for the Uganda Protectorate, he transferred to the East African Medical Service and was Mentioned in Despatches. (Tribute to Pioneers by Mary Gillett)

7 This would have been written in the 1930's. It later became The New Stanley Hotel.

8 The East African Standard was always known as 'The Standard'.

were the only important buildings I can remember. Within the last few years quite beautiful buildings have been erected, the more important being the McMillan Memorial Library, the Standard Bank of South Africa, the National Bank of India, the splendid Market and the very large Avenue Hotel, to say nothing of theatres and rows of garages on either side of Sixth Avenue[9].

When I arrived in 1915, motorcars were as rare as the eggs of the Great Auk. The few roads that existed were little more than tracks and all conveyances were drawn by ponies, mules or oxen.

My sister's coffee plantation at Kabete was ten miles out from Nairobi. When shopping had to be done in Nairobi it was an all day job. We could get into town in an hour since it was down-hill; then the ponies had to be rested and fed while we tramped about in the heat and dust making purchases and doing our business, lunched somewhere, inspanned the team and drove around collecting packages. The return journey being up-hill all the way, it was seldom that one got home before teatime.

Now we can get to town in a quarter of an hour and back in about twenty minutes. Truly the petrol engine is metamorphosing the world.

My first journey to Kabete was in a Cape cart with a couple of nondescript ponies: one was an Arab with a cricked back and partial paralysis in both hind legs and his mate was a much smaller animal, a South African mare evidently heavy in foal. A road of sorts had been made as far as the Veterinary Laboratory and the last two miles consisted of a grass track through low bush. The journey was all up-hill, and it took us an hour and a half to reach the house. I truly felt I was in the wilds of Africa and little did I dream of what was still before me.

I found that my sister had dug herself in very comfortably indeed. The tiny mud and stone house, somewhat resembling a pagoda, was dwarfed by a large flower garden in the making, surrounded by fifteen

---

9   Charles Rand-Overy was appointed Plan Examiner and Chief Draughtsman, Survey Department, East African Protectorate in 1905. We are told by his grand-daughter that he designed many of these buildings.

OLIVE COLLYER'S
'PAGODA',
NDUMBWINI

acres of well-grown coffee trees. The carriage drive boasted an avenue of Grevillea Robusta, the silky oak of Australia, grown as pot plants in our greenhouses at home. The trees were then two feet high, the lower branches being carefully removed with a pair of nail scissors. During the last year (1934) these trees have had to be felled, as they were fifty or sixty feet high and smothered everything.

The rapidity of tree and plant growth at Kabete and the surrounding districts is phenomenal, the soil being rich red loam of unlimited depth. It seems a crying shame that thousands of acres of this valuable coffee land should have been handed over indiscriminately to the Kikuyu tribe. More than three parts of it is a native reserve, meaning that the land is unpurchasable by Europeans. The railway ran right through this fertile country which increased its value enormously as far as the white settler was concerned; but it in no way helped the native who merely grew crops for his own consumption, and would have been quite as well off and just as happy if his *shamba* (smallholding or garden) had been a distance from the line. I am the last person who wishes to see the native denuded of his rights; but when one knows that land further afield would have suited him every bit as well, why allow him to spoil, by inadequate and dirty cultivation, a part that by rights should have been bringing many thousands of pounds a year into the Colony?[10]

I had not been many months in Africa before I discovered that there would be no possibility of returning to England until the close of the war. Owing to mines being laid by the Germans, travelling was off and passengers were no longer taken on the mail steamers. My ticket was therefore cancelled and the money returned. Other plans had to be considered for my future. In the meantime I helped my sister in her big business of growing vegetables for the hospitals and I saw a little of the country. I later took on an unpaid nursing billet with the 2nd Rhodesians, who were in a Rest Camp near the veterinary laboratory.

Dr Ellis, who was in charge of something like four hundred sick and fevered men, asked me to help him as he had nothing but orderlies in the camp, nurses being unavailable. The hospital consisted of two or three large tents, and these were packed full of men suffering from malaria, minor injuries, pneumonia and a few cases of blackwater fever[11]. It being the rainy season, the camp was often flooded with

---

[10] This view was widely held by settlers at that time and feelings ran high between the Colonial Administration and the settlers over land demarcation: the former believing that the welfare of the African was paramount and the settler being caught up in the struggle to make a living in a harsh world. Before Britain administered the country that was to become the Colony of Kenya, the tribal demarcations were vague. Although the tribal numbers were tiny compared with today, there was continuous inter-tribal raiding. The new British administration demarcated the tribal areas in an effort to prevent this and, at the same time, an area was demarcated for European farming with a view to making the Colony pay its way, in order that it would be less of a burden on the 'patient, plodding, acquiescent milch cow, the British tax payer.' (Elspeth Huxley: with thanks to C. S. Nicholls)

[11] A complication of a dangerous form of malaria which causes a destruction of the blood cells. The breakdown products find their way via the kidneys and into the urine. One person who had blackwater fever described his urine as looking like Guinness.

water and many of the tents leaked. It is surprising that a lot of the men didn't die; but I only lost one case from blackwater and he made a gallant fight for life. Just as Dr Ellis and I hoped he was on the turn towards recovery, the former was recalled to Nairobi and a doctor just out from home took his place who knew nothing at all about blackwater fever. He instantly altered the treatment, insisting that the man should be fed on meat juice. This started the sickness again, and that was the end. I tried so hard to save that man's life. For eight days and nights I never went to bed, and gave the injections every four hours myself. I still believe that if Dr Ellis had stayed on we should have got him through between us.

My sister, meanwhile, had been making up her mind to go and look at some land beyond a place called Gilgil. Coffee did not interest me and she thought that running a cattle farm would be more in my line. Kabete was not suitable cattle country, being full of east coast fever. It was a poisonous place for cattle and we only managed to rear two calves during the two years I was there.

Horses were also scarce, the Army having commandeered every available horse of any worth. We only had the two already mentioned and an old white Somali gelding for both riding and driving purposes. We managed to get an enormous lot of work out of the three, for we were constantly attending cattle sales and often had long distances to ride to reach them. My sister chose to ride the corky old cripple and I was given the Somali.

The cattle that were put on the market then were all native stock, small humped creatures of variegated colours. The cows gave very little milk, but it was of high quality. They would not milk without their calf, so when buying a cow you had to keep a sharp lookout that she had her own calf with her. When buying native cattle my sister always pitched on the loudest coloured ones she could find. The more splodged and spotted they were the better she liked them and some looked as though they had been hand-painted for a child's Noah's Ark.

Olive did a good deal of trading in those days and made it pay quite well. The thing was to pass the animals on at once, for unless regularly dipped they died like flies. It is curious, though, that the humped cattle, long since indigenous to the country, do not seem to be much more immune from disease than the high-grade and pure-bred stock we run on the farms today.

The sale-yards were always surrounded by a dense crowd of Kikuyu and Somali buyers, the former oozing castor oil and red clay with which they painted their bodies. Their hair was long and into it was twisted grass, the whole being bound together and worn in a queue; the forehead was decorated with a leather band embroidered with coloured beads. The head-dress, when completed, was thickly pasted with oil and red mud and lasted a long time without further interference. Some people who were less smart, just oiled and redded their locks, letting them hang in dripping strings loose about their face. Others wrapped their heads in the skin taken from the stomach of calves, the skin being dressed with the oil and paint. But the methods of hairdressing changed continually, the Masai, I fancy, setting the fashion.

The Kikuyu tribe have no originality and no initiative; they are imitators and copyists in everything they do. The Masai, being a far superior race, copy no one, but take their own line and stick to it. Nowadays, at the time of writing, thousands of Kikuyu wear European clothes and cut

A MASAI WARRIOR
Painted By Sir Harry
Johnston[12]

---

[12] Sir Harry Johnston GCMG KCB was appointed to the Special Commission to Uganda in 1899. During a period of unrest in the country his unfailing tact and wide knowledge of Africa and its peoples enabled him to effect a complete reorganisation of the Uganda Protectorate and this led to a happy regime. He was a prolific author and talented painter.

their hair short like the white man, parting it on one side and combing it into a fuzz. It is rare to see a Kikuyu with a decorated head.

The Masai, on the other hand, have not altered an iota since the advent of the white man. They still wear skins or blankets, stain themselves with clay with the hairdressing as picturesque as ever. Very few either understand or speak Swahili. Their attitude is one of 'Go to hell and be damned to you'. So long as I have not got to work with them I rather admire their attitude.

'Toe to Toe with Africa'

Chapter II

One evening, sitting by the fire in the dining room, we reached the crossroads and an important decision had to be made.

The position was this: if we bought the Gilgil farm I should have to look after it, which meant spending the rest of my life cattle herding in Kenya and giving up all idea of going back to England.

My sister and I have always been close friends. I disliked the idea of leaving her and as I had no ties in the Old Country, I decided that I would stay, take on farming and throw my lot in with hers. Putting aside my aversion to coffee trees, we had a good deal in common, both being animal lovers and quite horse-mad. We therefore considered there was every likelihood of a happy time in front of us.

Olive and a friend of hers went up to Gilgil to explore the district round about and to find a farm on the Syndicate land that might be suitable for cattle[1]. They eventually pitched on one of about 1,100 acres, lying between the Oliondo and Simba rivers and facing the range of the Aberdare Mountains, where no human foot had trod since the big Masai move in 1911[2]. The place was viewed under the most propitious circumstances; the big rains being on, both rivers were full of water and

---

[1] Some land allocated for European farming was bought by syndicates and then sold on. (*Red Strangers: The White Tribe of Kenya* by C.S. Nicholls)

[2] See Appendix II

LT. COLONEL
ALGERNON LINDSAY
ERIC SMITH CBE

the grass was three to four feet high. My sister returned to Kabete overflowing with enthusiasm and delighted with her purchase but, owing to the war and lack of essentials, I was not destined to see my future abode until January 1918.

In the meantime, in Kabete, there was a dearth of horseflesh in the colony and we saw the advisability of starting a horse-breeding establishment. Numbers of remounts for the troops were being brought up from the South, and a large depot was being formed at Kajiado, where horses were dying in hundreds from horse-sickness and tsetse-fly, some only lasting a few weeks. Many of the mares were in foal and therefore could not be worked. Others proved to be unrideable. A big sale of these Army rejects was to be held on the Nairobi Polo Ground.

Prior to the sale being held, my sister sent me off with a tent and two men to Naivasha, partly to see the stock of the Government Farm and, incidentally, to make some sketches of the Morandart River. I was provided with a Kavirondo[3] cook, who was usually stupefied with Bhang,[4] and another boy who did all the work while the cook enjoyed his smoky dreams.

Having already viewed the Kabete Experimental Farm with its imported pigs too fat to breed, and its acres of lucerne choked with weeds, I had not formed a great opinion of the Agricultural Department. I was therefore interested to see if the stock farm was better run than that of the cereals and porcines.

---

3 Now known as the Luo tribe.
4 Bhang – a Hindi word for the hemp plant and the source of the active agent in marijuana.

I arrived at Naivasha after dark and was obliged to spend the night at the hotel where I met an elderly man who offered to drive me out to the farm in his mule-gharry the next morning. I knew Naivasha from sketches done by Col. Eric Smith[5] before the railway was built and my disappointment was great when I witnessed its desecration by the hand of man. Nothing, of course, could spoil the beauty of Mount Longonot, from whose foothills flowed the azure waters of a wondrous lake, nor could it interfere with its colourful bordering of blue water-lilies, papyrus grass, and flat-topped acacia thorn-trees. But the wild foreground I remembered from those sketches had given place to iron buildings scattered amongst the rocky slopes of the veldt.

The Government Stock Farm lies some miles out from the township and, as I was driven there, my charioteer droned on and on about someone or something called 'Tommy'. At first I thought he was speaking of a little boy but as the creature was always falling through barbed wire and half drowning itself in water-holes, I decided it was a pet goat he was talking about. Next day I learned that Tommy was his daughter and I was amused to recollect asking if it butted dangerously.

Having pitched my tent not far from the house, I was taken by the manager to see the stock. There were one or two imported bulls, which were good enough, but because I was freshly arrived from England, the grade cows found little favour in my eyes. It took me some time to get used to low-grade cattle. The largest and best bull was killed by a lion the very next day and I was shown what a lion is capable of doing with

---

5   Lt. Col. Eric Smith CB of the 1st Life Guards was a relative, by marriage of the Collyer family. His brother was married to Margaret and Olive's eldest sister, Helen (see Book One.) He was the first Commandant of Fort Smith at Kikuyu where buildings were built with the first burnt brick. He is said to have lost an arm and an eye to Africa and his great nephew, Mr Jeremy Smith, told us that some members of his family believe he amputated his arm himself. He holds the record for the most marches from Mombasa to Uganda. After his first journey on the newly built Uganda Railway he was asked what he thought of it and he replied 'Better than walking. Better than walking' [*The Permanent Way* by M.F.H.Hill. *Early Days in East Africa* by Sir Frederick Jackson]

one stroke of its paw. It had sprung from behind on to the animal's back, and with just one swipe had broken the bull's neck.

I found myself toe to toe with real Africa now, for while lying on my camp-bed I saw a long pair of legs with naked pink thighs, standing just outside my tent. That cock ostrich led me a dreadful life. He persisted in following me wherever I went and stood a few yards behind my back all the time I was sketching. As I expected an attack from the rear at any moment I could not paint and asked the manager what he could do about it. The bird was at last rounded up and driven into a yard. At one time ostrich farming was becoming an industry in Kenya but when war broke out most of the settlers joined up and the tame ostriches were turned adrift, the cock birds becoming rather a menace.

One early morning a couple of cheetah got amongst a flock of sheep and played havoc until we ran out and drove them away. My eyes were gradually being opened, for up to now I had only seen wild animals behind the bars of cages.

I believe that I was the first woman to be invited to an Agricultural Dinner in Kenya, and at the time it seemed that I might be the last, for I put my foot into it badly. This annual function took place while I was in camp and I was sent an invitation to attend. Having so recently arrived in the country, I knew no one and did not in the least appreciate the importance of the event. The guests numbered only about twenty (most of the farmers were at the Front), and there were several heads of departments whom it was taken for granted I should know.

On the verandah before dinner I was introduced to a Mr MacDonald, a tall gaunt Scotsman with greying hair and a moustache[6]. I had not the remotest notion who he was, but he took the head of the table and I was placed next to him on his right. Opposite me was The

---

[6] Archibald MacDonald MRAC, FMAS came from South Africa to the Agricultural Department East African Protectorate in 1903 and became Director of Agriculture in 1907. [Mary Gillett]

Hon. Galbraith Cole[7] whom I had met before. In the course of conversation Mr MacDonald asked me what I thought of the country and inquired if I had visited the *beautiful Government Farm at Kabete*. Thinking the man was pulling my leg I laughed and said I had not seen much of the country, but I certainly knew the Kabete farm and considered it a pity that the Director of Agriculture had so little knowledge of farming.

At this point Mr Galbraith Cole went into chuckles of laughter. Conversation ceased and everyone glared at me. Not knowing why, I happily continued my strictures, mentioning the acres of weed-choked lucerne and the fatness of the pigs. 'Why,' said I, 'how can the man be a farmer when he does not even know that lucerne must be kept clean, and that fatted sows won't breed!'

At this point the manager hastily rose from the table and suggested a game of cards. Not being a card-player I was escorted to my tent by the man who had sat on my right. Outside the house he exclaimed in a horrified voice, 'Do you know who it was you were teaching to farm? Mr MacDonald himself is the Head of the Agricultural Department!'

There was a cattle sale the next day in the township and the least I could do was to go there, see Mr MacDonald, and tell him how sorry I was. My only way of getting to Naivasha was to mount a tiny chestnut mule which was almost unrideable. I felt so guilty that I thought I would risk it. So I saddled up the mule who went quite nicely until we

7   A son of the Earl of Enniskillen (and brother of Berkeley) Galbraith Cole took up land at first at Laikipia but this he relinquished as it was incorporated into a native reserve. In 1906 he obtained a large area of land on the slopes of the Eburru Mountain and on the shores of Lake Elementeita. He was tried for murder of a suspected sheep thief on his farm and acquitted. He was deported to Britain in 1911 but was allowed to return in WWI to help in the war effort.[*Moving the Maasai* by Lotte Hughes] Over the many years he was in Kenya he did great work for the development of sheep farming, some of the finest flocks in the country being on his estate. He also built up a valuable herd of cattle, many of which had been imported. Many acres were put under cultivation and all the chief crops were grown, as well as a large variety of fruit trees. His main hobby was shooting and his reputation of being a first class shot was known throughout the Colony. He died in 1929 at the early age of 48. [Mary Gillett].

were through the first gate, when he then put up a performance worthy of the breed. Luckily I had shut the gate or I should have been taken home in two twinks.

It was a witty private soldier who said, 'You never know what a mule is going to do 'til he done it.' Never was a truer description given. After a series of acrobatics my mount got busy on the top bar of the gate, standing on his hind legs and hammering it with this forefeet. He would have been doing this still if a mule-team of six and their drivers had not come along and driven him off with ox-whips. He then ran away with me over fearsome country consisting of rocks and holes but, as he was heading in the right direction I let him go; not that I could have stopped him if I had tried. He ended up in the back yard of the pub where I left him to look after himself and walked the rest of the way to the sale yard.

Mr MacDonald was on the rostrum talking to the Provincial Commissioner, to whom as well as to others he had evidently been pitching the tale about me. Accepting my apology he remarked that an outside opinion was occasionally useful. Being a Scotsman he naturally wanted something out of it and claimed one of my water-colour drawings of the Morandart. I was glad to make the peace-offering.

Wheeling and Dealing

Chapter III

KENYA'S PRIDE

1916

I soon discovered that my sister was nearly as good as I am at collecting animals. For some reason known only to herself she had bought no less than five stallion donkeys. They were never used, but they helped to keep the cattle warm in the yard at night.

We were going to call on a man living about four miles away who ran the best coffee *shamba* in the district. I suppose we had become rather bored with riding quiet respectable ponies, for that evening we decided the donkeys wanted breaking. We caught the two largest and proceeded to saddle them. Bridles were out of the question, for no donkey is ever bridled in East Africa. If you are stupid enough to ride them you guide them with sticks, one in each hand, and bang them over the side of the head. You also employ a boy to run behind with a long whip and yell at them.

Neither of us had even thought of a donkey ride since the old sea-side days when we were small children but we now mounted these mokes with joy, meaning to get some amusement out of them. We must have looked a funny couple as we rode down the steep decline to the main track that led through the Government Experimental Farm, beating and shouting with all our might to make the donkeys move. The little beasts made short sharp dives to right or left, dropping their heads and kicking like mischief at intervals, while a wild-looking native flew about here, there and everywhere behind us, his greasy locks flopping, uttering uncouth howls, flourishing a long stick and hurling a vast flow of incomprehensible language at the donkeys' tails. He had his work cut out to keep them headed in the right direction and it was all we could do to remain on their backs. We were laughing so much that our knees kept getting weak.

The boy was really doing his job well and had got the animals going at quite a fast jiggling trot when, rounding a corner where the road was very narrow, we met a full team of oxen drawing a wagon. Both donkeys made straight for the leaders of the team. With a mighty clout on the side of the head, and a pull at his near side ear, I managed to steer my mount to the side of the road. My sister's steed turned broadside across it, completely blocking the passage and holding up the traffic. Nothing would induce the little brute to move and in her anxiety and fear of being prodded by the leading oxen, she lost her temper and went for the wretched drivers in extremely fluent and emphatic Swahili, requesting to know what they meant by taking up the whole the road, whether they had ever driven oxen before and, if they had, why had they not got proper control over them? She wound up her tirade by threatening to report the lot of them but still the donkey remained perfectly immovable and after this unseemly burst of fury she had to get off its back ignominiously and allow the ox-drivers to *lift* the obstruction out of their way.

Really it was no bad effort, for we actually arrived at our friend's house. While we were there we collected another horse. This was a chestnut who was a near match with the decrepit one for the Cape cart. He was a young horse and he had been broken to the saddle, although he had never been in harness. In those days we neither of us took much account of what a horse did, so long as he was decent to look at and could go a bit. We turned one donkey adrift and I rode the horse home.

The next day my sister was extra busy with the coffee and requiring some stores for the house. She suggested that I should put the two chestnuts into the Cape cart and go and get the things from Kikuyu, which was the nearest place where you could buy anything.

Kikuyu is about six miles from Kabete and there was no particular road, only a very rough wagon track. Had I known how rough it was and what the hills were like, I doubt if I should have taken on the job so readily with one of the pair unbroken to the collar; more especially, I had never yet driven a Cape cart, which is far more difficult to control than any motor-car ever invented. You need to know its nasty ways. The axle, mercifully, is very wide so that it is not easily upset but the pole plays such tricks that it is apt to make a nervous horse bolt.

We harnessed up, inspanning the unbroken horse on the off-side under the whip. The old horse was a nice-tempered fellow, but hot stuff and fretful if anything upset him. Moreover, in his youth he had damaged his back and had very little power behind.

We started off gaily enough. I had a *syce* (groom) and my sister's old brown spaniel beside me; but at the first corner, out of the drive, which was a sharp right-angle, I saw what I had to look out for. The young horse resented the pole swinging against his shoulder and when going down the steep hill, it flew up with a jerk and caught him a nasty smack on the mouth. This did not make matters any easier. He began plunging and kicking, endeavouring to get rid of his harness and for a while I had my hands full. It was not, however, of very great moment, for there was a biggish bank on the right, which helped to keep him straight and I began to get the knack of balancing the cart and keeping the pole low.

Most of the way to Kikuyu Station was pretty severe collar-work, of which I took advantage, and where the going was least bumpy I sent the horses along at a spanking pace. With only one or two narrow squeaks we reached our destination in safety and loaded up the cart at the Indian *dukas.* (shops)

Just out of Kikuyu the track used to run alongside the railway line and about a mile towards home there was a large pit-like place where they had dug out all the earth for the railway embankment. The road lay close to this precipitous little crater and there was an extra steep downhill pitch for some distance before we came to it and for some way beyond.

The horses, now having their heads towards home and feeling the cart swinging easily after them down the declivity were getting out of hand as we neared this dangerous spot. In my haste to steady them I forgot about the Cape cart pranks and stepped on the footbrake as hard as I could.

The wheels were now practically locked, so up went that horrible pole as high as the blinkers. This so alarmed the young horse that he began pulling away to the right, edging towards the precipice. The *syce* and I made frantic efforts to get the pole down, so that I could steer past the danger. The old horse also did his best to steady the cart but his poor feeble back prevented him doing much against the younger stronger animal.

The offside wheel was already just over the edge when I realised what would happen if they bolted down that awful place sideways. One's brain works quickly at such moments and in an instant I changed my tactics. Letting go of the brake I jammed both my feet hard against the footboard and, getting the strongest pull I could on the offside rein, I swung both horses round, head on to the pit. It was our best chance. The weight of the cart gave them no hope of stopping. Over they went with leaps and bounds straight to the bottom where they landed in thick bush which checked all further progress.

At the first wild leap over the edge out went the *syce*. Then the stores and cushions flew in all directions. I had my feet well forward and managed to remain until the final mighty bump as we hit the bottom when I was catapulted clean over the splashboard and landed between the horses across the pole. The only thing that remained aboard was the old fat spaniel. The horses were so astonished at what had suddenly happened that, for the moment, they forgot to kick and stood quietly while I crawled out under their heads. The *syce* appeared, unhurt, a second or two later and we proceeded to outspan the horses and find out how much of the harness and cart had been broken during our rapid descent. Not a strap had given way and the cart was perfectly whole. The only thing that had suffered at all was the whip which was snapped in two.

We extricated the horses from their scrubby landing place and with a good deal of slipping and sliding, we got them up onto the road where I held them. The cart was our difficulty. I only knew a very few words of Swahili and could give no directions about it; also, while I had my attention engaged in quieting the horses, the *syce* had gone off into the blue without saying a word. I waited for a very long time and was beginning to think that, not having enjoyed his drive with me, he had run away. Then I saw him returning along the road with a small army of his own tribe that he had collected round about the station.

They started by cutting away the bush around the cart; then, inch by inch, blocking each wheel as they moved it, they began pushing and pulling it up the side of the incline. Force of numbers and patience did it and after a considerable time they deposited it safely in the middle of the track.

With gentle persuasion we got the horses inspanned again, collected our lost property, *backsheeshed* the helpers and started off, to arrive home later without further mishap. We had been such an almighty time doing that twelve mile trip that my sister was on the point of starting out to find us and to pick up the pieces, when we arrived with a flourish and pulled up in style at the front door.

By this time I had embraced the noble profession of horse-dealer and was attending horse sales to take home a few useful beasts I knew I could find a market for. At that time, if you wanted to see your money back and a bit more, it was wisest to pass them on as soon as possible.

Already horse-sickness was taking its toll of many mares from the first sale and a troop that had gone to Limuru were dying from dik-kop like flies. As the owner of these mares was fighting at the Front, directly I got back from Nakuru I rode over to his house to see if I could be of use to his wife, who knew nothing about horses and had two small children to look after besides.

I found the lady in great distress and much afraid that their thorough-bred stallion, 'Guardsman' would succumb. He was well stabled and not turned out to graze, as the mares had been, so I had every hope he might escape. I rode the twelve miles to Limuru and back every day for a week or more, taking the temperatures of the horses and doing what I could; but there is very little one can do in cases of horse-sickness. I have seen animals recover from dik-kop, but never from din-kop[1]; in a few hours they start to blow, and that is the end. They drown in the fluid that swamps the lungs.

---

[1]   We believe din-kop and dik-kop to be different strains of tsetse fly-borne diseases.

GUARDSMAN?
Taken at Ndumbwini

I was alarmed to find 'Guardsman' running a slight temperature one morning. After this I was asked to take the horse back to my own stable and keep him under observation, and this is how he first came into our hands, although we did not buy him until many months later. He proved to be a good sire.

At one sale at Nakuru I had let slip an Indian country-bred mare when I had asked her owner what he would take on his deal. He said he would toss me a fiver or nothing. I lost but later she came into our hands anyway because she ran away with everyone. Mr Christopher Monckton[2], whom we often mounted, renamed the mare 'Non-stop'; I called her 'Moshi', which means 'smoke'. She was the sweetest-tempered creature in the stable with no wish to hurt anything; but once set going, she could not stop.

Bitting was no good; she snapped curb chains like thin string. One day Mr Monckton and I were riding back from Dagoretti across country. He

---

2   Christopher Cecil Monckton. Born in East Molsey. He established a business in Nairobi dealing largely with the export of coffee.

was on my ewe-necked mare who was hot enough in all conscience and I was riding Moshi. We started to canter, which shortly became a wild gallop. At the bottom of a ridge we came to a swamp which his animal jumped and nearly cleared but dear old Moshi, head in air with white mane and tail flying, went straight into the morass up to her shoulders, flinging me face downwards into the middle of it.

Blinded and saturated with mud and slush, I managed to wriggle to shore on my tummy where Mr. Monckton, between fits of inane laughter, tried to clear my eyes, nose and mouth with an inadequate silk handkerchief. Both the mare and I were in such a disgusting mess that I saw nothing to laugh about at all. The mud that covered us was so thick and slimy it was impossible to mount again so I had to walk home.

One evening we wanted a doctor in a great hurry to help with a sick animal. The nearest doctor was six miles away so two horses were saddled up. I rode one and led the other who happened to be Moshi. I bundled the doctor on to her back and was in such a hurry to return that I forgot to tell him that the mare pulled rather hard. No sooner was he in the saddle than there was a flash of a white tail and the doctor was out of sight before I had remounted. He must have done that journey in record time.

Sir Northrup McMillan tried to buy Moshi in order that he could have her shot before she killed one of us. But his alarm was quite unnecessary. She was a gorgeous ride, and we soon discovered that ridden in a short standing martingale on the bit, tight enough to prevent her getting her head beyond a certain height, we could hold her easily in a snaffle. This gallant old mare died foaling, which nearly broke our hearts, but we had her a long time before this happened.

To accommodate my horse purchases I set about building some stables; in particular I was preparing for a large sale of South African casters. Nearly all the ponies commandeered from the Kenya farmers had died at the front and most people had been left without horses, so there was some excitement over this sale. Olive and I were pretty sure that good mares would be an investment and we proved to be right, doing extremely well with our horses for many years.

To build the stables I wrote on a gang of natives and was conducting the work myself with the aid of the headman called Kago. As he was destined to play a big part in my future life I must describe him as he was when I saw him first.

Kago was a raw native of superior class. Extremely strong and well made, his skin, profusely stained with red ochre, was of satin texture with finely developed muscles rippling under their delicate covering. His ornaments were many and varied in design. A band of bright beads worn as a filet across his brow helped to control a mop of very long hair reaching below his shoulders and dyed brick red with mud and grease. In the lobe of one ear he carried a cigarette tin which contained snuff. His well-shaped arms and small wrists were decked with bands of brass wire and beads. Chains and beads hung round his neck and on his fingers were many rings. His clothing was slight and consisted of a scarlet blanket. From a belt around his waist hung *rungu* (knobkerry), knife and *simi*. His mentality being superior to most of his tribe, he was a good and energetic workman and took some interest in what he was doing.

The stables were built of black wattle poles laid close together, and the gabled roof thatched thickly with dried reeds was comfortable enough for a hot climate. I have always voted for cool stables and clothing when necessary.

From up-country I had several commissions to buy horses at the sale for various people and, knowing the sort of animal we were likely to see in the sale-ring, I considered it advisable to visit the lines to try to get reliable information from the sergeants in charge of these remounts. I therefore rode into Nairobi and made the acquaintance of Sergeant McGregor, who took me through the enormous tents that housed the stock. Each horse was branded on the neck with a number and it took several visits before I got my list complete. For my clients I had to make as certain as possible that the horses I picked were rideable, non-buckjumpers, of useful age, sound and in good condition. This was not an easy business at all but finding McGregor to be a dog-lover as well as a good horseman, he soon became my ally and he spared no pains in pointing me out useful mounts.

McGregor was always shadowed by a cross-bred greyhound-deerhound dog, a fine fellow that he had brought with him from Rhodesia. The dog was a trained hunter and exceedingly fast. He was called Big Man and so devoted was the Sergeant to the dog that he asked me, if anything should happen to him, to promise to take Big Man myself and keep him until he died. I gave him the promise which he entered then and there in his notebook. A few months afterwards I received a letter from a Sergeant Denys telling me that McGregor had died of blackwater in Tanganyika and almost the last thing he said before he died was, 'Send Big Man to Miss M. Collyer; her address is in my notebook.' So Big Man became mine and he too played his part in my future life.

Journey to Uganda

(c.1916)

Chapter IV

Having received an invitation from Sir Frederick[1] and Lady Jackson to visit them at Government House, Entebbe, I began to make preparations for the journey. I meant to kill two birds with one stone and do a little horse-hunting near Nakuru on my way. A man who had started a stable somewhere between Nakuru and Njoro had either died or been killed, and I was given to understand that his horses were for sale. He had imported a thoroughbred from Australia: a horse called 'Scottie' by 'Great Scott', and I had thought of trying to buy this horse.

In East Africa one never travels anywhere without a personal servant. Up to the present I had no servant of my own and was dependent on my sister for the loan of one of hers. On my arrival she had had to add a second houseboy to her staff, and the way she set about doing this amused and astonished me. She went round her labourers and just

---

[1] Sir Frederick Jackson KCMG, CB. In 1889 the Imperial British East Africa Company equipped a large caravan to journey towards Uganda in search of Amin Pasha and to trade. Mr Jackson, as he was then, was in charge of the transport for the expedition and so able did he prove himself that other commissions quickly followed. [Mary Gillett] Some of his exploits were fictionalised in Rider Haggard's book 'She' (C.S. Nicholls) He became an official in the Uganda Administration in 1894. He was Governor of Uganda in 1911–1917 and was also a keen and knowledgeable naturalist. He was author of 'Birds of Kenya Colony and Uganda Protectorate' and 'Early Days in East Africa'

picked out the best-looking, who happened to be a ploughman – long-haired, much be-jewelled, be-mudded and be-redded. He was told to stop ploughing and become a footman at once! The native is extraordinarily adaptable and never refuses to take on any job he is ordered to do. This savage looking fellow was brought into the house and taught his work by a Swahili houseboy. It was wonderful how quickly he learned to wait at table. Imagine taking a Sussex yokel off the plough and turning him into a valet and footman in two days!

Mbuthia was a quick learner; but he also possessed a quick and violent temper. One night after dinner we were watching him clear the table. When it came to removing the cloth, he was told to fold it carefully corner to corner and in the creases already made by the iron. Never before having folded anything, the task was too difficult for him. After making several futile attempts he suddenly lost his temper and crumpling the whole thing up in his arms, he flung it into the corner of the room. On another occasion he was given a new pair of khaki shorts which he carefully examined. Finding the pockets not placed as he wished, he threw them down in the mud and stamped on them. Mbuthia became an educated Christian and remained in my sister's service.

SIR FREDERICK
JOHN JACKSON

He it was who attended me on my visit to Uganda. He had never been in a train and never seen a boat; but he remained quite impassive and expressed no surprise at either, while that vast sheet of water, Lake Victoria Nyanza, made no impression on him at all. The only thing that caused him shock was the Kisumu Market, when he saw the Kavirondo women stark naked bringing in their wares. This really horrified him, for the women of his own tribe are kept heavily clothed.

On my way to Nakuru I shared a carriage with a white-haired old lady who crocheted mats all the way and kept winding herself up in the cotton. She was painfully thin, dressed in a ragged black frock, her shoes being much the worse for wear. I felt sure she was starved and dreadfully poor. When the train stopped at Kijabe for dinner I waited to see if she was coming along to the restaurant to dine, but she made no movement and continued her work. Thinking she was probably penniless, I asked her to join me as my guest but she curtly refused my invitation. She had no blankets with her and the night was cold. I wondered if I would dare offer some of my mine. All my sympathy was entirely wasted, for on returning to the train I found her feeding sumptuously from a luncheon basket with a bottle of burgundy beside her; and wearing a magnificent sable coat reaching from neck to feet!

At Nakuru I detrained, walked across the road to the pub and took a room for the remainder of the night. No sooner was I in bed than there was a bang at the door. I was thankful I had locked it, for the manager was demanding admission for some woman who he said had booked the other bed in my room. I refused to open the door and told him to put Miss......... into the bath, as no stranger was going to sleep near me. A lot of clamouring went on in the passage, then more persuasion was used to make me unlock the door. But I remained firm, saying that possession was nine points of the law and that I did not care in the least where Miss .... slept, so long as it was not with me.

When I paid my bill the next day the manager, having taken the money, fell on the back of his head in the most violent epileptic fit it has been my lot to see. I stuffed my handkerchief between his teeth and ran for help. Finding two white men who seemed to know all about it, I then hired a rickshaw and went off to see the horses.

The chestnut stallion 'Scotty' proved to be a savage, nearly eating the *syce* who went into his box to bridle him. I gave up all idea of buying him and purchased a two-year-old filly by 'Royal Fox' instead. She was a bit of squib, but better than anything I had so far seen in the Colony. I arranged for her to be boxed to Kikuyu and wrote to Olive to meet her. 'Scotty' was bought by Mr W.B. Thompson[2] a little later and for a while was a most successful sire, getting many a winner from very indifferent mares.

I now continued my journey to Kisumu. At the last stop before the terminus I saw a most delicious sight that immensely pleased my English eyes. When we pulled up at the station, it was pelting with rain: sheets of water falling from a cloudburst. The platform was deserted but for one gigantic Kavirondo man, black as ebony, and stark naked except for a small trilby hat perched on top of his head, and carrying an open green umbrella.

At times the African shows more wisdom that we do. The heavier the rain the more clothes we put on. The native does the reverse; he takes his off and keeps them dry until the storm is over. The sun dries his skin in two minutes and there he is, clothed and complete without further trouble.

On our arrival in Kisumu that luxury ship, the *Clement Hill*, was alongside the pier, and we went on board at once. I carried an introduction to the captain, who was such an exact replica of Hayden Coffin that I expected him to burst into song at any moment.[3] But really he was a very beautiful young man, with a perfect stage manner who might have been taking me for a trip on his private steam yacht. The *Clement Hill* could not see at night, so at dusk we anchored in the Kavirondo Bay, proceeding early next morning to Jinja. Here 'Hayden Coffin' took me for a walk and I had the new experience of falling over a crocodile. First, we viewed the Rippon Falls, which are so enormously wide they

---

[2] Known as 'John Bull' because of his remarkable likeness to the imaginary character, Thompson opened a saddlery business near Nairobi. He served locally in WWI and after the war worked with Sir Northrup MacMillan's racing stud.

[3] Hayden Coffin was one of the most popular stage baritones of the late 19th and early 20th Centuries. Good looks and a powerful voice made him a favourite with audiences.

look no height at all. Here we saw lots of the big Nile perch leaping like salmon when trying to negotiate a fosse. I wondered why a ladder was not cut for them so that they could get to the lake. Owing to the size of the place, the fish looked no bigger than quite ordinary salmon but I believe they run to over two hundred pounds.

At the foot of the falls, fishing paths had been built which went well out into the water and were very little above it. Here we watched innumerable hippo bathing and playing; baby ones standing on the backs of their mothers, being dipped. It was a sight reminiscent of the old bathing women at the seaside who used to dip howling children. One immense bull hippo was lying quite close to us and evidently in the throes of a liver attack, for each time he rose he yawned and gave a splendid display of his enormous mouth and ivory tusks. Hundreds of crocodiles were showing their heads above water and I was gazing at them as I strolled along in front of my escort. Not looking where I was going, I stumbled against a log lying across the path and recovered my balance in time to see it leap into the water. I had kicked a sleeping crocodile of about seven feet long.

A HAPPY KAVIRONDO (NOW KNOWN AS LUO) COUPLE
Photographed by Sir Harry Johnston c.1900

On reaching Entebbe I was met by an Aide-de-Camp and conveyed in a rickshaw up a remarkably steep hill to Government House. It is not a very imposing building, being too closely related to a villa. In the entrance porch Sir Frederick Jackson was waiting to receive me, not looking a day older than when I had last met him twenty years before, catching butterflies in an English garden. A born naturalist and a

A Wakefield's Green
Pigeon
*'VINAGO WAKE-
FIELDI WAKEFIELDI'*
Painted by Sir Frederick
Jackson

delightful companion, no living thing was too
small for his closest observation; he was the
greatest authority on African birds, as is shown
by the complete collection he left to the Natural History Museum. He had also got all the
Uganda birds but one, when I went to stay with
him and he had servants out all over the place
trying to find this particular specimen. One day
after breakfast I was sitting on the verandah
outside his office and noticed a small bird flying
into a bush growing against the railings. There
was a nest in the bush, so I called Sir Frederick
to come and see it. His joy knew no bounds when he discovered it to be
the very bird he had been searching for, nest and eggs complete.

Except for naturalist strolls every evening with Sir Frederick I found
Entebbe deadly dull, and it was sweating hot. The damp tropical heat
was so enervating that nobody did anything, and the idle life did not
suit me at all. I made one or two sketches and gave my host a water-
colour head of his pet dog. This he showed to his old Goanese cook,
who had been with him many years. The cook, after looking at the
sketch for some time said, 'Yess sah; it's very nice shape.' He had no
doubt got a blancmange on his mind.

East Africa's Teeming Zoo

Chapter V

About this time Olive and I became acquainted with Mr and Mrs McMillan[1], an acquaintanceship that grew into one of the deepest friendships of our lives. Northrup McMillan is too well known and too closely connected with the early days of British East Africa to need any description from my poor pen. His memory will flourish just so long as Kenya exists, for his generosities and good works are untold. Many a settler owes his present prosperity to Northrup McMillan's kindly aid. He received the honour of a knighthood at the close of the war and no man more richly deserved it.

After Sir Northrup's death, Lady McMillan generously presented the Colony with the beautiful McMillan Memorial Library, which has been the greatest boon to all the white inhabitants of this their adopted country.

It was not until I stayed at Juja, Northrup McMillan's private game reserve, that I began to realize what a teeming zoo East Africa really is.

---

[1] Sir William Northrup McMillan KBE 1872-1925. He married Lucie Webber. He was a huge Scot, raised in St. Louis, Missouri, USA. He arrived in Kenya in 1901 for big game shooting, playing host to President Roosevelt in 1911 at Juja Farm, Donya Sabuk. He bred cattle, ostriches, sheep, pigs and horses and later grew sisal. Both Sir Northrup and his wife were philanthropists, contributing generously to the Colony of Kenya. Not only was the McMillan Library bequeathed to the Colony but also the Louise Decker home for aged Europeans. They were buried on Mount Kenya. It may be of interest that amongst their wide circle of friends was Karen von Blixen who wrote *Out of Africa*. (C.S. Nicholls and Mary Gillett)

Juja, which is an immense tract of veldt land forty miles from Nairobi, was strictly preserved, and the joy of its owner's life. No promiscuous shooting was allowed to be done there; only special visitors were permitted to collect their trophies from the vast herds of antelope, rhino, buffalo and elephant that inhabited this large estate. Lion and leopard found a sanctuary, crocodile and hippo lived at peace in the deep warm pools of the Juja river; a hunter's heaven and a naturalist's paradise. But oh! The ticks!

I went with Lady McMillan to Juja for the purpose of making a couple of watercolour drawings of the great dome-topped mountain that dominates the rolling plains surrounding it. A lone mountain, majestic in its solitude, the green rock-strewn slopes rise direct from an ever-waving sea of copper-gold prairie grass and its summit is crowned with forest. El Donyo Sabuk or Kiliman Bogo, it is called 'the hill of the buffalo'.

The subject was pleasing enough, but the agony while painting it was beyond description. The grass on the plains is swarming with a minute red tick that buries itself in one's skin and causes an almost unbearable irritation. They attack in their thousands and my legs from ankle to knee were a mass of them and their bites. The irritation lasted for days, and the hotter one got the worse it became. I had a bad go of fever caused by the poison from these ticks.

When the sketches were finished Lady McMillan collected three or four children from somewhere and took them for a day's fishing and a picnic on a river about twelve miles from the house. We went in a car with a chauffeur to drive and, there being no track, we bumped gloriously over stones and holes. The veldt was alive with game which were quite unflustered by the presence of the car. Enormous herds of tommy, wildebeeste and kongoni were everywhere. The comic gambolling of the latter was most amusing to watch; they don't look like real animals but funny toys made by hand to please the young.

A small mob of giraffe thrilled me to the marrow; the gigantic bulls with less tall wives and their ridiculous-looking children, stood placidly by as the car jolted past them. Their wooden gait is of the strangest, for if startled, they go from stand to clumsy canter in one movement. I have never seen a giraffe attempt to trot and do not believe they have any intermediate pace. Usually they move very slowly but when chased by lion and really extended, their pace is tremendous, the stride being over twenty feet. (I was told this by a white hunter who had seen a big bull chased by a lion and he measured the stride.)

At times a couple of wart-hog would jump up in front of us and rush away for a short distance, their grotesque heads carried high and tails stiffly pointing to the heavens, then they would stop dead and turn to stare at the disturber of their peace. Duiker, stembuck, dik-dik, jackal and several lesser bustards all appeared for my benefit. This was my first introduction to this particular Noah's Ark of the world.

The African-born children with us, who wore neither shoes nor stockings, watched this wondrous animal life with the utmost indifference. One small boy, who was armed to the teeth with hunting knives and other implements of torture, showed murderous propensities and wished to shoot or stab anything within range. He saw no beauty or interest in the creatures of the wild; his only idea was to kill, and later in the day he had the pleasure of cutting off, with his largest knife, the head of a snake that crossed our path.

The picnic was a great success and the children enjoyed fishing and catching nothing much. I enjoyed watching them rather less than one might expect, because there were crocodiles in those rivers and I had lately been given a graphic description of how these reptiles attack both human beings and animals that unwisely stand on the banks of watercourses. Crocodiles give no warning but come with a rush from the pools, sweeping their prey into the water with their scaly tails and afterwards tearing it to pieces with those fearsome jaws. I felt afraid for the children but being a novice at African picnics I suffered in silence. Lady McMillan, who knew far more than I did of the danger, was perfectly indifferent as to where the children stood to fish.

Sometime after tea we all packed into the car again for the journey home and had not gone a hundred yards before the chauffeur hit a hidden rock and smashed the sump. He was given the only rifle and told to hasten home and bring the mule-gharry to meet us. No sooner had he got well away than we heard a rush in the bush near at hand and a nerve-racking roar. A lion had made his kill unpleasantly close to where we were standing. Even this did not excite the children in the least, but Her Ladyship thought it advisable to move off. So we started to walk home. The veldt is rough walking and although the stiff, dried grass must have tried bare feet pretty badly the elder children stuck it well; but the youngest had to be carried. Soon after the beheading of the snake, which took their minds off personal discomfort, we were picked up by the buckboard drawn by six white mules. It was truly a delightful after-noon's amusement, with just that soupçon of danger, without which life becomes monotonous.

On my second visit to Juja a little later I was shown what a hippo, when annoyed, could do to a rowing boat. The house had been turned into a convalescent home for sick and wounded soldiers.[2] Two of the patients launched the boat and one evening paddled down the river. Rounding a corner hidden by tall reeds they came upon a bull hippo standing in the water enjoying his supper of lush vegetation. The boat was close on him before the men could turn it and row upstream, which they proceeded to do quickly, but not fast enough to beat a hippo under water. They got a nasty surprise when an enormous head rose from the river a few yards in front of the bows and, opening cavernous jaws, rushed at the boat. The hippo seized the fore part in his teeth, and crushed it to atoms as easily as a dog would a biscuit. Oblivious to croc-odiles, the men hurled themselves over the stern and got ashore.

If unmolested, hippo are usually peaceable enough but they prefer to take their meals in solitude and resent uninvited guests.

---

[2] These men would have been soldiers fighting General von Lettow-Vorbeck on the Kenya/Tanganyika border during the First World War.

Lonely and Unnatural Lives

Chapter VI

While I was on a short break with friends who lived on the far side of Lake Naivasha, I came across an ape, 'Douli', whose life was both interesting and heart-rending.

The East African trains could be most obliging with a little coaxing and the one I was travelling on stopped at a farm-track between Naivasha and Gilgil, allowing me to get out. Here I found myself in the middle of an empty part of the great Rift Valley in the late evening, with no one to meet me. I had to wait a very long time before a pony and milk-float made its appearance.

While I was at this farm I rode over to Mr Paul Rainey's[1] place, which was then being run by Mr C. Harvey and his sister, to meet 'Douli'.

'Douli' had been caught when very young in the Congo forests and had been given to Mr Rainey as a chimpanzee. When I first saw Douli he was still supposed to be of this species. At that time he was about three feet six inches in height, possibly a little more, for he could walk with his arm around my waist. He had a stone house of his own in the compound and a servant to wait on him. Miss Harvey took me to call and he met us at the door of his house with his empty breakfast things in his hands. He had already rolled his mattress up and put it neatly into a corner.

---

[1] An American by birth, Paul Rainey was a professional hunter, and he had a farm at Naivasha. He bred ridgeback lion dogs and had a gift for training chimpanzees. [Mary Gillett]

ROGI
She was picked up by
Arthur and Olive
Collyer when on safari
on the Larogi Plateau

The stories of this extraordinary ape are innumerable. He went everywhere about the farm with Mr. Harvey and could open and shut gates. He sat at table and behaved like a perfect gentleman, drinking his tea out of a cup. Afraid of missing any of the sugar at the bottom, he sluished round the last drop of tea to make sure he got it all. He was exceedingly gentle and affectionate and was loved and looked after like a child for many years. He was given a bath every week, in which he would wash himself with soap and wash Miss Harvey too if given the chance. He disliked tame monkeys and one day a lady came to see him, carrying one in her arms. She was warned about Douli's dislike, so during lunch, she chained her monkey to a tree. Douli spotted it and, picking up a large stone, hurled it at the animal and killed it on the spot.

One of the best stories told of Douli is when he was thought to be ill. Miss Harvey, being very anxious about him, took him into the house and put him in an empty bedroom with his mattress and blankets on the floor. So long as she was near he played up to being a very sick monkey, lying on his bed covered up with blankets, too feeble to move. Thinking he would sleep, she left him; presently, peeping in at the window to see how he was, she saw him throwing his mattress in front of him and turning heels over head all round the room.

He was an awful drinker and if he got hold of the whisky bottle, drank until he was blind. He made a mistake one day and took a bottle of lime-juice instead of the whisky and drank the lot which made him very ill.

There are some wonderful photographs of him lying in a deck-chair reading a newspaper and smoking a cigarette. He had a cat he was very fond of, whom he stroked in the most human way and gave it food out of his dish. The chickens he also fed, but in a different manner; he threw the food about, stood by with his back to them, and when they were busy feeding he reached round with his long arm, grabbed a bird, pulled its head off and threw the remains away.

He could open padlocks with keys and when no one was about would loosen the pole in the ground to which he was sometimes chained. He would then put all the soil back, patting it down so that no-one would know what he had done. The next time he was chained up he just lifted the pole out of the ground and slipped the chain off it!

I could write a small book on Douli's doings, but enough. There was a tragic end to this semi-human creature. I never forgot him and was most anxious to see him again. Many years after that first visit, I did but I saw such a different Douli from the merry affectionate ape I remembered. He was no longer a chimpanzee but had grown into an enormous gorilla. Twice he had done his best to kill his friend Mr Harvey, who had had to go to hospital with the awful wounds inflicted by Douli's teeth. On another occasion he had grabbed and stopped Mr Harvey's motor-cycle in the yard, causing a nasty smash.

Douli was now extremely dangerous and had to be kept chained. All stones had to be put out of his reach, for he threw them at anybody and everything. When no more stones were to be found on the ground he took to loosening the wall stones of his hut and throwing them. His best friend was the person he most hated and would have killed if he could have got at him. He still tolerated Miss Harvey and it was she who took me to see him on my last visit which made me sad. Douli was quiet and shook hands with me, and I ventured to put a measuring tape round his forearm which measured, when limp, sixteen and a half inches.

But, in the end, there was nothing for it but to have the animal shot. However, nobody could do it; it was far too like murder. By this time the history of Douli had reached New York. A naturalist from the New York Natural History Museum came all the way to Kenya to see the ape alive, then afterwards to shoot him and to take the skin and skeleton back to America and have it set up by a taxidermist.

Poor unhappy Douli, who wanted a mate. He was given a peach and while he was eating it, was shot with a revolver through the back of the head.

It is strange that for so long a time no one seemed to realize that he was other than a chimpanzee. Not until nearly the end of his life did the Harveys conclude that he must be a gorilla; yet when I last saw him he must have stood all of five foot six inches. Of course he had not learnt gorilla ways, never having seen one of his own kind. He just looked sullen and unutterably miserable. Having had his liberty for so many years, being heavily chained was a dreadful punishment.

I have seen much the same thing happen with tame lions out here. There comes a moment after a year old when they are no longer safe. They cannot be returned to the wild; for if they managed to live, which is doubtful, they would probably become man-eaters. It becomes a case of either shooting them or putting them behind bars for the rest of their existence. I have often longed for a lion cub but I know too well that within one short year the cub would suffer, and so should I.

Some years later, in a good illustration of this, I found myself in a risky position at the hands of a young half tame lion. I had met a married couple who were strangers to me. These people had bought a place on the foothills of the Aberdares and had just returned from a shooting safari and had with them a tiny lion cub in a basket which was being reared on a bottle. It was then no larger than a small cat. The land they had bought was not more than fifteen miles from my farm, as the crow flies, and they had a car in which they intended to drive over and buy one of my horses. They came and bought a horse and six months later sent me an invitation to lunch with them one Sunday to see their lion, which was now very large and extremely beautiful. A tame lion was a safe draw for me and I went to lunch.

When I arrived I found that my host had both arms bandaged as far as the elbow and both in slings, the lion having attacked him the day before and mauled him pretty badly. When I saw him, the animal was standing about in a patch of nettles; he was about as high as a large retriever in splendid condition and already growing a frill round his chin. I was advised not to touch him, in view of his recent display of temper, so after watching him for a while we went into the house and I sat down in a large armchair.

A few minutes later in walked the lion, came straight to me and, having sniffed me all over, decided it would be safe to sit on my lap. So up he got, laying his great heavy body across my knees and resting his head on the arm of the chair. His owners, thinking I might be alarmed, simultaneously whispered: 'Don't push him off, he may resent it!' Not that I had any intention of pushing him anywhere. He was talking nicely, as lions do when their ears are being scratched and tickled. Lunch-time came and still he lay across my knees with no intention of moving until he had taken his midday siesta, which my hostess informed me lasted until four o'clock. I was offered a cutlet to eat where I sat, but this I sternly refused, having no wish to share it with my companion.

I had to go without any lunch and remained a prisoner until exactly four o'clock, when the lion stepped down and strolled into the garden, taking no further notice of any of us.

Having once attacked and drawn blood from his master, he was no longer to be trusted and had to be caged. If he is still alive, he is residing in England; for he was sent to the zoo by Sir Edward Northey[2] when the Government House menagerie was broken up on Sir Edward's recall to England.

That lion had always been fed on raw buck and zebra meat. My sister's tame lioness, Rogi, was never allowed raw meat and remained perfectly gentle even after she was sent to Hagenbeck's Zoo.

---

[2] General Sir Edward Northey was Governor of Kenya from 1919 to 1922 and presided over the country's change of name from the East Africa Protectorate to Kenya in 1920. A delightful man with no liking for protocol and ceremony, Northey kept a zoo of wild animals in the Government House grounds and let his wife raise chickens in the attics. [C.S. Nicholls]

GENTLE ROGI

She was a year old when she left Kenya and I heard of her much later from one of the managers of Hagenbeck, when they were giving a display of wild animals at Olympia. 'Larogi' was not brought to London with the exhibition lions; being still so gentle, she was never caged but kept as a pet. I was informed that she was very under-sized, no doubt from having been fed on cooked meat not properly reinforced.

My firm belief is that lion could be quite well reared and well grown on cooked food, provided plenty of phosphates and other necessary ingredients were mixed with it and I should very much like to try the experiment.

There is only one of the big cats that can be tamed and kept with impunity and that is the cheetah. These make adorable pets and they purr like motor-cars when stroked and scratched. But they can never be broken of killing poultry, sheep and calves and, like a leopard, they not only murder when they are hungry, they kill for the fun of catching. Best leave them to their happy forest life and watch them as I have often watched them, in the early dawn, stalking buck through long grass or, having breakfasted, lying in a shady nook lazily licking the blood off their paws.

Idiosyncracies

Chapter VII

Wanting to buy more South African mares, I journeyed to Nakuru to attend a sale. Nakuru was a tiny township of wood and iron buildings overlooking a beautiful lake sheltered on all sides by rolling hills. Being in a basin it is one of the most grilling spots I know. The population was very sparse, because the inhabited farms lay at considerable distances from the station. The pub was the centre of the universe and a very rough house it proved to be.

I was alone, except for a young native I had taken on as a *syce*, who was more bother than he was worth. Never having been away from his own village he was afraid of everything, and terrified of getting lost, he clung to my heels like a hungry leech.

Arriving at Nakuru about teatime I left my things at the hotel and went down to have a look at the lake. From a distance the whole of the shoreline appeared to be pink, and I was interested to see what kind of rock or stones it was composed of. Pushing my way through bush to reach the water's edge, the pink shore rose up before me on innumerable wings as thousands upon thousands of flamingo circled around my head before making for safety at the opposite side of the lake. It was a wonderful sight and well worth the long hot walk I had taken to see it.

After the roar of those many wings had died away, the silence of the evening became almost tangible and for the first time in my life I experienced a sensation I have felt many times since being in Africa; that of being alone in the world. Creeping along in and out of tall reeds through narrow paths made by I knew not what, the damp ground was imprinted with a variety of tracks which, in my ignorance, I failed to decipher. When again coming out on to clear space, I found myself staring wide-eyed at a family of hippo going down for their evening bath. I was so near I could have hit them with a stone. Hardly daring to breathe but sinking slowly to the ground, I continued watching them until dusk reminded me that I was some distance from the township and, having far overstepped the track I had come by, I had to find another. Once out of the scrub the lights from the houses guided me safely back.

There were comparatively few people about because the majority of the horse buyers were expected to ride or drive in the next morning, so my sleep was undisturbed. Seven o'clock found me amongst the horses and I bought a privately owned brown filly before breakfast.

I was the only woman present at the sale and the only one at the pub that night, having to dine amongst the biggest lot of toughs I had ever encountered. Towards the end of dinner that evening crockery and glass were hurled haphazardly about the room. I have never had the smallest wish to break china even in my wildest moments but it was the fashion in East Africa then, even at the best Nairobi clubs, to throw plates about. I retired to my room but the noise became so uproarious that I packed my things and carried them across to the station. As I was leaving the house, a very fat man had just been stuffed into the service hatch through which drinks were handed from the bar. He was completely stuck and could not be pulled out either forwards or backwards.

At the station I found my horse-box by a siding. I had already loaded my purchases, as the train was due to leave early and I had left the *syce* in charge of them. I slept the night in the box with the *syce*, who reeked of stale castor oil but this was an improvement on a night at the hotel. Oh! The weary hours I have spent travelling horses on the Uganda Railway and no place is more uncomfortable to sleep in than a horse-box especially when one has to share the accommodation.

At that time the Nakuru Hotel was noted for its rough nights. On one occasion on a later visit, my sister and I were staying there for an agricultural show and we shared a room looking on to the verandah. The early part of the evening had been noisy but as night went on it became far worse. Even furniture was being thrown from the rooms and smashed. Just outside our window two men started to fight, one getting an arm broken, while his elderly wife rushed up and down in her nightgown, shouting 'Murder!' at the top of her voice. The noise was that of Bedlam let loose. The yell of 'Murder!' partially woke Olive, who sleepily murmured, 'This is not a fit place for ladies to stay at.' And promptly went to sleep again.

Having now a stable full of horses to look after at Kabete, as well as my sister's large vegetable business and the coffee *shamba*, there was plenty to occupy us both.

The native *syces* gave us a lot of trouble; none of them ever having had charge of horses before, it was necessary to teach them everything. So little did they know of horses they had never even seen a foal and when the pony mare had her baby, half the people in the Reserve came to see it.

The boys were quiet in the stables but had no idea of strapping or feeding. Bridles and saddles were put on in the most remarkable way; I have many times found my saddle facing the tail. They would do the thing correctly for a few days, then return to their own method. When asked why, the reply was ever the same: 'I have forgotten.'

During one very wet season we could not use the Cape cart for about three weeks. Next time out, every atom of the harness was put on wrong. Not a single strap was in its right place. The only thing they had done right was to face the horses' heads the correct way. While this obtuseness could be amusing at first, it shortly became exasperating to have to repeat the same orders day after day. Some of the men were passive resisters. They did not actually refuse to do what we told them, but ignored the order and just did not carry it out; nothing would move them as they stood sullenly by not uttering a word.

THE COLLYERS'
MARES AND FOALS
WITH THEIR SYCES

The petty pilfering that went on was maddening; brushes, combs, rasps, bandages and everything else they had use for disappeared and it was impossible to lay one's hands on the culprit. The Kikuyu would never give one of their tribe away, not necessarily from any feeling of loyalty, but because they were afraid of the consequences from their own people. The only things they ever thought about were food, goats, cattle and women. They were fond of their children but took no care of them and they were dirty in their person.

The circumcision dances – or ngomas – were the bane of our existence. The noise at night was awful and the whole community became mad and out of hand. The Missions had gained no control at all in the Reserve and had not the power to stop these rites. There were drunken orgies, after the performance of disgusting mutilation in both male and female. There was also mutilation of the lobes of the ears and searing the body with hot irons: possibly as tribal marks. They later took to burning the pattern of a daisy flower on their cheeks. This they found they could do with mustard less painfully than with a hot iron, so tins of mustard were stolen. Every girl at one moment had a daisy burned on either cheek.

The young footman Olive had established in the house used to come to me to have his face painted for these dances. My paint-boxes interested him very much and tubes of vermilion were constantly disappearing. This was most annoying for artists' materials cost a small fortune at that time in Kenya.

The painting of the face had to be done to a prescribed fashion; I was not allowed to improvise in any way at all. A broad white line extending from the top of the forehead to the point of the nose was the beginning, then spots and stars of white or red had to be placed at certain points. The young warrior in full war paint was a picturesque and savage-looking man. Learning of the existence of wrist-watches they began to cut straps for their wrists and copied the watch in beads. Football stockings they painted on their legs with white ash, utilizing the colour of their skin as the groundwork. These stockings were very cleverly done indeed and were a perfect imitation.

The Askari Kangas – the un-uniformed police detectives who pretended to find out where stolen property was hidden – considered it very smart to disguise themselves. One, on duty for us, borrowed a white shirt from my sister but this not being quite a sufficient disguise he also borrowed a long ostrich feather which he arranged with wire to stick straight out behind like a tail. Now, disguised as an ostrich, he could go safely amongst his own people without fear of recognition, although there was nothing done to alter his face.

We had one ultra-smart gardener who was always elaborately painted and he posed himself in statuesque attitudes for our benefit. He was too beautiful to do any work but unfortunately he got chicken-pox which much disfigured him for a while. Not knowing what it was, he made up his mind to die and was determined we should see him do it. Every morning he lay in the middle of the lawn in blazing sunlight with a blanket over his head. We did all we could and assured him it was nothing serious. Every day he went to the river and smothered himself in mud. Eventually he decided he would rather die in his home which was only a hundred miles away; he also wished to kill a goat there, as a last chance of recovery. So off he went one morning to accomplish this little trek on his own legs, putting off death for another four days.

Although this strange people are fond of children, it was their custom to kill twins at birth. I had an experience of this while I was living at Kabete. Just at the back of the stables and close to the Mission there was a very bad village. One day my sister's headman, who was a Cormoro man and a good Mohammedan, came to tell us that a young girl in this village was likely to die in her confinement and, as dreadful things were being done to her by her own people, would we come and stop it?

Olive had a visitor in Mr. Northcote[1], the Provincial Commissioner, so I said I would go with the headman and see what could be done. They had already taken the girl out of the hut because no Kikuyu is allowed to die in a house; they are put out in the bush. She was naked and the colour of ashes, cold, and with no perceptible pulse. After getting a little brandy between her teeth I examined her and found she had had one child a few minutes before and the twin to it was still to be born. The first baby had disappeared and of course nobody knew anything about it. I could not get a word out of them, neither could Ali. The second baby yet to come I felt certain was dead and the woman was so exhausted I saw little hope of her recovery.

The natives around me were being very hostile so I went back for

---

[1] Sir Geoffrey Alexander Stafford Northcote KCMG. After serving in the East African Administration he became the first Speaker of the Central Assembly. He then served in N. Rhodesia and the Gold Coast followed by his appointment as Governor of British Guiana and later Governor of Hong Kong. He returned to Kenya during WWII when he was appointed Chief Information Officer. He died in 1948. (Mary Gillett)

Olive and the PC, telling the *bibis* (women) not to touch the girl again until I came back. When we returned we found they had pitched the wretched woman into some bushes at a distance from the huts. While she still lived they were tearing the rolls of brass wire out of her ears, breaking away the lobes in their violence and unbinding in all haste the wire from her legs. Mr Northcote stopped this brutality but the girl died while we were there. Mr Northcote then cross-questioned them as to what they had done with the child that had been born. They refused to answer any questions at all so we searched the bush ourselves but without success. As we could not find the corpse it was not possible to take action and we had to leave it at that.

I suppose the Missions have done a lot of good amongst the tribes but I am heathen enough to think they have also done a great deal of harm. There is one story that perhaps illustrates my point. A native, who had been sixteen years in a Mission school and who was a Christian, was asked what he thought God was like. The reply was, 'One big sheep.' 'Why do you think he is like a sheep?' 'His son is a lamb, therefore he must be a sheep.'

It seemed to me crime and wickedness increased as time went on. Murder, rape, house-breaking and bag snatching became much more common than they used to be when I first arrived in the Colony and they were committed with far more knowledge and cunning than of yore. Criminals began to wear gloves and were careful to see that no finger-prints were left behind. If possible they armed themselves with their white victim's guns before holding him up in bed and opening his safe. They were perfectly aware that black people seen in uncertain light were difficult to identify. Many could read English and study trials in the Criminal Courts, learning all sorts of tips that would help them in the perpetration of crimes.

During the last year there have been a number of shop-keeping Indians murdered by Africans and at least two brutal murders of Europeans, including the attempted murder of a white man and his wife at a farm at Naivasha. He later died and a gang of seven Lumbwa were arrested, tried and hanged.[2]

In severely cutting down the expenses of the Colony, police supervision has been considerably lessened. The criminal elements are fully aware of this folly. I foresee a great deal more trouble in the near future, especially in the vicinity of towns and townships. I have given much thought to this question which is perhaps natural, given that I have lived alone for so many years.

The ignorant nonsense that has appeared in the English papers from time to time about our treatment of the tribes has often infuriated me. The English officials and those of higher degree who visit this country for a few weeks or a few months can have no knowledge of the African or of his feelings at all and therefore possess no right to criticize. It takes years to understand the African mentality and then it is hard to say how far one has got in the study of such a strange psychology.

I can say this for a fact, however, that the present generation of the Kikuyu on whom most of us depend for our labour, would be completely lost now if left to their own devices. They have become entirely dependent on the white man for both health and maintenance, even to the extent of settling many of their tribal disputes.

As much of this subject is bound to appear in later chapters I shall say no more for the moment but return to life at Kabete and our preparations for my move into the wilds.

---

[2] Confusingly Miss Collyer has skipped to the time she was writing her book in the 1930's, whereas the events she described up to this point took place during the First World War in 1916 or 1917.

'A Greeting by the Gods of Wilderness and Wild'

Chapter VIII

KIPIPIRI IS THE NEAREST MOUNTAIN
AND THE ABERDARES ARE BEYOND THE RAINBOW
Painted by Margaret Collyer on her farm.

Nothing pushes time along so quickly as a life of routine; days are unmarked, and months fly by like a breath of wind. We at last awakened to the fact that the year 1917 was on the wane and that in January 1918 we intended getting busy on the Gilgil property.

Never in my life have I come across a worker to equal my sister. Her Kikuyu name is *'Niawera'* ('the woman who works') and natives have a clever way of adjusting a name that fits. Notwithstanding the time and labour Olive expended on the coffee plantation, vegetable growing and the flower garden, she always seemed to have some in hand for other matters as well. I was called *'Nakanoona'* by the Kikuyu, which I believe means 'a woman of no words'. Do not smile, my friends, for it was given to me when I knew very little of the language.

A lot of preparation was necessary before we could move off to Gilgil. Some stock had to be bought and a team of trek oxen secured. I could be of little help, for never having seen the Gilgil farm, I did not know what things would be required.

Olive and I went together to a sale at Naivasha and bought thirty cows for a beginning and parked them there to be picked up later. The transport at the war front was now mostly mechanical and trek oxen were being sold off by the Government at sales held on the Nairobi racecourse. We attended one of these and picked a team of white native animals, mostly young and unbroken to the yoke. I knew nothing about ox breaking or I should have stuck out for a trained team. Olive said that oxen were broken easily so I took her word for it and, for the moment, was content with what I had bought. Woe is me! But we had a lump of trouble with that little lot!

Tents had to be sorted out, chop-boxes made and stores bought. 'Are there no shops in Gilgil?' I timidly enquired.

'Of course there is an Indian *duka,* but the farm is some distance from the township and we don't want to starve.'

'Can I get any labour on the farm?'

'Certainly not; the whole country has been uninhabited since the

Masai move[1]; we shall have to take men along with us; six will be enough for you. Your head-boy, Kago, is a reliable sort of man, and I will give you an old servant of mine as cook, so you will have two you can trust.'

Tools had to be purchased: one hammer, one saw, one cross-cut saw, iron wedges, two axes, *pangas* (machetes), a spade or two and *jembies* (a type of mattock) for breaking ground. No nails, for these cost a small fortune, so did iron roofing. It was also a year of famine. Maize meal was seven and a half rupees a load[2], a load being only sixty pounds which was a month's ration for one man.

Then there was the question of transport for me. I could not risk taking up horses, for we did not know if they would live at the altitude.[3] Olive suggested I took a mule or two, and one evening I met her dragging along a minute brown mule mare with only one eye. She had bought it from a Somali she had seen on the road and considered it good enough for a beginning. It was a bad-tempered creature with a sore back who kicked at you when being mounted. No other mule being available, the old white Somali pony was to be taken up for Olive to ride just for the week she intended staying with me.

Lady McMillan had given me two young Airedales and Sergeant McGregor's 'Big Man' was to be sent up after me. In addition I took a shot-gun and a 9.7 rifle, a camp-bed with two or three old blankets, a tin bath and some chickens. These were selected by my future cook, Kichoki, as he was chicken boy at Kabete and supposed to know the best birds. He selected six old hens, his favourites, that he did not want to leave behind, one speckled hen was so ancient she could hardly get about – no cock but we did not discover this until we reached Gilgil.

---

[1] See Appendix 2

[2] One rupee was worth one shilling and fourpence until 1920 when the Government fixed the rupee at two shillings and the rupee was dropped as currency in the Colony. (C.S. Nicholls)

[3] The farm that they had bought, later known as Chatu Farm, consisted of a roughly oblong stretch of land of 1,100 acres. At the highest point the altitude was about 8,000 ft.

A great friend of ours, whom we called Kangangi[4] – his native name – said he wanted a short holiday and would like to trek up to the farm with us. We were glad of his company as an extra man is always of assistance and also he would be company for Olive on her return journey.

We bought a small light wagon and tried to teach the white oxen to draw it but most of them refused to learn. I think we got six to go fairly well before starting them off by road – or rather track – to Gilgil. (This was years before the main road from Nairobi to Kisumu had even been thought about.) All the men, with the exception of my personal servant, accompanied the loaded wagon. They were to pick up the thirty cows that had been left at Naivasha and meet us at Gilgil station a week hence. From Kabete this was a distance of between seventy and eighty miles.

I suppose the men took the old safari track over the escarpment and very rough going it must have been. Kago was in command of the party, bringing them through quite safely and up to time.

The day arrived when we ourselves had to make a start. No *syce* being capable of driving the cape cart, we rode to Kikuyu station, and the luggage was carried by porters. The train left at about 4 p.m. Olive by that time hated us so much that she insisted on travelling by herself, Kangangi and I sharing another carriage. We dined at Kijabe round about eight o'clock and reached Gilgil two hours later. There was a hotel being built but it was only at the foundation stage at that time and so we spent the night in the station *dak*-house.

The next morning I saw my future local township of Gilgil and I was not favourably impressed. The station itself consisted of a wide platform and a small tin shanty. Just at the back, across the road, were one or two Indian shops, built of iron and very dirty, one fair-sized goods shed and that was all. A mile or more across a plain was a house of sorts, belonging to the manager of the Syndicate who had sold Olive the farm. He had promised to meet us, but he didn't, and I rode the pony across to fetch him, as we had no idea where the farm was or how

---

4 E. B. Horne. A member of the Colonial Administration.

to get to it. Presently he arrived in a motorcar with his wife and a white woolly terrier. My Airedales instantly resented the pink bow tied round its neck and pulled it off.

At the *dak*-house maps were spread on the table and we were shown the position of the farm and the road that would take us twelve miles on our way. Thereafter it would be a cross-country trek with nothing to guide us so he lent us a native called 'Snub-Nose', who had been with the surveyor of the land when the farms were marked out and who knew where the boundary pegs were placed.

There had been a long and severe drought and the country all around Gilgil had been burnt out by grass fires. There was not a blade of green to be seen and the scrub had been reduced to charred sticks with scorched and shrivelled leaves clinging to them. It was dismal, dreary country indeed and my spirits dropped to zero as we endeavoured to catch the oxen and yoke up the team. There were still only six that would come to hand and the wagon was heavily laden. At the first sharp rise out of the township two of the beasts lay down. Their nostrils were then held until they were nearly suffocated before they would get up. It is no use beating a sulky ox for the more you beat the longer he will lie.

We pushed and pulled to the top of the hill when Olive, seeing it was pretty hopeless, said she would walk back to the Syndicate and try to borrow four trained animals. In the meantime we were to go on as far as we could and she would catch us up.

It was a terribly hot day and clouds of dust, inches thick, kicked up by the cattle ahead of us, blew back and smothered us. On either side of the road grass fires were burning merrily which very much added to the heat. We had the pony and mule but riding was out of the question for it needed every man of us to keep those wretched oxen moving at all.

After shouting, beating and pushing for a couple of hours I suggested stopping to brew some tea. We then discovered that the water tin had been forgotten and there was not a drop of water to be found anywhere, neither did we know where we would be likely to strike any. There was nothing for it but to keep going and trust to luck, for we could not camp without water.

As the day drew on our thirst became intolerable. The dogs and cattle suffered badly and we began to despair of finding a creek that night when, rounding a bend, we came upon a bridge over a river. There wasn't much water in it and what there was, was very muddy. That did not worry us; we filled all our available vessels first then turned the cattle loose to drink their fill. As the only working oxen obstinately refused to come up to the yokes again, we decided to camp where we were and wait for Olive. It was nearly six o'clock and we had done a hard day's work but we had no idea how far we had come or how far we were expected to go. The journey had been at a funeral pace owing to the behaviour of our beasts.

After some tea I left Kangangi to pitch the tents and I rode out to see what had become of the thirty cows who had got far ahead of us. A further four miles on I found the men comfortably camped with the herd close to a small house marked on the map as Top Farm. Telling the men to bring some milk along in the morning, I rode back to the river and found the tents ready up and a meal cooking. Still no sign of Olive and she didn't turn up that night.

The following morning, no milk having been brought, we ate a sketchy breakfast and set to work catching the oxen again who ran in all directions. Our training of the day before had had no effect and they were as unruly as ever. The dogs enjoyed it, having great sport heading them off and I, being utterly sick of oxen, did not care in the least if their noses were bitten.

We were just shoving the last one under the yoke when Olive galloped up on a smart little mule she had probably stolen, full of wrath that we had not got further the night before, but bringing the good news that a wagon was close behind with a full team of good oxen, four of which she had every intention of borrowing for a few hours.

I should have been diffident about taking animals from a wagon, the owner of which I did not know. Not so my sister. She had a splendid method of getting anything she wanted. As soon as the wagon was alongside she told the drivers we just needed their four leaders to help our lot up the hill and before you could wink she had unhitched them and hooked them on in front of the white beasts.

We now got on swimmingly: the borrowed animals not only walked but pulled, and our lazy devils had to put their backs into it. On reaching Top Farm the mob of cows was waiting for us. We cursed the herdsman for not bringing us milk but he told us that a lady and gentleman who had stayed the night at the farm, had insisted on milking our cows and had gone on with all the milk they could get.

The wagon from which my sister had borrowed the oxen was off-loaded at the farm and the drivers began to clamour for the return of their beasts. But Olive had not done with them yet and had no intention of parting with her commandeered relief force until we reached our second camp. She claimed one of the drivers as well, saying that he could bring the oxen back to the farm later.

It was lucky that we had not far to go. A short two miles on and we struck the Olioba River where the wagon track ended as far as we were concerned. From this point we had to strike off the track and make our way across country. Wheeled traffic was no longer possible and we were therefore forced to outspan and pitch camp.

The place was pretty and here bushfires had not destroyed the grass so there was plenty of food and water for the animals. The Olioba, flowing from a ready swamp above us, twinkled refreshingly over a shallow bed below the tents. Across the ford rose a high escarpment of wondrous coloured rock from which fallen boulders lay strewn about on the grassy slopes below. The cart-track ran under the lee of this mighty wall but where it led we had no idea.

Here was the sticking point. The wagon was no good to us and we had no porters to carry our stuff. Not a single stray native was to be seen and none resided in these parts. We were up against a problem that required some thinking out.

The next morning we left Kangangi at the camp to stop any men he chanced to see while Olive and I took the pony and mule, with Snub Nose to lead us, and we started off to hunt for our elusive property. At the top of the first slope we were again blockaded by solid rock, up which a cat could not have climbed. Scrambling along the side, we came across a narrow opening made by water. It was too narrow to get our mounts through so we set to work to widen it sufficiently. The stone was softer than it looked and we were soon able to lead them over to the opposite side.

We found ourselves wandering across a huge tract of swampland, bone dry at the time and terribly rough riding; our poor little conveyances stumbled almost at every step. To save them and their legs, we got off and walked. Snub Nose trotted on ahead annoyed at such delay. A native usually walks about five miles an hour, as later I found to my cost.

Just as we reached a bit of better going and were looking forward to being carried once more, we came upon a mass of flattened rock leading steeply down to what appeared to be a creek, heavily treed on either side. We led the animals over the stones and through the strip of forest until we reached a river bed with clear shallow water wending its twinkling way through a lovely fernery of maidenhair, osmunda, hart's tongue and other ferns. The rocky bank on the other side was far steeper, rising hundreds of feet above our heads. The only negotiable passages were narrow watercourses where riding was an impossibility.

We staggered and slithered to the top of this fortress, dragging our animals after us and eventually arriving at the top in a dripping and exhausted condition.

From this point, although there was a hill ahead of us, we could see for a considerable distance. In every direction the place was black and smoking. The beautiful tall herbage that had so enraptured my sister had now been reduced to ashes from unchecked veldt fires, desecrating the whole country in their windswept flight. We were appalled. Many hundreds of square miles of black, black blackness. Ridge upon ridge of great rolling downland with scarcely a bite of grass to be seen. Twenty miles due east loomed the Aberdare mountain range where the dense cedar forests flickered fire and belched smoke that veiled the summits and intermingled with pearly clouds of distant sky.

Thus my future home deigned to greet me and the gods of wilderness and wild bid me welcome, admitting a demon desolation to the soul and wringing all remaining courage from my sinking heart.

For a while we gazed upon the destruction of our immediate hopes until Snub Nose brought us back to the necessary business in hand.

We were not yet on our own farm however. The boundary pegs, long since overgrown with bush, required to be searched out. This took a very long time for we had to leave our mounts at the top and scramble down through dense forest and vines to the Oliondo River which was our western boundary. The surveyor, having a treasure hunt in his mind when he had marked out these farms, had successfully hidden every peg in the most obscure places.

It was nearly dark when we arrived back at our camp, weary, worn and somewhat sad. But Kangangi's news put some life into us. Whilst we were exploring, a farmer had come along who would buy the wagon, and sell us four well-trained oxen. He had also offered to lend us a couple of men to help with the porters' work. His farm was nine miles further up the road and we decided it would be a good plan to visit him as soon as possible. We went the following day, taking it in turns to ride.

The house was in the middle of a forest, thickly inhabited by leopard that were for ever killing his dogs and calves, and the trees were alive with the small Sykes monkey who jeered at us from the branches as we trudged along.

We bought four oxen of great antiquity and a few more cows as well as a grade shorthorn bull and drove the lot back to camp, assisted by the two men on loan.

From the top of the rock fortress to the Simba River, where we intended to make a permanent camp, was three to four miles of rocks and gullies. Some of the heavier things could be taken on a sleigh by oxen, and Kangangi and I were told to go and make one from a small cedar growing on the far side of the rocky creek. It was a whole day's work making the sledge for neither of us knew in the least how to do it and we were quite sure it would in no way meet with Olive's approval. Neither did it when she brought the safari across to load up. But I escaped before the worst happened as I was obliged to take the cows across.

Driving cattle over strange country with no track to guide them is difficult work. They scattered all over the place and by four o'clock I was lost. Then a cow saw fit to calve and so I was obliged to leave the main herd in order to look after her.

There was nothing to show me the position of the camp; the burnt ground made every bit of the place look exactly the same. I wandered on and on, following the cattle until I came to a forest I had not seen before. I was wondering if I should ever be found again when there was a fearsome roar right ahead and a lion stampeded my charges who came racing back on top of me. I did all I could to head them off and stop the leaders who were wild with fear and took no notice of my waving arms and stick. Making sure the lion was not following on, I sat down on a fallen tree and, I ought to add, wept. But in fact I didn't, I only laughed until I cried. The contrast of life struck me as being so intensely funny. Here was I, lately an artist in London, now lost in Africa trying to stop a mob of cattle being stampeded by a lion.

The sun had gone to bed and dusky eve was fast enveloping the landscape when suddenly a native stood before me and, strangely enough, he was someone I had known at Kabete. Like all black folk he knew everything that was going on for miles around him. He knew where our camp was to be, knew that our safari was having difficulty in getting stuff across to the farm and even knew how to soothe frightened cows. He helped to collect them and then showed us an easy way to get into the farm camp.

One lion meant lots of lions. Tired as we were, bush had to be cut at once and a *boma* (stockade) made for the stock before we could get to bed. Bonfires were lit around it and the natives slept by the fires. But nothing less than an earthquake would have awakened any of us that night.

In most places it is more unusual than usual to see either lion or leopard, and to take a walk on the veldt was as safe as taking a walk in an English country lane. But in my case it was rather different, for I took up land in a part of the country that had never before been inhabited by either natives or Europeans. Years ago the Masai herded their cattle here during the rainy seasons where grazing was good: but they were not settled residents and since 1911 nobody had been here at all. It was really little wonder that almost all the animals in existence had made it their home.

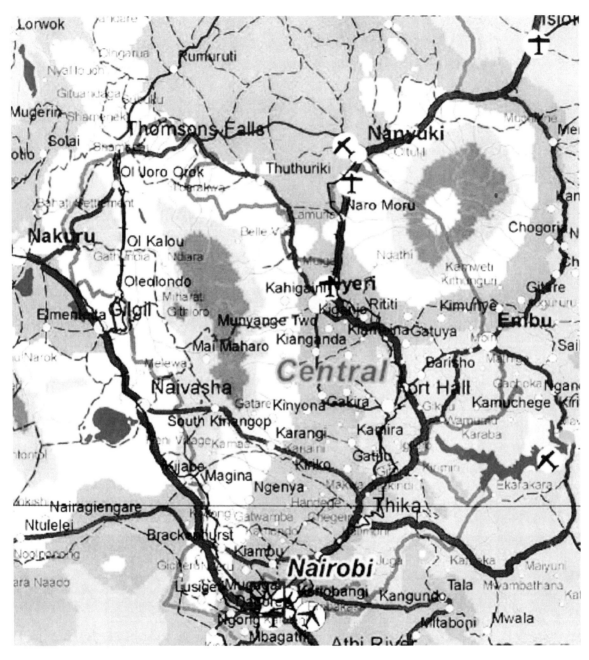

MARGARET'S FARM WAS BETWEEN GILGIL AND THOMSON'S
FALLS, JUST SOUTHWEST OF THE LOZENGE SHAPED
LAKE OL'BOLOSSAT WHICH ITSELF CAN BE SEEN SOUTH OF
THOMSON'S FALLS

'A Terrific Fight'

Chapter IX

MARGARET COLLYER'S TENTED CAMP ON THE OL'KALOU FARM

Dawn – the sun slowly topped the ridge to throw his rays mockingly on our untidy camp. We were in a hollow, below the hill on the far side of the river. Mercifully here the fires had jumped the grass and left us some grazing to carry on with. There was also water still running in the Simba, which my sister had been assured was a permanent stream. This turned out to be a land agent's fib, for this creek is only fed by soakage water from the surrounding hills, and is always empty during dry seasons. Such little drawbacks were left for me to discover later on.

Kangangi now became rather troublesome, for he could not countenance the idea of leaving me alone with the natives in such a God-forsaken place. He persisted in protesting at all hours of the day, declaring it was unsafe, quite unfit for a white woman and that we were both mad to attempt a pioneering job so entirely cut off from help of any description. His prayers for my reprieve met with no response from either of us; the farm was bought, we had managed to reach it, and I was determined to carry on, no matter what.

There are so many faults in my character they fall over each other; but God be thanked, fear is not one of them or my life on that farm would indeed have been a hell on earth. I make no boast when I say few women would have stuck it out; but I had abilities to help me which the large majority probably would not have possessed. No credit is deserved for physical courage; a person is either born with, or without it. It is an inheritance one has little right to be proud of. Protection for me lay in my love of animals and animal life. It was such an immense interest to watch their ways and habits in a world so much their own that I never tired of learning all I could about them. It was an absorbing occupation and a safeguard against occasional attacks of loneliness akin to insanity. I dreaded these rare occurrences more than words can express.

Artistic training also came to my aid at such times, where beauty reigned supreme all around me, and though I had no leisure to paint with my hands, my mind was ever painting brain pictures which far excelled anything I could have put on canvas.

Our safari to the farm had taken more time than we had calculated and Olive was unable to remain longer than two or three days at the camp; business at home was calling and she had to get back to Kabete.

When she and Kangangi were about to leave me I had terrible qualms and weakly asked what I was supposed to do next. Her reply was a stimulating tonic. Utter scorn both rang in her voice and looked out of her eyes.

'*Do next!* Why, you build a house, of course. There are plenty of trees about. You've got a saw, wedges and a hammer; what more do you want?'

It was on the tip of my tongue to say: 'But I've never built a house. I don't know how to fell a tree.' But sheer pride forbade the utterance of such words to so indomitable a being. Instead I wished them a cheery goodbye and a safe journey back to civilization – and a ready-made house.

Having tidied up the camp and arranged things to be more ship-shape, I then counted up my possessions. Two dogs, one mule, six old hens (no cock), thirty-five cows, one calf, one bull, sixteen white and useless oxen and four conscientious antique oxen. There was also Kago and Kichoki plus four other strange blanketed fellows.

I called Kago to my tent for a conference and we discussed future plans. It was quite certain I could not build without first getting labour and no men were to be found nearer than Rumuruti, forty miles away on the other side of the mountains. Kago undertook to go over and collect a gang, also a few women, which was possibly a wise move on his part. He said he could return in under a week. I gave him some *posho* (maize meal) for the journey and let him go.

My difficulty now was to feed them all. Everything I needed had to be brought up from Gilgil by porter and Gilgil was eighteen miles from my camp. Nowadays eighteen miles sounds nothing at all but back in the days of no roads and no cars it was a very long way indeed. It took a day to go and a day to return and, being short of men, I could only send them once a fortnight for my mail. This was the one link I had with civilization for the next three years. Once or twice I went more than five months without sight of a white face or speaking my own language.

One curious thing struck me the first day I was alone and that was the absence of bird life. Except for a few plantain birds with their blood red flight feathers, there were no small birds in residence at all. They came later, for where human habitation exists, there will birds be gathered together.

I was glad when Kago returned with his several followers, for lions roared around us every night and I feared a raid on the cattle, who were always trying to break out of the boma and bolt for it. I got little sleep because the fires had to be kept going and I did not trust the men to do it. The dogs were chained to my bed, for I had been warned of the danger of leopard.

While poking about with the cattle one evening, the cook, Kichoki, came to tell me that there was 'an animal of the forest' walking round the camp which I had better shoot. He mentioned its Swahili name, which I did not know. Asking him to describe it, he said, 'Its ears are on the top of its head and its tail is behind very.' An excellent word portrait of our friend the jackal.

Most of the grazing having been burnt out, the herbivorous game had retreated towards the mountains, but the place was still teeming with monkeys and carnivores. I never went twenty yards from the tent without seeing some creature spring out of a bush. It was not safe to move without a gun. The grass that had escaped destruction was dry and above my head; a proper lurking place for denizens of the wild. I set to work to cut a clear space all round the encampment, feeling safer when things could not jump out on me unawares.

Within a fortnight I received another small mule from Olive. Also McGregor's dog 'Big Man' and very glad I was to have him, for he had forgotten more about hunting than I ever knew.

The house was not the first thing we built by any manner of means. We felled trees and split logs for a twenty-yard square cattle-yard. Lion were coming closer every night and the cattle were getting more and more restless. We pushed the work on apace and soon made a very solid wall seven feet high around the enclosure, mudding up the cracks to a height of four and a half feet. If a lion cannot see where he is going to land he will not risk a leap. We then put up a hut for the herdsmen just outside the gate and it was while we were thatching this hut that I got into my first bit of trouble.

I had been splitting logs all day in the heat of the sun and went back to my tent for a late tea. Being tired, I took off my gaiters and wide belt, on which I carried a hunting knife and whistle.

The dogs had had a dull time watching us work and now came crowding round with wagging tails and smiling eyes requesting me to take them for a proper walk. Never having been able to refuse a dog anything, I dragged myself out of a chair and decided I would give them a run after a bush-buck that was usually to be found nearby.

'Dona' my favourite Airedale, was the older of the two terriers: a reliable huntress and under control. 'Prickles' was the reverse; a self-willed, unruly little devil who was ever getting into trouble. 'Big Man' was all he ought to be and a bit more.

With gleaming eyes and trembling sterns they now waited for me to make a move. The evening was cool and beautiful as I strolled down a game-track to the edge of the wooded creek. Monkey life having dozed during the heat of the day was now gambolling and chattering amongst the branches of the tall cedar trees, the black and white colobus galumphing from bush to bush. Masses of white jessamine, were in full flower and the air was filled with its delicious perfume. Life was well worth living as I mooched along between avenues of golden grasses.

The bush-buck was not where I had expected to find him and, having no gun with me I contemplated turning back, but three eager faces looking up into mine bade me go on and try for something else.

I was still so English that I scarcely believed that danger lurked in every bit of cover. On nearing the edge of the forest I struck into a well-defined game track which led me across a dry watercourse about half a mile from our building operations. Dona and Big Man had come back to heel but Prickles was ahead by himself. I heard him give tongue some distance away and urged the others on to his opening. Away they dashed when I heard Prickles' yaps of joy turn to yelps of agony. I was climbing up a steep incline and I started to run as I have seldom run in my life for I felt sure a leopard had got him.

His screams suddenly ceased and I could hear the other two dogs baying something they could not tackle. As I got to the top of the rise where a twist in the stream brought it close to the side of the path I was running on, an appalling sight met my eyes. On the rocks and only a few yards from me was a huge python with three of his coils around Prickles' body. The brute's head was raised and its mouth open, while the other two dogs were barking and dancing frantically round it unable to go in.

All I could see of Prickles was his head. Blood was oozing from his mouth and eyes, and these eyes were now glued on mine, pleading for help. For one ghastly moment I was panic-stricken and that moment felt like an hour. My brain ceased to function and I could not think of any possible way to release him without a knife or gun. The dog's expression of agonized terror must have recalled me to myself and I looked around for some weapon with which I could attack the snake for the dog was being squeezed to death before my eyes. Mercifully I spied a heavy burnt short log which I seized with both hands and, rushing at the snake, I hit it as hard as I could across the back of the neck as the head was raised.

The blow made no impression on it at all, except that the beast dropped its head and made a lightning dive for me. I bashed it again and again; and at each blow it came at me like a flash and I had to give ground. All the time I was encouraging the other dogs to help and Big Man got hold of its tail and hung on. Dona was with me at its head, barking and jumping at its neck. Again I went close and hit with all my might and main. It made another rush and got me in the thigh and Dona grabbed hold and tried to pull it off. The snake appeared to make no perceptible movement but in an instant the dog was flung yards into the air.

All this time, it had been a running fight and yet the snake had never loosened its coils one iota. It was by now thoroughly enraged and kept following me up in lightning darts. To avoid one I jumped up on to a low ledge of rock; but still the brute came on and this is the strangest part of the story. To reach me it had to get its head over the edge of the ledge on which I was standing, with the log ready and every muscle taut. By the merest fluke in the world I struck at exactly the right moment. Just as the throat of the reptile was against the sharp edge of stone I smote and to my utter amazement the head dropped to the ground as though badly hurt. Dona instantly fixed it by the back of the neck and I saw the coils round Prickles slowly, slowly relaxing their mighty grip. I yelled to Dona to hold on and worry whilst I sprang off the rock, seized hold of Prickles' collar and, pushing the coils off him, dragged him out and threw him into a patch of grass. Then I ran back to pull off Dona and, ordering Big Man to let go of the tail, I waited breathlessly to see what would happen next.

To my astonishment this enormous reptile lay for a minute perfectly still, then very slowly it turned its head round and glided back to where I first had seen it, disappearing down the watercourse.

It had been a terrific fight from start to finish and my strength had all but given out. I could not have carried on for very much longer and all the time I had felt like a pygmy, utterly powerless to hurt a monster of such strength and agility. Since I was a child I have always had a terror of even a little grass snake but the moment I picked up that log and went in, all fear completely left me; my one thought being to save the dog.

I saw the end of the python's tail slide down into the bed of the stream and watched it go a short distance down the gully and then coil up under the root of an overhanging tree.

Then and not until then did I call for aid. I think my 'view holloas' would have reached the next world and a man thatching his hut heard me calling. He blew the alarm whistle for the rest of the men who came tearing along armed with spears to my assistance.

Kago had the sense to bring my rifle for he quite thought a lion had got me. His relief when he saw me yet alive was something to be remembered. Explaining what had happened I scrambled down the stream with my rifle. Its head was lifted as it saw me and I knelt down about ten yards off and put an explosive bullet into its coiled body. It came at me with a hissing lunge and I had to run. I then got four more bullets into the middle of it but failed to hit its head which kept swaying about. It was badly chopped up and could not get away, surrounded as it was by the boys with their spears. So I sent back for my shot-gun and, when this arrived, blew its head to pieces with a No. 5.

The Kikuyu will not handle snakes dead or alive but with two or three hooked sticks we got this fellow up on the bank. He was still wriggling notwithstanding his head had been nearly blown off. I measured his length roughly. Pulled out straight he would have gone every bit of seventeen feet.

Kago carried Prickles home in triumph, the rest of the men giving forth war-whoops and throwing their spears to show their joy at the death of the enemy. Prickles had been bitten rather badly in one or two places and he was constantly sick for a few days as a result of the squeezing, but his ribs were intact. I put him into a hot bath, and rubbed him well to disperse the stiffness I felt sure he would suffer from. In a few days he was as full of buck and wickedness as ever.[1]

There is a sequel to this story and how to account for it I am not sure, but I think I can make a good guess. About four days after the event, when I had more or less recovered from the shock, I was digging a patch of ground for a vegetable garden with the cook, when it occurred to me that some day I might like to have a relic of such a splendid fight. So I suggested to Kichoki that I would give him five rupees if he would pull out some of the snake's teeth. He remarked that he had passed it the day before; it was smelling horribly and the skin was now useless. Five rupees being a tempting offer, he stopped digging to think about it. So I said, 'Come on Kichoki, I will go along with you and we will get the teeth this evening.'

Imagine our surprise on reaching the place to find *no snake*. Not a vestige remained. If hyena had eaten it there would have been tracks and signs of them and bits of bone lying about. We searched all round and not a particle of it could we discover. Kichoki declared that hyena would not eat snake. Now, snakes invariably go in pairs and my only

---

[1] Margaret named her farm 'Chatu' which is the Swahili word for python.

conclusion was that its mate had come along and swallowed it. Python are known to be foul feeders; the only danger from the bite of one is that the wound may go septic from its dirty teeth. I have already given an account of one snake swallowing another in the zoo and I believe this is the solution to this mystery.

All the years I have lived up here I have neither seen nor heard of another python. But a week after destroying this one I was riding with Kago down to Gilgil on the mules when, crossing a bit of swamp land, I saw what looked like a thick log lying across the road. I was a little in advance of Kago who was carrying my rifle. I took no notice of the obstruction until my mule turned round with a frightened snort and galloped in the opposite direction. The other mule of course followed suit and as it takes a donkey engine to stop a startled mule, it was some minutes before we could turn round and go back.

The log was still there and nothing would induce our mules to approach it. I got off and took my gun to see if some wild beast was lying up in the reeds. I walked right up to the log before I noticed that it was moving slowly. That was enough for me. I turned and fled. We waited at a distance while a far bigger python than mine had been, cleared off. It was not my land and of course it would have been poaching had I shot it. That one belonged to Lady Colville[2] and I left word at her house that I had spared her pet.

To complete this story of Prickles and his snake – instead of it warning him off them for life, he became a snake-killer. Yet it was months before he would cross that watercourse. I often rode that way with the other dogs but he would go a mile or more round to avoid the spot where he so nearly lost his life.[3]

---

[2] Lady Colvile was married to Maj. Gen. Sir Henry Colvile KCMG. Described as 'the slightly dotty niece of the Duke of Marlborough' she farmed in the Gilgil area. She also built a small hotel in Gilgil. Lady Colville was believed to have died in 1930 [James Foster and Peter J. Ayre]

[3] This episode was published in *The Field* shortly after it occurred.

Early One Morning

Chapter X

The longed-for rains had come and in one short week the aspect of the country had changed from sooty black to verdant green. With the fresh young grass came herds of antelope, many varieties giving us the pleasure of their company. Never having been molested, they knew little fear of human beings and being obliged at times to kill for meat, I have shot kongoni as close as twenty yards. These uncouthly shaped, glassy-eyed creatures, so like a taxidermist's specimens, just stood and stared with expressionless faces when I raised my gun to shoot them.

Zebra in their hundreds ate everything we planted. Ostriches laid their eggs on the warm flat rocks and hatched out quaint curly-quilled chicks in no way resembling their parents. Jackal, serval cat, cheetah and wild dog abounded in the forest creek. Hyrax called, monkeys chattered, leopard and bush-buck coughed and the king of beasts nightly roared his challenge, which echoed from hill to hill.

It was one of those gorgeous mornings that you only get in the Highlands of Kenya. Beauty and nature calls to the soul that loveth both. Solitude is not loneliness; the mind is absorbed in the wonders of the vast wild world and for the moment companionship is neither needed nor wanted.

The labour were not yet out of their fuggy smoky huts but the wanderlust was upon me when I went to Kago's tent and routed him out of his blankets, telling him to get the gun and come.

Much to their disappointment I left all the dogs in camp; I was in no mood for murdering anything. The first light of dawn and the fresh clean air were so indescribably nice that I wished to live and let live.

We walked down to the small path that I had, by that time, cut through the belt of forest, crossed the Simba river and climbed steadily to the top of the grassy ridge on the far side. Here, at the height of eight thousand feet, I sat down by a patch of bush, lit a cigarette and feasted my eyes on the view that lay before me. From this point of vantage I could see Lake Naivasha glimmering in the distance far away to my right, guarded by the deeply seamed and rugged Mountain Longonot. To my left, under the foothills of the Aberdares, Ol 'Bolossat Lake was distinguishable. Between these two sheets of water, a distance of forty or fifty miles, lay immense grassy plains with the big Malewa river running through the centre.

Behind the plains and ridges rose the mountains, the sun just clearing the peaks of Kipipiri and Satima, the pinky glow softening their ragged outline and blending them into the pearly grey of the morning sky.

I was dreaming of my paint-box and idly wondering what my old friend David Murray would have made of all this on one of his notable six-foot canvases, when my attention was arrested by the strange behaviour of a herd of kongoni who had been peacefully grazing at no great distance from where I sat. The posted sentinels of the herd were evidently becoming uneasy; instead of standing as though stuffed, they began moving round in small circles with heads held high, trying to wind the approaching danger which their sensitive nerves had already detected.

I took up my field glasses to get a clearer view and after a while, I spotted a couple of cheetah crawling along on their stomachs through the long sparse grass. They were yet some way below the kongoni, and out for a succulent breakfast of young buck meat. As they approached the herd, they separated, their evident object being to get the antelope between them. Although there had been uneasiness amongst one or two of the lookouts, no real alarm had been raised and nearest to the crouching, stalking cheetah was a half-grown doe feeding a short distance from the main body of the herd. I could easily see that this was the one they had marked down to try for.

Slower and slower, nearer and nearer crept the spotted cats; but by now all the kongoni were on the alert, with heads up and crowding into a pack. All indeed but the youthful doe, who was too intent on a nice patch of green grass to notice the movements of her friends. It was a most exciting thing to watch although my sympathy was with the little doe. I was praying that she might perceive the danger before it was too late when at that moment the cheetah made their rush and spring. For a second there was a mix-up, then I saw the doe going like the wind after her terror-stricken companions. How she managed to escape I cannot think; but she did, though no doubt carrying some wounds that would mar her beauty for life.

In my joy at seeing her safe I had taken my eyes off the cheetah and when I looked again they had both disappeared. They certainly did not give chase, as I had expected them to do. Having made their stalk and rush and somehow missed their mark, I suppose they wandered off to find something smaller and easier to kill. I was contemplating getting the dogs and going in search of them when Kago pulled my arm and called my attention to something he was staring at with all his might. He was pointing away on our left to a high rock-covered bluff. With the naked eye I could only make out a lot of moving black objects. Again I pulled my glasses from their case and even with these, was still uncertain what the animals could be, when Kago, who had the eyes of a hawk, said '*Nugu* (Baboon), and hundreds of them coming this way.'

This promised to be far more interesting than hunting cheetah, so I settled down for a long wait. Between the ridge on which we were sitting and that on which we had sighted the baboons, was a deep wide coombe with a stream at the bottom. They were travelling slowly and as they dropped into the gully we lost sight of them; it seemed a long while before the first of the large army reappeared on the top of the rise. We crawled deeper into the bushes and lay in silence and watched.

Hundreds and hundreds of baboon were on safari, moving from one forest to another in search of food. They were travelling in a complete circle. All the old men were on the outside, forming a wall of protection around the women and children in the centre. They were moving at a leisurely pace, walking on all fours with their tails hooped downward in the dignified way they possess when alone and unfrightened. The women were carrying tiny babies, while the older boys and girls skipped about amongst the crowd; these at times would break out of the circle, only to be chased and driven back by the guardians of the party. They came trooping past us so close I could have hit them with a stone. Little did they dream that possible danger lay so close at hand. They were lords of all they surveyed and had been in undisturbed possession of the forests, ridges and valleys where scarce a human foot had trod for numbers of years. Though they were now trespassing on my land, I felt myself to be the real intruder, not they.

Their mode of travel was kept up until they reached my piece of forest. Then they broke up, the big monkeys diving beneath the shade of the trees, barking and quarrelling, whilst the children romped in the sunshine amongst the lower bush at the edge, playing hide-and-seek and catch-who-catch-can. It was a pretty sight, so full of happiness. Once a very old man came out of the bushes and began bullying and scolding the babies. I half thought of shooting him; but his ugly wrinkled face looked so worried and concerned about things in general I had no heart to fire. He roughly caught one or two of the children and hunted them over in a desultory fashion for fleas; but that was not the cause of his trouble. It lay far deeper, I thought. He was old, nearly worn out, and maybe expecting and dreading the day when he would be put out of his tribe and be compelled to end his days alone and lonely.

Perhaps he was a king and feared that the rising generation was about to dethrone him. Or he may have been puzzling in his mind over the laws of nature that are essentially cruel and have no use for the aged and feeble. It is the same thoughout all the wild life; there comes a time when Might is Right, a fierce fight ensues and the old rulers are beaten and turned adrift to fend for themselves as best they can. Their young and beautiful wives are taken from them by stronger and better men; their children know them no more. They are driven away without guard of any sort and, as I shall show, they usually meet their end by violence.

After this enjoyable morning I went back to breakfast and work. After tea, when it was the dogs' hour for recreation, I took them to a maize *shamba* (field) that had just been planted and there we came face to face with the old man baboon. The dogs made a wild rush at him but he was close to a tree, up which he ascended at great speed until he reached a safe branch. Here he sat, with the pack barking and leaping beneath him. This did not in the least disturb his equilibrium: he amused himself by picking off the dry twigs and bits of bark and throwing them at the dogs below. Never have I seen dogs more furiously angry. I thought the terriers would start having fits from pure rage. They eventually tried to cut the tree down with their teeth, so I had to call a boy to help me get them home.

A day later I was riding out in the open through some tall grass when Dona got wind of something and streaked off with the rest of the pack at her heels. I had got a glimpse from the top of my mule of a large shaggy back and had carefully not mentioned it to the dogs until I could be sure what it was. However, Dona's nose beat me to it and the bobbing black back, with the hounds after it, disappeared down a slope out of sight.

Kago and I urged our mules on after the hunt and soon we heard howls of rage just below us. We left the mules and ran on to the scene of the fight. Surrounded by dogs was an enormous old man baboon standing on his hind legs struggling for his life. He had got Dona by her collar, holding her off his throat with his long hairy arms and sinews of welded steel. The bitch was mad with anger but helpless to resist. Big Man and Prickles were tearing the animal in pieces from the back and sides. We stood close and watched the fight for a few seconds; it was too unfair so I took my rifle to shoot. Because the dogs were all over the monkey, in my anxiety not to kill one of them, I made a mistake and broke the hind leg of the poor beast. He collapsed, rolling over on his side and lay groaning with one hand holding the broken limb. This was too much for me, so we pulled and whipped the dogs off as quickly as possible and I finished the disgusting business with a shot through the head.

No sooner had we completed this murder and started skinning operations, than away went the dogs after another monkey, evidently an old friend of the one we had killed and who ventured back to see what had become of his mate. This, I am sorry to say, we also had to shoot.

These two were quite alone and no doubt, from the look of their teeth, they were very old and had been turned out of their troop in the way I have already described. The larger of the two measured five feet from the tip of his tail to the back of his head. He had an immensely long and shaggy coat, and the canine teeth were one and a quarter inches in length. I preserved both skin and skull because of his great size.

I believe baboon to be entirely vegetarian. They live on grass and what maize and vegetables they can steal. Yet their teeth are almost the teeth of the carnivora, which is rather strange. Away from rock or trees they are extremely inactive and do not appear to be able to go any great pace. My dogs caught them very easily. When in numbers they are dangerous to dogs but the two we killed had not a ghost of a hope against my pack.

The following incident happened at the Ngong Forest and it was repeated to me immediately after the happening by two natives who had played a part in it.

A lot of Kikuyu women were collecting firewood on the edge of the forest. Several of them had tiny babies which they had left lying about on the ground while they were at their work. One baby had been dumped under a big tree. The mother was getting wood not far off when she heard strange noises and, turning, saw a female baboon grip her baby by one arm and bolt up a tree with it. All the women began screaming, as is their wont, and the more they screamed the higher the monkey carried the baby, until it was on the top-most branches, dangling the infant by one of its arms over their heads. Every second they expected to see the child dropped from this great height to the ground.

Their screams had brought some of the men to the spot and amongst them was Kago, who usually had his head well screwed on. At once he stopped the women yelling and sent one to a hut to fetch a bunch of bananas and a bowl of milk. These he placed beneath the tree where the monkey could see them and then he herded all the natives a distance from the spot and awaited events.

The monkey, seeing this tasty array of food it loved, gathered the baby more firmly under its arm and carefully made the descent, depositing the child on the ground and getting to work on the fruit. As soon as it had moved a few yards from the child, all the men rushed at it and it fled with the edible trophies. The baby was quite unhurt.

This story sounds incredible; but I have since learnt that it is not at all an uncommon thing for a female baboon to steal babies left unattended while the mothers are working or gossiping.

The cultivation of land bored me to tears. I had to make myself watch oxen dragging a plough up and down the *shamba*. I dislike seeing cattle work and have never become accustomed to it; the heavy crack of an ox-whip still sends a shiver down my spine. I am not a farmer and have never had the smallest inclination to grow crops but I like the animals connected with a farm and have enjoyed looking after their welfare. The rest has been forced labour which I have carried out to the best of my ability, even though my heart may have been elsewhere.

My recreation from the drudgery of everyday routine work was to get on a horse, ride out into the blue and watch the wild life that surrounded me. In this way I learnt some curious facts about the game that I should never have known had I not constantly been amongst them. For instance, Thomson's gazelle never frequent ridges at eight thousand feet, neither do impala or blue duiker. A mile or so from my farm, a few hundred feet lower in altitude, I found both impala and Tommy living happily. Just outside Gilgil township, a good deal lower still, plenty of blue duiker are to be found. I have never found klipspringer on my rocks, but two miles away there used to be plenty. I did not know that leopard caught or ate rats and moles until, in the course of an early ride, I watched one for a long time doing both.

All these matters pleased me greatly. The smaller mammals too are fascinating. Zorilla, the white and black striped skunk is a superb little creature and as fierce as the white-tailed honey bear when cornered. The ratel is so tough skinned that he is practically dog-proof but the slightest tap on the nose with a stick will kill him at once. The greater and lesser mongoose, hyrax, porcupine and antbear, serval cat, kaffir cat, the gennet, both small and large are all beautiful things but dreadful chicken killers. All these and many more besides I had as residents on my farm.

As soon as I was settled here for good, birds began to make their appearance. The blue pigeon came first, then the doves, African robins, bul-buls, mousebirds, waxbill, endless weavers, a large variety of hawks and kites and a fine eagle who is a snake killer. I have seen him holding down a puff-adder with his claws. After killing it, he cuts the reptile into chunks and eats it on the nearest bough of a tree.

The secretary bird walks slowly and solitarily about the plains. Since his children take six months before leaving the nest he gets very bored, and looks it. The big ground hornbill stalk about like fat metropolitan policemen and have to taxi twenty yards or more before they are able to get on the wing. Partridges of several varieties live in the bushes and last, but not least, the pretty black and white river duck float on my dam.

Pioneering Adventures

Chapter XI

MARGARET COLLYER'S FIRST HOUSE WHICH
WAS BURNT DOWN IN 1927
The tall lurcher is almost certainly Big Man, and two
of the Airedales could be Donna And Prickles

How to build a house without nails puzzled me very much. Then the simple idea of using wooden pegs dawned on me and I set to work, spending all my evenings whittling these out of a very hard wood we found in the forest. It all took a long time. Holes had to be drilled in every rafter to push these pegs through and as none of the men could use an auger I was obliged to do this work myself. I was beginning to learn that nothing was impossible; if it could not be done one way it could be done another. What I had always considered the necessities of life were not really necessities at all; they had to be omitted and one ceased to worry about them. I do not think any of my friends in England would have greatly envied me my new house but anything is better than a tent and I was glad enough for the shelter it gave me.

The floor was pounded mud. Across the centre a six-foot log wall divided bedroom from sitting room and on this wall were hung my bridles and saddlery. A few flat stones formed the fireplace. My furniture comprised a camp-chair or two, a deal table, a cupboard, a camp-bed and a bath. It was a long time before I had a looking-glass.

The window holes were barred across; the doors, made of split timber, were solid enough but extremely draughty and the hut was dreadfully damp and cold during the rainy seasons. No matter how deep I dug the ditches round it the floor was never dry, and I had to sit with my feet on a box.

I lived in this hovel for ten years until it was burnt down in 1927.

In 1919 the Soldier Settler Scheme[1] was put in motion and towards the end of that year the farms were balloted for. Ex-soldiers, unable to get work in England, were told that with £500 capital they could come out

---

[1] The Soldier Settler Scheme was introduced by the British Government to offer land for farming in Kenya after World War I. C.S. Nicholls writes: 'In all 2,540,000 more acres were made available for white settlement. For the ex-servicemen there were to be 500 A-farms, of approximately 160 acres each and containing a high proportion of arable land, and 850 B-farms of from 500 to 3,000 acres each. The farms were distributed by raffle. Men and women who had served in the army, navy or air force for at least six months were allowed to submit a series of numbers, in the order of their choice.'

to Kenya, stock a farm and live happily ever after. Whoever encouraged such an idea could have had little knowledge of what the colony was like after the war, for everything needed for farm work stood at ruination prices. Ploughs, harrows, rollers etc., even if they could be bought, were enormously dear, so also were wagons, trek oxen and native cows. I have paid as much as Shs 180/- for a native cow and calf.[2]

A great many of these farms were miles and miles away from the railhead, and nobody saw fit to warn these unfortunate people of the difficulties and expense of necessary transport which was mostly in the hands of Dutchmen (South African Boers) who charged exactly what they felt inclined. A lot of the 'B' farms selected were worthless tracts of land with no permanent water and no timber at all on them. One of these 'B' farms was allotted to me and, knowing the vicinity, I never bothered to go and look at it as all that land was rocky, dry and hardly fitted to carry goats.

In December the following year, the country was again burnt out by grass fires and the poor folk waiting at Gilgil could not get up to their farms since there was no feed for the oxen *en route*. I well remember riding down to the township one terribly hot day and meeting two families being taken to God knows where by Dutch transport. On the first wagon, sitting on top of a load of household furniture, was a woman with a small baby and several older children. Her husband was stalking along ahead of a team of miserably starved cattle belonging to a Dutchman I knew.[3] The country on either side was black and there was not a drop of water in any of the usual watering places. I told the

---

2   This would have been some £9 in English money: which has been computed at approximately £275 today.

3   C.S. Nicholls writes, '…the Boers were reluctantly accepted because they were crucially useful to the British farmers of the EAP during these years before tractors became available. Since they were the only ones who could train and handle teams of oxen, they undertook all the contract ploughing for other farms … and they specialised in training oxen. Others ran transport [carrying] goods and people by ox wagon.'

man he had far better turn back at once, especially for the sake of his children, as he most certainly would never get through and the oxen were quite unfit to trek. My interference was meant kindly but it was met with withering scorn and on they went, destined to return in four days with the children in a sad state, the oxen having to be left on the road.

This is only one of many such stories. At that time Kenya was in no way ready for this influx of European families. Just think of the risk of taking small children on to these isolated farms where there was no possibility of getting medical aid. No roads were then in existence and the only way of travelling about was either on horseback or by wagon. It was a crying shame that ex-Service men with wives and families should have been given such false reports of the Colony and encouraged to risk all and, in many cases, to lose all. Who was the politician in England responsible for these tragedies I wonder?

Quite a bit of capital was needed to start any sort of farm. When I came to this farm in 1918 and, for many years afterwards, the transport of our crops for market took all the gilt off the gingerbread; the cost of carting was not taken into anything like enough consideration.

All this was untried and untested land. It was for the unfortunate pioneer to discover what would grow and what would not. We could produce flax to some purpose and thought there would be a fortune in this. Before many of us had retted our first crop, the slump in flax was upon us, and what was sold did not cover the price of the seed. It cost us £100 in seed alone to sow sixty acres and I much doubt if we got half that amount back.[4]

After a time there was some sort of wagon track cut from Gilgil to Thomson's Falls, a distance of forty-eight miles; but where it crossed the Simba river I do not know, for I had my own way of getting to Gilgil on horse or mule back, striking into the old Somali path along which I often met Somali caravans with their accompaniment of sheep, goats

---

4 In June 1921 the price of flax dropped from £500 to £50 a ton. [C.S. Nicholls]

and camels. These caravans travelled to and from Isiolo and were a charmingly picturesque sight as they rested for a few hours near a river. The bright coloured shawls and other garments hung on bushes to dry, the camels lying down with loads still piled on their backs, sheep and goats grazing near the water's edge and their graceful coffee-coloured owners lounging about in sun and shade.

The camels so pleased me that one day I tried to buy one and was very surprised when it was offered to me for £5. It seemed such a lot of camel for so small a price. However, as it bit me in the leg when I wished to make friends with it I gave it a pass, especially as I was given to understand that if I bought the camel I should have to buy its boy as well. I do not love the Somali, except to gaze upon. They charm my artistic sense only, for some are very beautiful with their long slim well-rounded throats, on which the somewhat small head is set with dignity (or insolence). Their carriage is good and upright, limbs fine and cleanly modelled; the attitude of the whole figure representing *dolce far niente* to perfection.

The protection of my cattle against lion troubled me the most, for they were around us every night and bonfires had to be kept going on either side of the *boma*. Night watching devolved on Kago and me to replenish the fires every four hours. I dare not let the dogs loose after dark for fear

MARGARET COLLYER c. 1920.
The tents have gone

of leopard which were fairly numerous. Hyena strolled about in the moonlight like a pack of wolves, often coming close up to the huts.

The night calls of the wild were so strange to my ears: the yap-yapping of the zebra, not at all the sort of noise you would expect a zebra to make, the cough of the bush-buck, the gruff choke of leopard; worst of all, the unearthly yells of wild dog as they hounded some antelope to its death. I have only once heard hyena laugh, and hope I may never hear it again; it was the maniacal laugh of some fiend in hell.

I would that I were sufficiently deft with my pen to enable my readers to visualize this place as I first saw it, to give them some inkling of the complete solitude that surrounded and engulfed me.

Some time early in 1919 I was sitting outside the house by the camp-fire. It was fairly late, as the night before there had been lion around and I was anxious to keep the fire going as long as possible. With the exception of Kago, who was somewhere within call, all the rest of the men had long since retired to their huts. I had my rifle fully loaded by my side and was listening intently for the first grunt of the expected invaders when, without a sound of any description, out of the deep gloom into the firelight appeared five natives. They were dressed in khaki uniforms, all were armed with service rifles and they had bandoleers around their waists. A yard or two away from me they stopped and saluted.

I was taken very much by surprise for they were of a tribe I had never seen before. Big men they were, bearded with long hair touching their shoulders. And more evil-looking cut-throats it has never been my lot to see.

I addressed them in Swahili and asked what they wanted. One of them at least understood the language for he started to spin a good old yarn. He told me that they had come from an Englishman who was camping on the far side of the Malewa river, shooting lion which had been raiding cattle; that they had run out of *posho* (maize meal) for the men and had had nothing but buck-meat to eat for over a week. Their master had therefore sent them over to my camp to try to buy food from me. I asked them for the letter to me from their master and also wished to know why they had come armed. They replied they had no letter as their master had got nothing in his camp to write with. They had guns because they were afraid of walking in the dark without them.

I did not like the look of this at all. To begin with, there were no farms or cattle on the Malewa for lions to raid and no white man would send five heavily armed natives to ask for food from a lone woman late at night.

I had to do some quick thinking and in the meantime I quietly slid my right hand down, picked up my rifle and placed it across my knees. The men had all put the butts of their guns on the ground and were holding them by the barrels.

Said I, 'It is impossible for me to sell food to your master, as I have only enough for my own people. If you are hungry I will give you food now, but I must call my boy to get it. Before he brings it, you must unload your rifles and put them down in front of me. I do not feed armed *watu* (people).'

Evidently they were hungry for they at once proceeded to take the cartridges out of their guns and lay them at my feet.

The moment this was done I blew two sharp blasts on my whistle which I knew would bring Kago along at the double. Ages ago he and I had arranged that one whistle meant safe and that two meant danger, help required quickly. In less than two minutes he was by my side, spear in hand, staring at our visitors. I then got up, with my rifle at the ready and ordered Kago to carry all five guns into my house and padlock the door. I had not taken my eyes off the men, for I quite expected a rush on the store. There was a slight movement, but as I raised my rifle they thought better of it. Kago came back and stood like a statue by my side with his spear gleaming in the firelight.

I then enquired, 'What tribe are these men, Kago, and why do they come here armed?'

He answered, 'They are Abyssinians, *Bibi*,[5] and they are soldiers.'

I then gave them leave to sit down and told Kago to bring them some food. They must have been nearly starving, for they fell on the posho like wild beasts. While they were yet eating I took Kago on one side and told him to go quickly and call out the men with their spears. And to fetch my shotgun and load it. I said that we must see these strangers off the place at once or they would raid the store and there would be some shooting. Kago smelt trouble too. In less than no time I had my little army of spearmen lined up in the dark behind the Abyssinians and so silently did they come that the hungry men never heard them. It was not until they had eaten their fill and lay down to sleep by the fireside that they had any idea that Kago and I were not alone.

In the meantime I had handed their empty rifles to my men to carry, for I was determined to see my visitors off the farm myself and not give them back their weapons until they were well over the border.

When they had rested a little I lined them up and told them they were to march in front of me and if they looked back or attempted to turn round I should fire at once. Handing Kago the rifle and taking the 12-bore myself we started the two-mile tramp to the boundary of my farm. Here I gave them back their rifles with a warning that a guard would be put on the store and that if they returned I would shoot on sight. We then doused the lanterns in case they might take a parting shot at us.

Some of the boys and I kept watch all night, but nothing happened.

The next morning a man on a pony arrived at about seven-thirty. From the condition of the latter they must have galloped most of the way from Gilgil. He jumped off and, shaking me violently by the hand, said 'Thank God you are alive! I have never been in such a fright in my

---

5 Bibi means woman but not in a disrespectful sense. Both Olive and Margaret Collyer preferred to be addressed as Bibi. Most white women were referred to as Mensahib which meant the woman of the gentleman (and the term came from India), which the Collyer sisters were not.

life. I quite expected to find your camp bust up.' This man was an old Stock Inspector from Rumuruti and a friend of mine.

It seems that the previous night he had been dining with the Provincial Commissioner at Naivasha, when mention was made of five Abyssinians who had deserted from the Kings African Rifles with guns and ammunition and who were reported to be making for the Northern frontier. My friend suddenly remembered me, living just off the direct route to the frontier and quite alone. The PC had entirely forgotten about my camp and was in a great fright when it was recalled to his mind. Not a moment was lost in getting to me. Police were ordered out and, as a goods train was shortly leaving Naivasha for Gilgil, they were stuffed into this. My old friend jumped on to his pony and managed somehow to get himself and it into the guard's van. On reaching Gilgil he came to my assistance as fast as his horse could bring him.

I am afraid I smiled at his intense relief on finding me whole. But he saw no joke at all when I told him of my midnight visitors.

We waited until the police arrived and then I took them to the place where I had left the Abyssinians the night before. A quarter of a mile further on, the guard came upon the dead bodies of two Africans who had been shot in the back. These were proved to be two of Lord Delamere's men carrying food and tobacco. They had been robbed of both and left where they fell.

I suppose I had really had an escape but I was annoyed that I had not caught and locked up the murderers. Had I only been notified in time I could easily have 'jumped' the lot. After disarming them I could have given them food in the store and just turned the lock on them. As a matter of fact they were taken four or five days later near Rumuruti, where they again endeavoured to get food.

No native is allowed to carry firearms, neither are they permitted to walk the country with spears and *simis* unless they have special permission to do so.

* * *

In 1920 the country took on a rather brighter aspect. Settlers were able to return to their long-deserted farms, stock up afresh and make the most of the life still left to them. Racing had begun again; good ponies were much in demand and were fetching high prices.

My sister, who had been breeding horses regularly from all the South African mares, now had a good supply of youngsters on hand and sold her surplus stock well without the smallest difficulty. She was training and racing home-bred stock, and winning her share of races with them.

Living so far away I did less in the training line and was mostly content to look on at my sister's successes. The first horse I galloped here was 'Grey Fox' and I trained him for the Produce Stakes, which I think he could have won if I had been allowed to ride him myself, for the colt disliked strangers and declined to gallop with a new jockey on his back.

I enjoyed the cut and thrust of buying and selling horses. Grey Fox was much too good for my work and I sold him to Colonel Durand for £120. At the close of one day's racing I bought a two-year-old filly by Fred Dunn for £60. She ran as a bad jade in her first race at Nakuru and I sold her on the course for £100 to a bookmaker. At the same time I bought a two-year old colt from Mr C. Clutterbuck[6] for £100 which the following year I put up for auction on the Nairobi racecourse and he was knocked down to a new owner for £200.

We were now able to invest in a few more cattle and one day I arranged to meet my sister at a sale in Gilgil and then the following day we would go on to another sale at Naivasha.

Those early days of cattle sales were most exhausting. One had to get a shake-down for the night any-old-where, a railway carriage on a siding

---

6   C. Clutterbuck was a well-known Njoro farmer and father of Beryl Markham – the first woman to complete the solo crossing of the North Atlantic in an aeroplane, East to West, in September 1936.

or the *dak* bungalow on the platform, and one had to cart about blankets and pillows wherever one went. If one bought cattle there was all the bother of getting them up to the farm. This necessitated taking a sufficiency of men to drive them home; they had to be fed, looked after and then given minute instructions as to the route the cattle were to be taken and how they were to be treated.

At these two sales I had been keeping a sharp look out for a horse that might suit me; in fact, I could not get back to the farm without one, since I had left no return conveyance at Gilgil.

After spending a whole day in the sale ring at Naivasha, I took a walk round to see what oddments were to be put up for auction after the cattle had been disposed of. I passed a collection of old wagons and saw a horse being held by a *syce* which was evidently going to be put up for sale. Walking across to where he was standing I had a good look at him and was rather impressed with his appearance. He was a chestnut gelding, not in his first youth, but just the kind of animal to be useful on a farm. He was quiet to handle and, as I could find nothing wrong with him, I called up Olive to ask her opinion. She too very much liked the animal and I was just remarking that if he went at a reasonable price I would probably buy him, when a voice behind me said: 'If you intend buying that horse I shall refuse to put him into the ring.' I turned to see a large man whom I had certainly never met before. We both got rather on our toes and asked him what he meant by saying that he would not sell his horse to us. He replied quite humbly that he was only trying to save my life, that the animal was scarcely rideable, quite unholdable, and at breakneck speed would either jump over, or fall into any obstacle that happened to come in his way.

I was arguing that I must get a horse and that I did not mind a tricky mount, when another man wearing dark glasses joined the group. He was as small as the other was big, quite smart in neat breeches and boots, and having the unmistakable cut of a horseman about him. He enquired tenderly whether it was I who was in need of a 'harse'. The moment he opened his lips it did not require a wizard to guess what 'counthry' he had been born in – that far away emerald isle, the birthplace of the most acute horse dealers in the world. The sound of the brogue was so pleasing to my ear that I listened to a truly artistic description of a 'little black harse' he had for sale in his stables at Nakuru, forty-six miles from Naivasha. This animal could do all but talk and with a bit of schooling, he would be able to do that right enough. The owner of this plum was driving back to Nakuru in a car that night, in company of another Irishman, and offered to take me with him and put me up in his own house. Although I had no clothes but what I stood up in, I decided I would go, so having taken leave of Olive, I climbed into the back of the car.

It was important for me to return to the farm the next day, to receive the new bunch of cattle we had bought and I was all out to do a deal if at all possible. But it would only be an Irishman who tried to sell a pitch black horse on a pitch dark night. When the loose-box door was thrown open with a flourish I could distinguish nothing at all. However, after a minute or two a *syce* came along with a smoky hurricane lamp which was placed on the ground. The horse was bridled and I examined him piecemeal by its dim and dirty light. As a whole, I could get little idea of what he was like, but my fingers told me he was pretty free of splints, spavins or curbs. I could also detect that he owned a particularly well-bred head and a really gorgeous shoulder. Not wanting a horse to look at, but to ride, I said, 'Put the saddle on and I'll try him round the show ground.'

I hardly saw the horse even when I was on his back, but the feel he gave me was enough for me. It was perfect; and before I had gone half-way round the ring I was quite sure the animal was going to be mine. It was a real Irish deal, starting on the verandah with much-needed drinks and cigarettes, then writing a cheque followed by a hot bath, the loan of a pair of my host's pyjamas and, at last, we all sat down to supper.

It had been a long, tiring day, what with vetting bovines and a rattling good horse deal at the finish and it had been too much for a highly excitable nature. Before the soup plates were removed, our host was fast asleep with his head on the table. Suddenly, to our consternation, there was a tap at the door and in walked the District Commissioner with another man in tow. They had come in haste to fetch the vet to a couple of valuable imported dogs who were desperately ill with tick-fever. For the moment the vet could not be roused and as I knew a good deal about ailments of the canine race, I offered my assistance instead. But I could not accompany complete strangers in borrowed pyjamas and, late as it was, I hustled once more into grubby riding kit. The dogs and their lady owner were occupying a tent in the DC's garden. One of the animals was already past help and showing signs of pneumonia but the other one was pulling through. I stayed until 2 a.m. and then went back to bed.

It was very early next morning when I went to the stables to have a daylight look at my purchase of the night before. The horse pleased me and I borrowed a saddle and snaffle bridle in which to ride him home that day – a little matter of over forty miles across country.

My Irish friend arrived to breakfast still in his night attire and dressing-gown and watched me eat from the depths of a cosy armchair. Notwithstanding having my cheque for £60 in his pocket he was not in the best of humours and the topmost rung of the ladder was reached when a messenger arrived with an urgent letter from a lady requesting the doctor to come immediately as her parrot was ill!

'And what the hell do you do for a sick parrot?'

This emphatic question being addressed to me, I remembered once in my life having owned a parrot that had had to be sprayed for some disease it had contracted. Said I,

'You spray it.'

'Sphray it? What do ye sphray it wid?' This I could not recollect, so I said,

'I don't know, but just tell the lady the parrot must be sprayed.'

Seizing a writing block and pen, he wrote,

'Dear Madam – I strongly advise you to spray the parrot at once. Yours etc.'

Having materially assisted a veterinary officer in the treatment of ailing parrots, I climbed on to my new horse and rode to the hotel, where I was to pick up a man who had promised to show me part of my road home. I had not the foggiest notion how I was going to get there and had no wish to lose my way in the forest on the Escarpment[7], for it harboured plenty of elephant and buffalo.

I was waiting patiently for my conductor, holding my horse by the reins, when out from the pub came one of the best trainers in the country. He seemed rather amused to see me with the Black, who had apparently been in his stable for a while. He glanced at the plain snaffle bridle which boasted no such thing as a noseband or martingale, asked how far I was going and hoped I was a very strong woman.

At last we started and, striking off the road on to the turf, both horses broke into a canter. Then I realized what was meant by the query concerning my physical strength. With head up and mouth wide open, away he went and, for a very little under nine miles I was a mere passenger. He didn't bolt but just galloped on and on and with no martingale I could not get any pull at him.

The Black must have been nearly a thoroughbred horse, and as my companion was riding a common-looking farm plug, he was soon left far behind. I began to despair of ever stopping when a turn in the track brought a house into view which the horse seemed to recognize for he steadied and pulled up outside a rough stable. Jumping off, I waited for my guide to arrive. He had a good sort of double bridle on his cob which he kindly lent me and with this I continued my journey.

Although I had very rough country to cross and several times I missed my way, we did the trek home in extremely good time. The horse was so easy to sit and so natty on his feet that I had no feeling of

---

7   This would have been one of the escarpments out of the Great Rift Valley. The steepest edges consist of rocky cliffs, while the less steep parts are covered in forest.

regret about buying him. At the end of that trying ride he came into his stable almost as fresh as when he had started. He very soon gave up the pulling game and a nicer horse I never wish to own. I rode him regularly for two years, galloped zebra on him and could shoot from his back. He was six when I bought him and I was stupid enough to sell him when he was eight for £20 more than I gave for him. He had been found during the war, wandering loose and unclaimed, so that £60 I paid was pretty nearly clear profit for my veterinary friend.

Galloping zebra is very good fun when riding a fast and sure-footed animal, for they take a devil of a lot of catching on their own ground. Some time later when I had a car I was anxious to find out how fast they could go. One day on the Malewa Plains I paced a herd with my car. Before getting amongst them the speedometer registered forty miles an hour and they looked like keeping it up for some distance. Not wishing to crash into a pig-hole, I slackened up after racing them for a mile and a half. If the small Burchell zebra can move at that rate, I wonder what his larger and finer brother, the Grevy, can do per mile?

I once had an exciting race with zebra. In 1925, when my sister went to England, I took the stallion 'Guardsman' and two yearlings up to the Gilgil farm and kept them while she was away. While Guardsman was with me I regularly rode him as a farm hack. He was an exceptionally nice ride, and being very quiet, he had no objection to standing about while I did my work.

One morning I was riding him alone, not having taken the dogs, and I crossed the road on to the plains where a herd of zebra were grazing. Two stallion zebra were yapping round some mares that must have been in season. As far as I know, Guardsman had never seen zebra before and as we approached the herd he let out a positive scream of rage, caught the bit in his teeth and charged the two stallions who simultaneously charged him. Having only a chain snaffle in his mouth I had no control over the horse at all as he raced through the herd with a zebra stallion at either shoulder: all three animals, open mouthed, striking and biting as they galloped on. I had nothing in my hand but a hunting crop, with which I tried to beat off the zebra, thinking every moment they would grab my legs instead of Guardsman's shoulders. They took no notice of me at all; for all they cared I might not have been there.

On we raced, keeping up a running fight with the two stallions while the mares streaked ahead of us, making for a gap in the rocks by the Lokolwa river. I knew the passage was very narrow and the riverbed was full of boulders. I foresaw where the inevitable catastrophe must take place if we rushed the gap three abreast. Even now I could see the mares dropping into single file in preparation for crossing the river, which was one of their usual tracks. The gap in the rocks loomed nearer and nearer while the fight still went on. I had long since stopped pulling at Guardsman's mouth and was clinging on to the saddle with both hands, tucking my legs up on the flaps as far as I dared to get them.

Now, my best chance of avoiding being crushed against the rocks was to pull the horse head-on into them but the zebra on the near side was the hindrance to this manoeuvre. Force of habit, however, caused him to drop back before entering the pass and this gave me the opportunity I had been waiting for. Risking a bite in my right leg, I dropped into position and hauled with both hands on the near-side rein. Seeing the stony wall in front of him, the horse propped and stopped dead while the two zebras followed on after the mares.

I was off in a second and I hung on like grim death to the reins, for the horse had gone crazy and was almost unmanageable, screaming and standing on his hind legs. Pulling him away from the gap I succeeded in leading him in the opposite direction, when he became more reasonable and gradually quietened down. But I kept off the stallion's back for some time yet and only mounted again when we were within sight of home.

I wonder what would have happened had he slipped me and got away with the zebra? Would there have been a fight to the finish or would the horse have recovered his senses in time and returned to his stable? It is a question that will ever remain unanswered.

ARTHUR COLLYER'S
ASKARIS
(with Frieze and friend)

* * *

I never succeeded in making my sister understand that this place was different from Kabete which was overrun with a big native population, and it was necessary here to take precautions against midnight marauders. She was inclined to laugh at my fears and considered it quite unnecessary for me to be escorted wherever I went. She had certainly been a long time in Africa, but until my brother's death at Nyeri, she had lived with him on stations. When on safari she had been well protected by Police *Askaris* and had never been entirely alone in the wilds. Nor had she hunted with a pack of obstreperous dogs.

On her first visit to the farm, I sent men and the two mules to Gilgil to meet her and expected her arrival at the farm somewhere around 6 p.m. There was much excitement at the thought of her coming and all the labour collected round my hut in the evening to make her welcome. Great preparations had been made and to me the day seemed endlessly long until the time came when I thought I might expect her.

The evening waned to dusk, and dusk to dark, but there was still no sign of her. I was getting anxious and wondered whether anything evil could have happened, when Kago, returning from the umpteenth 'look see', said he was sure whistles were being blown on the top of the opposite ridge. It seemed that the arriving party needed lanterns before crossing the gully that lay between it and the homestead. Hastily lighting up we went in search.

At eight o'clock we found Olive sitting complacently on a mule waiting to be lighted over the last rough bit of the journey. It was an eight-hour ride from Gilgil and she had loitered to have lunch somewhere en route, not dreaming that we should feel any anxiety about her crossing from the Oliondo river in pitchy darkness. She said that the mule had seemed rather nervous and that she thought she had heard a lion! The ground being wet, the next day we went to look at the path along which she had ridden and found fresh pug-marks of two lion that had evidently been following the mules.

She was quite kind about the work I had done and satisfied with my peg-built house, though I do not think she would have enjoyed living in it much during the rainy season.

She suggested we should put bells on some of the cattle so I bought a beauty from a native and hung it on the neck of the bull who was the only one I could catch. I fixed it while he was in the *boma*. In the morning the herd boy came to say the bull was very ill and could not move forward. He could only walk backwards. I discovered this strange sickness was due to the bell under his chin. He did come out of the yard tail first and continued to progress that way until I removed the bell. It showed great ignorance on my part to put it on him. No bull should be made to carry a bell. I suppose he already knew this and acted accordingly.

This bull was a low shorthorn grade called Karuli which, being interpreted, means 'The Father of many.' He certainly populated this district, for bulls were very hard to come by, other than native bulls. When I had no further use for him he was sold to a friend of mine who had taken up land a few miles from here, who also bred from him a lot. He was then passed on to a neighbour, on whose farm he stayed until he died.

On the day that Karuli's first calf was born a young Englishman turned up, riding through from Laikipia. He had seen my camp-fires from the hills and had come for a shakedown, since his ponies were tired and unable to get to Gilgil that night. This was my first white visitor and very glad I was to see him arrive. He looked a bit like a travelling tinker with both his ponies covered with pots, pans and kettles. Being a stockman, I showed him my first calf with pride and we duly and solemnly christened it 'Irrikisasi', the Kikuyu word for Firstborn.

This young man, who later put up many times at my homestead, was a Mr Llewelyn Powys, who wrote such books as *Black Laughter* and *Ebony and Ivory*. I was sitting outside my camp-fire latish one night, as I rather expected Mr Llewelyn Powys to come along. He was about due and I was anxious to hear particulars of the rising of the Masai. Little outside news filtered through to me but I had understood that the Masai had become extremely truculent and some soldiers from the KAR had been sent to quell them.

I was also watching over a sick cow, which was a favourite of mine, and she was lying by the fire at my feet, when I was suddenly surrounded by ten fearsome-looking men in full war-paint and elaborately painted on face and body. The head-dresses were made of feathers which formed a frame to the face. Monkey skins covered their loins and colobus tails were attached to their legs below the knee. The long, fine spears and large painted shields told me they were Masai warriors out for blood. They were a most imposing sight as they stood in the fire-light, immovable and silent, the dignity of pose being immensely impressive.[8]

It is, or was unusual for a Masai warrior to speak Swahili, but one of the group could both understand and speak it.

I asked him why they came to me in full war-paint and with no sign of peace on their spears. He replied, 'We are not at peace, we are at war

---

[8]   At Appendix I there is a photograph of Masai warriors.

with the English soldiers. We have been driven from our homes. We have no food and are very hungry. Will you give us food?'

Said I, 'The soldiers and police are after you. Why do you come to me for food and shelter?'

'We come because you are the sister of '*Colyon*' (Collyer)[9], who was the friend of the Masai.' A touching appeal indeed: could I do other than feed and help them?

We cooked them a big hot meal. Before eating they brought all their weapons into my house and piled them under the bed. I promised to return them in the morning before daylight when I would come and let my visitors out of the store in which I intended to lock them.

In the early dawn I un-prisoned them and, handing out their possessions, told them to get away as quickly as possible before my men were about, as they might give the show away.

Having saluted me in their own fashion they melted into space and I neither saw nor heard of them again.

* * *

Before the war and during the war, land was finding purchasers, and from 1920 to 1923 several owners arrived to take up their farms. It was quite a shock to me one morning, when exercising a couple of horses, to see two white men walking about, uninvited, on what I had come to look upon as my dominions. I was riding one horse and leading another; the dogs had treed a serval cat, and I was wondering how I could get it down for them when these men appeared.

Bidding them a pleasant 'Good morning' I asked them to hold my horses while I went up the tree after the cat, since there was no hope of the dogs leaving until they had destroyed it. When I was nearing the animal, one of the newcomers enquired whether it was not rather dangerous to climb up a tree after a tiger!

---

[9] See Appendix.II: Arthur John Morice Collyer.

These men were destined to be almost my nearest neighbours, but my closest neighbour was an Australian whose land marched with mine: Mr White. He had been a cattle farmer in Queensland, and at once commenced importing pedigree Ayrshire bulls from South Africa, and later a group of this breed from Australia, the foundation stock for a fine herd.[10] Unfortunately for him his manager refused to believe it necessary to protect the cattle against lion, in fact he laughed at me when I told him lion would claim the lot if he left them out at night.

Very shortly after the arrival of the South African bulls two were killed one night. The manager poisoned the meat, and I took a ride over the following morning to see the result. The place was a seething mass of dead and dying vultures, jackal and hyena; but no dead lion. Feeling pretty certain one lion had returned to the kill before the rest of the menagerie arrived, I said nothing about it to the manager, but I took Kago and the dogs, and we drew the banks on either side of the stream.

Kago viewed a very sick lion on his bank, which he said was coming over my way, so leaving my horse I walked towards the stream, rifle in hand. The bed of the stream was deep and narrow at this point. I was just climbing up a rock to get a view of the water when a gun was fired from the opposite bank. There was my friend of the morning sitting on a stone looking as though he had just shot a water-rat instead of a

LT. H.A.D. WHITE
DSO
*With thanks to his grand
daughter, Rosemarie
Armstrong*

---

[10] H.A.D. White D.S.O. (Bert) was born in Queensland in 1883. In WWI he served in the Second Australian Light Horse Brigade at Gallipoli before buying the land alongside Margaret's, which he named Curragilla. According to his son, Harold, the land was 'quite uneconomic' and it was later sold. Harold White himself went on to a long and distinguished career as a farmer and contributed greatly to the quality of agriculture in Kenya.

three-parts grown lion, which was lying dead at his feet. Luckily the lion was full of strychnine, or he might not have died so easily; more likely he would have sprung out of the river almost on top of me. My new-found friend and I laughed a good deal over this episode and went off to find some more but we only managed to bag that one.

* * *

I think that 1925 was about the blackest year I had so far experienced, although from a financial point of view the last four years have been the worst[11], for the locusts came in their billions and ate the country to the bone. But in the April of 1925 my sister went home for six months, leaving me like a lost soul crying in the wilderness.

Then came the news of Sir Northrup McMillan's death in the south of France. Not only was this a great loss to the Colony but a very personal grief to me, whose friend he was.

The breaking up of my sister's stable and the necessary destruction of all the horses, many of which were old friends, and the knowledge that this calamity would utterly spoil her long-delayed and well-deserved holiday at home, affected and reacted on me. Our racing days were at an end and another milestone had flown past.

I have been in this Colony under no less than five different Governors and the push that Kenya received in the right direction was during the reign of Sir Edward Grigg[12]. It was he who really started the ball rolling

[11] Apart from locust swarms, the end of the 1920's and early 1930's was the time of the Great Depression.

[12] Sir Edward Grigg succeeded Sir Robert Coryndon as Governor of Kenya Colony from 1925-1930. *'Tall and good looking, with charming, gracious manners, Grigg was possessed of imagination and enterprise.'* [C.S. Nicholls] He described the Kenya settlers as *'A very gay, a very gallant, and a very much misunderstood community.'* In a speech at Falmouth in 1927 Grigg said that Kenya was *'not conquered by force of arms. It was conquered by one of the greatest forces of our modern civilisation; it was conquered by the railway….The railway brought settlers and our Government in its track, and it was the railway which created Kenya as a Colony of the Crown.'* [M.F. Hill] However, he caused anger amongst some officials in the Government who suspected Sir Edward of favouring the interests of the settler over the African which was contrary to the Administration's obligations.

for, prior to his advent, we had been merely treading water and not advancing in the least. But he very soon got a move on, commencing operations on roads and railways, which opened up a deal of closed country in a surprisingly short space of time. If he ran the Colony more heavily into debt he did it for very good rhyme and reason; the improvement in all main roads was a boon to the general community, for our transport cost us less and we had access to many hitherto inaccessible areas.

The Gilgil-Thompson Falls railway line commenced early in 1928 and was opened in 1930, although at the beginning all the trains regularly fell off the rails two or three times in the course of a single trip. So far this branch railway has not added to the value of land in these parts but it has made dairying possible and cream can now be delivered fresh at the Co-operative Creamery which should ensure Kenya butter fetching a higher price in the London markets. The line has also saved settlers the worry and expense of ox-transport to Gilgil.

The railway runs at the foot of my land and the nearest station is Ol'Kalou, seven miles away by road. In the dry weather by driving across the veldt I can do the journey in four. What a difference from the old days when we had to trek to Gilgil either on foot or mule-back!

Black Arts

Chapter XII

There is rather a curious story attached to my ox-driver. The family has been here ever since I came. He was a little boy when I knew him first and he was very slightly removed from an idiot. I tried my best to teach him to work but it was hopeless, so I told his mother I could not employ him.

She did not mind at all when I said the boy was an idiot for, said she, 'When the stone is broken in three years' time he will have plenty of sense.'

'What stone?' I enquired.

'The stone he wears in a bag round his neck. He was born with this stone in his hand, and after circumcision it will be broken by a big doctor and the child will entirely recover his senses.'

I can only say that what the woman told me came to pass. The stone was broken at the ordained moment and the boy returned to me sound in mind. Today he is one of the brightest and most intelligent men on the place.

I have enquired of several doctors if they have ever seen or heard of a baby being born with a stone in its hand. They have all said 'No' and laughed at this story. But it is true all the same.

We shall never fathom the psychology of our black brother, for it is so mixed and contradictory. In many ways they are generous; they will lend money and often do not get it back for years afterwards. They will always give food and shelter to anyone of their own tribe. Yet during a famine their wives and children will be allowed to starve while the men remain fat as long as it is possible. They would sooner die than kill their goats for food. I have seen them next door to living skeletons, with lots of sheep and goats running about their huts.

They are rather sorry for the sick, although they do not do much to help them. They do not laugh at illness, whereas if there is an accident and someone gets hurt they yell with laughter. One day I saw a lot of men standing round a tree we were lopping some branches off before felling. They were in fits of laughter. Looking up I discovered a boy sitting across a branch, twenty feet or more from the ground and he was cutting it off close to the trunk. The men were delightedly waiting for him to fall and be smashed at their feet. If I had not come along at that moment they would have allowed this to happen and never given the lad a word of warning.

They are great philosophers and little worries them. I have often envied them their philosophy. If one of their people or children die, well, they are dead. There is nothing to be done about it. Why grieve? If locusts come and devour their crops, that is God's affair and cannot be helped. If anything evil happens it is always God's doing. Anything really good is entirely the doing of the Kikuyu himself.

During the first year of my life on the farm, there came a time when our mealy meal was nearly finished. Because many of the labour could not eat buck-meat, I decided to send Kago down to Gilgil with an assistant and both mules to bring up what he could buy in sacks slung across their backs. We were still short of labour and when two natives strayed on to the farm while Kago was absent, I set them to work on a piece of fencing I wanted done. They seemed fairly capable so I allowed them a vacant hut to themselves. I did rather notice that these strangers were avoided by the rest of the gang, but being so little versed in native law it did not strike me as very odd and I thought no more about it.

Before Kago returned we had completely run out of *posho*. The men struck work and for a day I was left to herd the cattle myself. On the night he got back I had promised everybody double rations. To my surprise no one came for food that evening except the two strangers whom, I told Kago, I had just written on, thinking he would be pleased to have the extra help. He did not enthuse at all and when again the following morning no one turned out to work I got on my toes and wished to know the reason for it. Kago drew a long face and said, 'It is because you have written on two '*Ndea*' – a witch-doctoring tribe that the Kikuyu were afraid of. 'All the boys will run away if you don't send these strangers off the place at once.' This seemed a great nonsense to me and, sending for my men, I told them they would get no food unless they turned out to work. The strangers meanwhile were carrying on with the fence.

On hearing what I had to say, there was that silent resistance so characteristic of the Kikuyu tribe and I felt I was likely to be up against it if I persisted in employing these *Ndea*. I therefore gave way and promised to dismiss them. At that particular moment I missed a hammer I needed and enquiring what had become of it, I was told that it was in the hut of the strangers. Every man in turn refused to fetch it for me. Kago acted as spokesman and said the hammer could not be collected as the *Ndea* had put a bad snake to guard the door of their hut so that nobody could pass in.

'Well' said I, 'I must get that hammer myself since you are all afraid of a snake.' And I proceeded to walk towards the hut with the men following behind at a respectful distance. Just as I reached the door, Kago seized my arm and pulled me back, crying, 'The snake will get you! Don't you see it with his head up ready?' Of course there was no snake. I then faced the crowd and told them to look straight at me. As soon as all eyes were on mine, I repeated twice, very slowly and distinctly, 'There is no snake here,' and after a minute or two bade them look again. This time they saw nothing, and I walked into the hut and brought out the hammer.

I have come across this hypnotic practice by a few natives several times since. But I have succeeded now in dispelling the influence amongst my own people by demonstrating to Kago what hypnotic suggestion really means. He is naturally intelligent and his mentality has developed considerably during his eighteen years of faithful service with me. He now laughs at things that years ago alarmed him very much indeed.

The petty stealing that was always going on nearly drove me distracted and, seeing no way of stopping it myself, I consulted Kago as to what we had better do. He said that if I would give a sheep for sacrifice, he could get the thieving stopped for some time, but that he would have to call a council and make arrangements. The council sat for a whole day when not a stroke of work was done and, towards evening, I produced an old sheep that I handed over to them. The ceremony, whatever it was going to be, was to take place the next day when again no work would be done. It was all very secretive and very mysterious.

The drumming that night was worse than usual. I could not sleep at all and went to Kago's tent to find out what it was all about and whether I could witness the happenings on the morrow. At first he would not hear of my being present; no white man had ever been allowed at any of these ceremonies and he evidently did not think it very safe. The sacrifice was to take place in the forest where a clearing had already been prepared for it. After reflection Kago said I could go with him, but that we must both hide in a deep ditch near the spot and I was made to promise that, whatever I saw, I would not cry out nor say a word to stop the proceedings.

The following day there was a great to-do; everyone turned up in full war-paint with skins and beads, carrying spears and drums. Both the men and the women were smeared in ochre, the faces of the former bearing the white nose-line with stars and stripes decorating their cheeks. War-whoops, spear throwing and leaping went on for some time until two elders, arrayed in hyrax karosses, led up the sacrificial lamb (my poor old sheep).

Before the procession formed, Kago and I cut along down to the forest and hid in a ditch, brambles being bent over the top of us. Again I was reminded of my promise that on no account would I utter a sound. I gathered that on these occasions everyone went mad and was apt to see red. If discovered we might get rapped on the head.

It was eerie waiting in the gloom of the trees listening to the muffled beat of drums as the procession solemnly and slowly approached the forest edge. Here for a time it halted while the shrieking women were dismissed and the drums stilled. Now they came on again, marching silently; except for the occasional snapping of a dead stick there was no sound to indicate that upwards of thirty men were within a short stone's throw of our sanctuary. So silently did they come that I was wondering what had happened to them when the lamb and elders suddenly appeared and took the centre of the leaf-strewn stage. After these, there followed in single file, the procession of *Morans*, who squatted in a circle around the three principal actors in this dramatic scene.

How I wished I understood the Kikuyu tongue, for two long speeches were delivered by the elders, each in turn standing up during the course of his oration.

What followed immediately afterwards nearly caused me to break my word to Kago, to seize the heaviest stick I could find and clear the forest of those brutal savages. I made a desperate effort to get onto my legs but Kago, anticipating my move, threw himself across my shoulders with his hand firmly held over my mouth.

For the next half hour I was forced to witness the most dreadful cruelty it has ever been my lot to imagine. The sheep was thrown on its side. One man pulled back the head, the other slit the skin with a knife between the bones from chin to joint of jaw, then he drew the tongue down through the cut. Each warrior in turn was called up and on taking the oath, bit off a portion of the living tongue. Then the legs of the animal were broken with sticks, each man repeating the following words (or as near as I can translate them) – 'As I break the bones of this sheep, so may I be broken if I steal while on this white woman's farm.' Having smashed all the sheep's legs to pieces, it was killed by cutting the throat. The body was left where it lay, the procession reformed and disappeared as silently as it had come.

By that time I was so sick that Kago had to fetch water in my hat before I could stagger home.

Whatever this extraordinary ceremony meant, it certainly had the desired effect and for a long time afterwards not a thing was stolen.

I have enquired often but never met any white man who had seen this oath taken. Possibly Mr John Boyes[1] who styled himself 'The King of the Kikuyu' could tell us more about it.

When influenza was raging and the natives were dying like flies, we closed the whole of the farm to strangers in a most simple way, though it took several days to accomplish it. It entailed the killing of two sheep but, as they were killed mercifully, I did not mind. We packed all the entrails into a sack and cut both skins into thin strips. Wherever we found a track on the extreme outside of the farm, we dug a hole and buried a small portion of the entrails, putting poles on either side of the path and stretching a strip of the skin from one to the other. In this way we closed every path on all sides of our boundaries. No stranger would come within our gates and we escaped the scourge that took such a heavy toll on the other farms.[2]

Now that I am writing about the ways of the African, I will relate one more incident before resuming my narrative.

I was awakened at two o'clock one morning by the dogs barking and by being prodded in the back by a long stick which had been pushed through the door. On enquiring the reason why my dreams had been disturbed, I was informed that a woman had just died in one of the huts.

---

[1] Born in Hull in 1873. He was 'John Boyes, King of the Wa-Kikuyu'. What is now Nairobi was uninhabited when he arrived. He was admitted to the Kikuyu blood brotherhood and became their uncrowned king. After a roving and adventurous career, he settled down as a coffee grower and dairy farmer. He died in 1951.

[2] The 1918–1919 influenza pandemic killed about twenty million people worldwide.

Since she was dead I saw no cause to turn out at that hour and cursed the man for waking me to no purpose.

At seven I met Kago and asked what he was doing about burying the woman or putting the body out of the hut. He said it was impossible to touch a dead body but as the door was open the hyenas would go in and finish it off. Not content, I went up to the hut and on hearing a feeble whine, I went in. The woman was dead but, lying in the curve of her body, was a live baby two or three weeks old. The husband and bigger children had fled and left the infant with its dead mother.

Picking the child up I took it home and tried to feed it with warm milk. I then sent for its father and told him what I thought about him. His excuse was that the baby was too young to eat anything but its mother's milk so if he had taken it away it would have died. It was better that it should die where it was.

Kago found another woman with a baby to take the poor little motherless one; but I have every reason to believe that she killed it, for I was never able to find it again.

There then arose the question of the corpse which the hyenas declined to pull out of the hut, and it was too close to mine to be pleasant. After three days and nothing having happened, I said I would burn the house down and cremate the body. I was then told that if I did this my people would run away, as to burn a corpse was all wrong. I said, 'Well, let them run if they want to. I am going to take some kerosene and set light to the thatch.' This I did, but it took me a whole day to collect extra wood before I could reduce that corpse to anything like ashes and I had to work alone, as not a man would come within a hundred yards of the place.

In those early years, no other European lived within miles of me and there was no possibility of getting help had I needed any. I was queen of all I surveyed, my subjects being such as I have endeavoured to describe them and these incidents will give the uninitiated some idea of the kind of folk with whom I was destined to live and work.

With Best Wishes

for

Christmas

and the

New Year

Corgi Puppy

Sealyham

Working with the Cultural Divide

Chapter XIII

MARGARET COLLYER

In working native labour I have found it is far better not to mix the tribes. The only real trouble I have ever had here was when I was obliged to get a gang of Kavirondo down from Kisumu to do some heavy road-making, which is too hard for the lightly built Kikuyu. I would never do it again, for the Kavirondo are not fit subjects for a woman to employ; they need a man over them and a strong one at that. I had no peace while they were here and most of them were bhang smokers, which I did not like at all.

Kago now had enough money to buy himself a wife, and he had his pick of two nice-looking sisters who were half-bred Kikuyu and Masai. He chose the younger and went away for a few weeks to make arrangements about his property. While he was away the girl gave the glad eye to my personal servant and stayed with him in his hut. This matter was reported to Kago on his return and he asked me if I knew anything about it. On hearing that I did, he said, 'It does not much matter. I'll marry her sister instead. They are both good workers.'

On another occasion I said to Kago, 'Keep your women away from me; they are so stupid they nearly drive me crazy.'

'Yes,' he replied, 'they have no sense at all; they are like the beasts of the forest.'

The native laws take a little understanding. For instance, the girl that played Kago false went utterly to the bad and had four or five children, all by different men. No one of course will have her as wife. She lives with her brother, who is one of my ox-drivers and the five children are his property. He has the right to sell the girls and pocket the money they fetch. Actual money seldom passes hands; the women are paid for in sheep and goats. The market varies quite a bit, and in some places the women are cheaper than in others.

A great help to me in controlling my employees was the *Kiama* or Native Council which was appointed by the labour themselves. All the years that I worked with natives I can honestly say I have never hit a man myself. If it was necessary to punish for disobedience, stealing or cruelty, the case was always put to the *Kiama* and I usually abided by their decision. I must now relate an incident that will in some way show the sentimentalist at home what farmers in this country have at times had to put up with from their labour.

Once, when I returned from Nairobi, it was raining very hard indeed. I had a disgustingly nasty ride up to the farm, and had some difficulty in getting the horses to ford the Oliondo River because the amount of water in it was heavier than they cared to face.

Kago met me with news that the Simba River had also risen many feet and was running a foot deep over a bridge that we had just managed to put up. It was nearly dark before I got home and I did not look at it that night. Still more rain fell before morning and at dawn heavy storms were threatening all around us. That day I was obliged to ride over to see a man living some distance away and I hurried off early, intending to get back before milking time in the evening.

On crossing the bridge the water was over my horse's knees. The flow was so strong that I turned back and cantered up to the house to warn the herdsmen on no account to take the cattle across the river to graze but to be sure to keep them on the house side. I foresaw that if another cloudburst occurred, the ford would be impassable. Having left strict injunctions with regard to this matter I continued on my way.

Before I returned that evening there was another tremendous storm and torrential rain fell above our farm as well as on it. I urged my horse to do his best as I doubted whether I should be able to get across the bridge. The water was now four feet deep on the roadway and my animal had considerable difficulty in keeping on his legs.

As I was galloping up to the stables I saw to my horror that my orders had been ignored and that about three hundred head of cattle were on the far side of the river where I had told the herdsmen on no account to take them. Being milking time the leading cows were already heading for the one and only ford which I was now sure they could not cross without many being drowned.

The rain had stopped any work being done and, on hearing my horse, Kago and his gang of labourers came out of the store to meet me. The cattle were not Kago's job and he had not noticed the herdsmen crossing the river. I sent two men flying down to try and turn back the leading cows and, after throwing off coat and skirt, I got together all the ropes and chains I could find. With Kago and the remaining boys we ran as fast as we could to the ford.

The stream had risen six to eight feet. It was tearing down in full spate, bringing with it logs of trees and boulders of stone – a terrifying sight. The cattle, anxious to get home, had refused to be checked and were crowding down to the water through the narrow entrance to the crossing.

There was nothing to be done but to let them come and see how many we could save. They plunged into the water pushed on by the crush following behind. We stood on the bank with ropes ready noosed to throw over their horns.

The first six cows were instantly swept down the narrow gully below the crossing place. I managed to catch the horns of the first cow and, getting a turn of the rope round a small tree, held her head above the water. Her body was swept round and the whole strain came on to her neck. Kago and the boys secured three or four more and with others washed up against these, the gully was blocked and the rest of the herd swam and plunged over to safety.

The cattle we held formed a living dam and our best chance of saving the rest was to keep them there, water pouring over their backs and heads. All I could see of my cow was her nose and by dropping into the water and clinging on to roots, I got the end of the rope noosed round her jaw above the nostril. Thus I could prevent her from drowning, provided that the rope held. The strain on it was becoming tremendous and although I wanted to reach for a trek chain lying just behind me, I dared not let go for a second.

The main body of the herd was almost across when I felt the rope crack and saw the wretched animal hurled down the river-bed in an avalanche of water heavier than ever; the bulk of the mob being through, there was nothing now to stem it. The boys were hard at it, dragging the cattle they had hooked upstream to safety, so I ran after the drowning cow, who was now fifty yards below the ford, her frantic struggles weakening every second as water got into her lungs. I was about to despair of saving her when her horns caught in an overhanging tree root and her rapid passage was checked. This root was on the opposite bank to where I was standing and her nose was under water. The strongest swimmer would have been mere flotsam in that narrow gorge, with such a torrent pouring through it; yet I had to save her somehow and hold her nose up until further assistance arrived.

I jumped, trusting to luck that a friendly root would be near to hand where I landed in the water, close to the animal's head. In the event I succeeded in catching the same one that was holding her and, pulling myself partly out of the water, got hold of her nose and held it up. It was no use calling, because the noise of the water and the bellowing of frightened cattle was deafening. But Kago had seen me start after the cow and he would come as soon as he possibly could. He not only came, but had the sense to put chains round the necks of a couple of trek oxen, on to which he had tied a long double rope. Throwing this over, I got it firmly fixed round the cow's neck; then as I was unable to free her horns from the root, I crossed on the rope myself to reach a *panga* which Kago was holding out to me.

As soon as she was cut free from the root, her hindquarters swung downstream, and the oxen started to pull her up. Still holding on to the rope, I had to go with her, for I could not climb up the slippery bank. She was dragged to land at the ford and lay like a dead thing for some time before making any effort to move. With the help of an ox we got her home at last and I was overjoyed to find that my loss consisted of one calf only.

It was pelting with rain. I had been in the stream for over an hour, but my work was not finished yet. I still had to round up the herdsmen who had caused us all this trouble. Kago said that directly the cattle were across they had both bolted, knowing what was coming to them later.

Cold, soaked and furious, I was determined to have those men before another hour had passed. Kago, two dogs and I went in search, and found them in a hut, that was not their own. At our approach they ran away like a couple of hares, in different directions; but they might well have saved themselves the trouble, for Bora marked one and Dona the other and both were pulled down within twenty yards. There was no need to tie them up with those two dogs on guard, so they came along to the store, where they were put flat on their faces and Kago laid on fifteen strokes each, with no mean arm, for he was as cold and angry as I was.

They were locked up for the night and I called the *Kiama* the next morning to sit on the case, which as usual took all day. The judgement was that, besides the fifteen strokes, they were to be fined twenty shillings each, or goats to that amount.

I have not the smallest doubt, in view of what I have read in the London papers, that my treatment of these men will be severely criticised and I shall be called bad names. Yet it should be remembered that they were beaten by one of their own tribe; they were also judged by a Council of their own tribe, and in my opinion they got off with far too light a sentence. It was no thanks to them that I did not lose a great many cattle, which I should have done had I not arrived home in time to anticipate what was going to happen.

On my farm I have always had as much labour as I required and my men never leave my service unless kicked out for some impossible fault. I have men working for me that have been with me for many years and my labour return forms for the Government are invariably sent in each month with 'No change' written across the document.

When casual '*kiboko-ing*' (whipping) on European farms was stopped by law, the native became at once more difficult to handle.

After one or two isolated cases of cruelty to natives by white men, which were disgusting, disgraceful and unpardonable, the law was forced into taking steps to try to prevent any such recurrence. But because God chose to put a few unmentionably cruel brutes into the world disguised as 'white men', it is unnecessary to take it for granted that the remainder are brutes.

Now that I have the opportunity, I shall voice a matter that has often been uppermost in my thoughts which others, perhaps, have not sufficiently taken into consideration. In the days when ex-soldiers and closer settlement became the cry, a class of people, amongst others, came out to East Africa quite unused to having servants to wait on them, many being of the servant type themselves. Since black labour was very cheap, these people were able to provide themselves with cooks, houseboys and personal servants, a luxury they had never before known and still less did they know how to treat their employees. A tribal native was to them a 'nigger' and to be treated accordingly. He could be hit, knocked about by the men and nagged at by the women, most of whom were afraid to be left alone with native servants at night.

Cases of outrage and insolence by natives invariably occur to white women of this type. A native may be ignorant of the white man and uneducated, but he is never such a fool as not to recognise at once those with educated manners. The outrages that have from time to time occurred when women have been left alone on farms are, nine times out of ten, entirely their own fault. I have myself seen women treat their personal servants, who have access to their bedrooms, in a most unbecoming and familiar fashion, allowing natives into their rooms when they themselves have been less than half clothed. Because the servant happens to have a black skin, they have ignored before him all the niceties of decent behaviour.

The African is not to blame if he takes every advantage under these circumstances. He comes of a people amongst whom women are kittle kattle. If he wants a woman he will take her; if she happens to be somebody's bought wife, he gets into trouble, but otherwise he has a pretty free hand. Is it therefore to be wondered at that if a white woman is fool enough to make herself cheap, she is apt to suffer for it at the first opportunity offered?

For all these years my men have had every opportunity of murdering me, stealing from me, or anything else they wished to do. I have always slept with my doors and windows unlocked or open; I have never owned a revolver and only kept my guns loaded and close at hand when lion were around. Yet I have never received anything but civility from my people and, in many cases, kindness. Certainly I have not felt the smallest fear of them, nor had any occasion to feel it.

The only man I ever had any cause to fear was an Australian employed on the farm next door. Not having seen him before, he arrived at my house one soaking wet night very drunk indeed and fell face down in a ditch full of water. My men saved his life by pulling him out and he then started fighting and throwing stones at them. I tried to send him home, but he persisted in coming into my house and sleeping on my bed. I chained the door and put a boy on guard and spent the night myself in the calf shed. Early next morning I sent a *syce* with a mule to ask a friend to come over and turn the man out of my house and off the place. I never saw him again. It was scarcely an example one wished to set to natives and I spent some time explaining to them that although he owned a white skin, he was no Englishman and therefore not of my tribe.

I do not pose as being particularly pro-native, but I am English enough to wish to see fair play. Given a little consideration as well as fair play, the native on the whole is not at all a bad fellow to work with.

* * *

I was always rather haunted by the idea of a possible lion or leopard maul; for with no transport or help at hand, it would have been a very

AN UNKNOWN DOG IN KENYA,
Painted by Margaret Collyer

unpleasant experience. I rarely rode any distance from the farm by myself, for much the same reason. A fall might have meant a broken leg and, away out on the plains, one would never have been found – a positive nightmare even to contemplate. One poor African was thrown from a horse on these plains and never located. I had my men out searching for him for days, and all we discovered was trampled grass and his hat. The indications told a tale that did not bear thinking about.

Preparatory to what at any moment might happen, I was constantly teaching Kago how to clean and dress wounds. Bottles of disinfectants were marked so that he should know what to use if the patient happened to be myself. I had also shown him how to stitch flesh wounds. Several men had cut their legs nearly off with axes. One day, I was sticking something together with gum and Kago enquired of me what it was. He was much interested and repeated the word 'gum' once or twice to memorize it. A day or two later he came running down from where we were cultivating to tell me that a man had fallen off the seat of the disc harrow and the plates had gone over him. I expected to find him chopped to mincemeat and when I reached him I found that his head and chest had been badly cut about. I told Kago to have him carried down to my hut so that I could stitch him up. I hurried back to get things ready for the operation. I waited and waited but the man was not brought in. Presently Kago came along to say that he had refused to have needles put through his skin, but he consented to be washed with disinfectant. I gave a bottle to Kago and thought no more about it. If he did not want to be stitched that was his own affair.

The next morning when I enquired how he was, Kago beamed with delight and said that he had mended him beautifully; he had gummed him together and I must come and look at his work. I have never seen such a lovely sight as that boy's face. Kago had cut strips of newspaper which he had covered with gum and stuck these all over the boy's head, face and chest. It was quite scientifically done, the cuts being well pulled together and a space left between each strip of paper to allow for suppuration. But gum mixed with printer's ink on deep wounds made me feel rather ill. They were all so entirely delighted with the effect which Kago had managed to produce that I let it go and hoped that the patient would not die of septicaemia. He apparently was immune from blood-poisoning, for he made a quick recovery.

Hunting to keep the Farm Working

Chapter XIV

BAR ONE
With thanks to Mark Jenkins

The difficulty of getting enough meat for the men was a great worry to me. The days of plenty were not yet and often we were hard put to it. On a well-remembered day Kago came to me with a long tale of woe. The porters who had been sent to Gilgil for posho were overdue, the men were hungry and had again refused to work. In fact the cupboard was bare and meat, if nothing else, had to be got somehow.

It so happened that I had been practically *hors de combat* for some time with a bad go of veldt sores[1]. For two or three weeks I had been struggling about on sticks with a number of these unhealable suppurating wounds on my legs. I literally could not get on ordinary clothes and I had to stick to mosquito boots and pyjamas. As I got a little better I would spend half the time trying to keep my legs up and the other half endeavouring to supervise the work. It was torture to move and it was also an impossibility to cross a horse.

I was resting my aching legs on a couch discussing the hunger strike with Kago when my personal servant, Buni, came in to tell me that he had just seen a herd of eland on our ground about a mile away, one bull and ten cows. I knew Buni's word was to be relied on and my duty was clearly defined. I had to make the effort and, if possible, shoot the bull eland to provide the starving with sustenance.

I considered it would be less painful to walk than to ride and I started just as I was, with men and my pack of dogs which had, by now, increased to seven. These were all coupled up and given to Buni to lead, while Kago helped me along and carried the rifle. It turned out to be a weary two-mile tramp before we sighted the eland. We were up-wind of them and had to make a wide circle and long crawl before we could get within two hundred yards of the animals.

Had I been sound instead of nearly crying with pain I should not

---

[1] Veldt sores are a form of tropical ulcer common in people who are malnourished. They can occur as a result of infection spreading as a result of a cut or more specific infections such as diptheria of the skin, cutaneous leishmaniasis and yaws. [BMA Family Health Encyclopedia]

have taken the shot so far away. The wind was strong and varying but I had a good 'lie down' and a perfect sight of the bull who was standing broadside on to me. I was taking a heart-shot and there was no need to hurry. Whether I did not allow enough for the wind, or had misjudged the distance I do not know, but I fired and broke the beast's foreleg. The cows galloped wildly about and covered the bull so that I could not put in another shot, and he began to move off on three legs.

I now loosed Big Man who would work to the wave of a handkerchief, and sent him to head off and bay the bull. He did his best but could not quite manage the work alone, so I let two more dogs go. I thought we should just about do the job when that little devil Prickles slipped his collar and went hell for leather straight for the nose of the bull which charged him and then made off as fast as he could after his ten wives.

Our best chance now was to loose all the dogs and gallop him down. I sent Buni ahead to signal Big Man and Dona to turn them towards me. The dogs and the man together held the bull up time after time but I was too lame to get up with them quickly enough. It was about 3 p.m. when I fired the shot and we chased after that wounded bull until 8 p.m., when it was too dark to go on; but the dogs had managed to keep turning him until we left him, nearly done for, only a quarter of a mile from home. It was a dreadful thing to wound a beautiful beast and have to abandon the hunt. Through my field glasses I had seen how shattered the leg was.

I spent a wretched night, what with the pain in my own legs after such a walk and the thought of what the poor bull must be suffering as well. Before going to bed I arranged with Kago to follow the animal up at daybreak. Ride I must and would.

I rode Askill, the Basuto pony and an excellent hunter. He was saddled up for me before dawn while Kago rode a mule, carrying the rifle and rawhide ropes. With all the men we set off to find our wounded quarry. We had marked the spot where we had left him the night before and soon found where he had camped. When we parted from him he had had all his cows with him but the following morning, around his sleeping place there was no trace of his wives and he himself had also disappeared. There was a good deal of blood about and we gave the dogs a sniff of it so that they should know what to follow when we loosed them. In the meantime they were securely coupled and chained.

I rode on to the top of the ridge where, with glasses, I could see for miles in all directions. Here I sat on my pony and, scanning the plains bit by bit, at last I got a sight of the bull. He was certainly a mile and a half away, plodding along, slowly making for the Aberdare forests. Not a cow was in sight but with him was *another bull* keeping half a length ahead and continually stopping as though encouraging his friend to come on.

I have often heard of elephant coming to the assistance of a wounded companion and actually propping it up but I had never heard of an eland doing the same thing for one of his kind. This is not the home of eland; they are occasional visitors only and when I fired that badly directed shot, there was no other bull within miles of us. And yet this one had somehow got wind of the mishap and had arrived out of the blue. If the wounded bull had had a hope of recovery I should have let him go but I knew he had no chance at all and would only suffer and die of starvation. I therefore had to shoot him somehow.

My idea was to gallop as hard as I could and get between the two bulls, heading the wounded one back. I left word with Kago to follow as quickly as he could, bringing along the rifle and dogs and to keep a close watch on what I was doing. So saying, I set my pony going at his best pace and a great chase it was, over very rough ground. The old Basuto stuck to it like a man, while that bull, although he was only on three legs, went very fast indeed. I managed to get quite close to the leading bull, a splendid old fellow; but he gave up as soon as I put my pony between the two of them and raced away for his life.

Now, with some difficulty, I turned the wounded one into some thickish scrub and deep *dongas* (gullies caused by erosion) to my left and did my best to press him hard but the going was so bad I lost sight of him and had to wait for the dogs to be brought up. They were soon with me and we slipped the pack, Dona hitting off the line at once and owning it well. The rest of them went to her cry and away they raced on a red-hot scent.

There then followed one of the most exciting hunts I have ridden in. Half the time the dogs were right at the heels of the beast, giving tongue like a pack of foxhounds. The country was so awful to ride over that I could not keep very near them. Once or twice I heard them all at bay and then on they would go again. I had quite lost Kago and all the men, but the Basuto was still going strong and he was a marvel over rock and gullies, never faltering or making a mistake so long as I left the reins on his neck.

The musical chorus of the pack sounded nearer and nearer, telling me that we were gaining and that the bull was fast tiring. Once he was stopped just in front of me and I viewed him for a second; yet he made one more gallant effort to shake off the dogs and get away. In the next rocky hollow they held him for the last time. He had got his tail against a wall of rock and the dogs had surrounded him on three sides. He was warding them off with his horns as they leapt for his throat.

How Kago on his tiny mule ever caught us I cannot imagine; but he did and arrived very shortly after I had jumped off my blown pony. But alas! A dreadful thing had happened. The mule had fallen headlong over a hidden log and the stock of my rifle was broken completely in two. It was a tragic moment. Here we had this enormous beast at our mercy and no possible way of killing it.

Then I thought of the rawhide rope. I uncoiled it and, making a noose at one end, after one or two misses I succeeded in throwing it over the bull's horns. I then got a half hitch round a tree and so held him. When the runners arrived I suggested we should pull the animal over but they, one and all, refused to help saying that he killed men.

I had a look at my broken rifle and, fitting the splintered wood carefully together, I bound it with strips of rawhide. I knew, as I slipped in the bullets that I was about to take a horrible risk but it had to be done. Walking to within five yards of the bull I pulled the trigger and shot him through the forehead. The rifle held so all was well.

We took the skin off while the animal was yet warm and the men filled themselves to the brim on the meat just warmed over a fire of sticks. The dogs took good care to get plenty too. My lunch was a cigarette and lots of water. After resting a while we cut the carcass up and with fourteen boys and one laden mule we managed to get all the meat home that evening. Everyone had a great feast. There was much dancing and rejoicing. The tom-toms continued tom-tomming even into the dead of night.

After the eland hunt I would rather not say what condition my veldt sores were in the next morning. I was one large bandage and more or less on my bed for weeks.

I have often ridden over the line of that chase since, on far better and more valuable horses, but only at a foot's pace and I have marvelled how my Basuto pony ever managed to stand up, going as hard as I could ride him. Since living in this country I have owned a few extra good horses but never one that could have cantered that course without getting an unholy spill.

I rode Askill for three years and he never once put me down. He was then sold as a polo pony at which game he did well.

My sister Olive joined me on one exciting hunt on one of her visits to the farm. She had brought with her a Swahili man from the coast. This was mainly, I fancy, to give him a holiday and a good fill-up of buck meat, for she was great on doing good turns to her employees.

Besides old Askill, I had now been lent a white stodgy gelding whose manners had not pleased his owner. He was here to learn better, which suited us splendidly. So, the following day, both well mounted, we coupled up the dogs and, with a retinue of boys, including the white-*kanzu'd* (robed) Swahili, we started off to destroy a kongoni or any other suitable animal we found on the plains. About two miles away we came upon a herd of the former feeding quietly. Taking my rifle I did a nice stalk and succeeded in shooting a big buck.

Now, the Swahili tribe, being Mohammedans, cannot eat meat that has not been '*chinja*'d': in other words its throat must be cut by a Mohammedan. It must not be touched by anyone else until this duty has been performed. My sister, who was back with the men some distance away, got very excited lest anyone else should approach the animal until the Swahili had got his knife into it. She started at full gallop for the carcass to protect it herself, her boy running full speed after her. Kago, well knowing the amount of lead a kongoni can carry away and, thinking it might get up and bolt at any moment, uncoupled all the dogs and let them go. Olive's galloping horse was quite enough to get them on their toes and they all chased after her. On the way they put up another kongoni that must have been lying asleep in some bushes. As they raced, the full chorus of the pack brought back English hunting days to Olive's mind. With a fine 'View Halloa' she set her horse going, cheering on the dogs with all her might and was out of sight over the brow of the hill before I had time to retrieve my horse and get into the saddle. And that is the last I saw of her for the next two hours. Meanwhile the Swahili boy had '*chinja*'d' his beast and, with the rest of the men, was busy skinning and cutting it up. I arranged with Kago about its transport home when, as there was no sign of Olive, it occurred to us both that the dogs were probably getting her into trouble. She little knew what they were capable of doing when their blood was up and she would be certain to try to protect them from getting hurt, with her naked hands if necessary, for she had no weapon with her but a hunting-crop.

I cantered on to look for her, telling Buni, the best runner I had, to follow after me if we did not return in half an hour. I rather guessed that the dogs may have headed for a swamp nearby where there were water-buck and I went in that direction.

Askill was feeling his way down some rocks that led to the river bed when I heard Olive shouting, yelling and whistling. Her shouts then became pathetic so I bustled to her aid and soon found the white horse tied to a tree. On the opposite side of the water, frantic with rage, was Olive beating and slashing in the midst of the barking pack who had got a large waterbuck cornered in a waterhole. She was angry with me and furious with the dogs who she designated as an unruly lot of brutes. She had tied Dona and Prickles up to a stump, where I saw their empty collars hanging, for they had instantly slipped them and returned to the fray. Big Man and the rest were springing for a throat hold and they were being continually cut over by the hoofs of a buck, who was savagely striking at them. Olive was in a frenzy lest they should be killed or drowned.

Having my gun with me I quickly ended it with a close-up shot through the head and the buck pitched forward into deep water, where I was all for leaving him, as time was getting on and we had far to go. But not so my sister, who owns an economical mind. A waterbuck's skin is very valuable for riems and she was determined to salvage this one. The body was in a deep hole and, by ourselves, we could not pull it out. Again there was a clamour amongst the dogs and they rushed at something else. This time it was a Kavirondo native whose life we saved between us. Afterwards we offered him the meat of the buck if he would help haul the body out of the river and skin it for us.

Where that Kavirondo came from was a mystery but he had heard the dogs, smelt the meat and intended having what we left behind. He had it all and probably sat for a week eating it, unless a lion got him first. That was no affair of ours, however.

Throwing the hide over Askill's saddle we were about to start for home when Buni turned up with a lantern. There had been some hitch about carrying the kongoni home and the stretcher was only just moving off when we got back to the spot. Olive wanted to go home quickly and cantered off by herself, quite in the wrong direction, as she had lost her bearings. I came along with boys, dogs and meat and it was as well I stayed behind, for no sooner had we left it than a pack of wild dog came down onto the offal. Having devoured that, they followed us right across to the Simba river, my hounds trying to break loose and go for them all the time. We took good care to couple and chain them securely. It was pitch dark coming through the creek and I should never have found my way had I been by myself. Where Olive got across I cannot think but she turned up all right soon after we had reached home. On the whole I think she enjoyed the day. It was a pleasant contrast to her peaceful existence at Kabete and no one relishes a hunt or a scrap more than does this very sporting sister of mine.

* * *

No proper human being could ever bear a solitary existence without a dog for company. I had seven and this was six too many if you wished to live a life of peace with no unpleasant excitements. For it is the dogs that start the trouble and then have to be helped out of it.

Of all the infernal little monkeys that ever got inside the skin of an Airedale, Prickles stands out as being the worst. He was a dog of great character, most of it bad, but he possessed a sense of humour peculiarly his own. He tried my patience to its utmost limits and I lived on tenterhooks lest he should get killed. But it was Simba who caused the first heartbreak from my pack.

We were out on one of our Sunday hunts on foot – Askill and the mules being allowed a day off. We had killed a wild pig and were making our way home. I walked in front of the pack with my hunting crop, Kago following behind with the pack between us. I was congratulating myself that with luck we might reach home safely and intact when, without an instant's warning, Prickles dashed off to the right and bolted another pig. Of course all the dogs saw it and away they went. Following them was Kago, who, of course, had quite out-distanced me. I could see him flying up and down in front of a dense green wall of forest, unable to force a way through.

As I approached, he threw himself face downward to try to worm his way under the tangle of thorn, vines and branches that had impeded his path. The strip of forest was narrow and we could distinctly hear the dogs putting up a mighty fight with the boar who, being hard pressed, had evidently fallen into the gully and could find no outlet on the far side. Every now and then there was a piercing yelp from a dog as the pig found its mark. The whole pack was charging up and down in this narrow ravine and although they were only fifty yards away, get to them I could not. Hearing dog after dog damaged I became crazy, struggling to break a way through the bush and getting completely entangled in unbreakable vines. Then I heard Kago calling to me in dismay:

'Come, come quickly! Simba is down and nearly killed. Some of the others are hurt. Lie down and walk on your face!'

It was good advice and I took it without hesitation, lying down and wriggling my way to where Kago was standing, half my shirt being torn from my back. I was then able to see the awful mix-up that was taking place eight feet below the bank on which we were standing. Kago had picked up a stone the size of a football and stood with it poised above his head. As the mass of dogs and pig rolled and tumbled, he let fly the rock with all his strength at the head of the pig, smashing its skull between the eyes and killing it stone dead.

A few yards away from the scrum, the whole of her side covered with blood lay my poor Simba. She was not dead but one tusk had gone deep into her groin. As I raised her she fainted and we bathed her head and side with water, pouring a few drops down her throat. Darkness was upon us as, with much difficulty and pain to the bitch, we got her out to the veldt and, leaving me with her, Kago ran home to fetch a stretcher, bearers and brandy.

Having thrown off a woolly coat before diving into the forest I now had this to wrap around the dog, for she was icy cold and I could only sit and rub her feet and legs. It was a long hour to wait in the dark with a dying dog until I spied the lights of lanterns bobbing towards me.

Simba was now more conscious so we poured a good dose of brandy and water down her throat and, covering her with a light warm blanket, we carried her slowly home.

TWO OF MARGARET'S LATER AIREDALES, BUZZY AND TAJ. 1931

With care and incessant nursing she recovered up to a point but the poison from the dirty tusk seemed to have saturated right through her system. She gradually became paralysed behind so, after many months, I thought it kinder to put her gently to sleep for good and all.

Simba was the first of many good dogs I was destined to lose on this farm. Wart-hog took toll of several, leopard two, kongoni one and others died from snake bite before I ever heard of FitzSimmons' anti-venine treatment which thereafter I was seldom without. When thought strays back to my lost canine friends I endeavour to console myself with the knowledge that although their lives were short, they were very happy. To die fighting is a better death than outlasting time and gradually failing and fading out of one's earthly existence.

A South African Interlude

Chapter XV

1923 was a year of drought and famine. Both feed and water gave out and I was forced to sell all the cattle which left me with nothing but cultivation and a few horses to look after. But growing cereals on a big acreage was ruinous work and we lost a great deal of money trying to make unsuitable soil produce wheat, oats and barley which it declined to do in sufficient quantities to become a paying proposition.

If the farms in this area are anything at all they are stock farms. Had we been content to stick to stock and not wasted money on agricultural implements with the necessary amount of labour to ply them, we would have done very well. But you must not forget that the object in all pioneer work is to find out by degrees what can *not* be grown, so that those coming after may profit from the forerunners' experience and start in on a certainty, without the expense and trouble of experimenting.

Also in 1923 I went sick. Not wishing to die alone and unaided, I journeyed down to my sister and was overhauled by a couple of Nairobi doctors, who sent me off the following week to South Africa, with orders to keep as near to the sea as possible. I was not permitted to come back to the farm to arrange about putting in a manager, so all this extra work fell on my devoted sister's shoulders.

I went to Mombasa, which sweltered in steamy heat. I went to Zanzibar and talked Art, for the first time since leaving England, with

Mr and Mrs Sinclair[1] at the Residency. From there I sailed to Beira which, set in the midst of beauty, should not be permitted to exist. The Germans, had they blown Beira to blazes, would have earned a substantial reward in heaven. Never have I seen such an ugly, dreary town. The heat and hideousness drove me quickly back to my cabin where even Edgar Wallace[2] and a bunk were preferable to anything that was in sight.

Mozambique amused me not a little, the quaintest little dab of earth imaginable. One wonders why it is there at all. Two straggling and struggling frangipani shrubs, a cactus or so, lots of brown and white spotted shells: the kind that the sailor lad brings home to his mother who puts them on a crochet mat under a glass shade. These and very large crabs held dominion on the seafront. Also there were horrid boys offering for sale small wild birds in tiny wooden cages, the poor little inhabitants beating themselves to death against the bars. I bought up one consignment and immediately broke the cages and let the birds loose, probably only to be netted again the very next day.

Lorenzo Marques is rather a dream of beauty. Its arboreal banks come right down to the sea and many trees actually grow out of the water. Robinson Crusoe and Friday might easily have lived there.

I then sailed south to Durban where I hoped to get good food, and did not. And why, in a town as hot as Durban, do they not have hotels properly ventilated? My bedroom, which was most expensive, was very small with only one window opening on to a street and no exit for the small amount of air that did find its way into the room. I have never felt heat in East Africa that could compare with the heat in Durban. However,

---

[1] J.H. Sinclair CMG CBE born on the Isle of Wight. An architect by profession, he prepared the plans for the building of the elegant Residency and served for 24 years as Vice Consul, Consul, Consul General and British Agent in Zanzibar.

[2] Edgar Wallace was a soldier, poet, war correspondent, reporter, author and playwright. He wrote more than 150 popular thrillers including 'Sanders of the River' about an administrator in Africa.

it was in Durban that my long unquenched thirst for music was assuaged by excellent concerts.

At the Zoo in Durban I came across a small English oak, doing its best to grow. This so consoled me in my loneliness that I could not tear myself away from it. We were both exiles; but on the whole I was thriving better than the little friendly tree. Here too I made the acquaintance of the most enormous fur seal I have ever seen. It was as tame and friendly as a dog. I went to call on him every day for a week, taking a basket of raw fish on which to feed him. He sat as close to the bars of the cage as he could get and took the fish gently from my fingers, his soft, round, luminous eyes looking straight into mine with a marked expression of 'Thank you for the treat.' The strong sun kept drying his back too rapidly and when he had borne it as long as he could, he flapped round and took a quick short swim in the tank and hurried back again to his position on the rails, fearful of missing the last bite of the fish my basket contained.

I was away from Kenya exactly six weeks and that is the one and only time I had left the Colony for nearly ten years. Although the South African trip was not particularly enjoyable, the rest did me much good and I returned to my farm a different being from the feeble creature that had left it two months before.

Safaris

Chapter XVI

Years passed, the roads improved, the old Cape-Cart, in which we had had so many merry drives, was dead. In its place my sister bought a second hand car of which she was inordinately proud, notwithstanding that it cost as much in oil as would have kept two horses on oats for the same period of time. It did not go very fast but a bit faster than the horses and everything was beginning to speed up considerably.

A road was built between Gilgil and Nairobi. It was very bad in parts and the great Escarpment hill into the Rift Valley was a hair-raiser of considerable merit. Yet the motor cars could beat the trains every time with an hour or two in hand.

I acquired a second-hand Ford motor car. It was a murderous contrivance, for if the gear jumped out going down a hill – and this was continually happening – everything including the brakes became detached and there was every chance of going to glory quickly. The hills here are not be trifled with. When the roads are wet it is like driving on butter for they are only composed of mud and even with chains, cars shoot all over the place and a bad skid in certain places might land one at the bottom of an unpleasant precipice.

In January 1933 my sister and I took a fortnight's holiday, and drove to Kakamega where Mr Johnson had discovered pockets of alluvial gold and his find had been a rich one. This was shortly after the locust invasion had ruined so many people and many farms were deserted. There was a rush to Kakamega which the *East African Standard,* very rightly, did its best to control, but without much success, for many went up with their last few pounds and soon returned without a penny. The word 'gold' is like a magnet to many people, but when I saw the very amateur and laborious work being done to get enough even to pay for food and labour, I had not the smallest wish to join it.

We spent four days going round the various 'claims'. These were small round holes punched in the earth like those one punches in a cheese with a cheese scoop. They were in every direction and it was leg breaking country to walk over after dusk. Some of the larger holes were possibly twenty or thirty feet deep. There was one very indifferent stamp mill that apparently lost more gold that it recovered from the quartz. The man who owned it went broke soon after we were there.

When we were there alluvial gold was no longer being found in paying quantities, and only very small reefs and stringers had been discovered underground, the paying proposition of which was then extremely doubtful. The Piccadilly Circus Claims seemed to be the most hopeful, and a little later they were bought and made into a company known as 'Risks Ltd', which I heard is going ahead with a lot of new machinery being brought out from England to work them.

I had very little doubt that there was plenty of gold in Kakamega and the surrounding country but it would need a mint of money to get it out of the ground. The whole field was bound eventually to get into the hands of large companies with big capital at the back of them. The day of the small man was even now past and those who held claims would have been wise to sell them.

That the mining operations were harming the native population was an absurd idea. Hundreds and hundreds of them were being employed in the mines and they earned a good monthly wage which their employers were obliged to pay regularly. Before gold was discovered these people merely sat on their plots of cultivation and did nothing. It was extremely fertile country and the surplus stuff they grew found a ready market amongst the European settlers. Every plot of cultivation destroyed by claim holders had to be compensated for; and the natives were treated very well and very fairly.

When the washing for alluvial gold first commenced, the Maragoli tribe had no idea what it was and thought that washing mud was yet another form of madness in the white man. But it did not take them long to jump to the value of the yellow metal, and last year gold was already being stolen by the labour and sold to the Indians. Probably by now the claim-holders have a method of searching the men before they leave their work, but nothing of this sort was being done when we were there.

When Olive and I were in camp (of course I mean our usual way of camping with no camp at all) I had all my clothes stolen one night. I awoke one morning to find my suitcase gone, and all they had left me was a hat and overcoat. They would have taken these as well, but I suppose we roused a little which disturbed them. Luckily they missed the real plum, for all our cash, amounting to £15, was in my sister's suitcase, which was under her bed and they did not see it. Anyhow they got away with two pairs of nice velveteen slacks of mine, and several new shirts, to say nothing of smart silk pyjamas. I had to drive the car to the police station in my night attire. They got their sleuths on to the line at once and my suitcase was found thrown away in a ditch, with my sketching things, brush and comb, and my shoes still in it. Olive, having done herself rather proud in the clothes line, had to fit me out for the remainder of our holiday.

If the gold fields were to prosper, as I hope and think they may in a year or two's time, the treasure found would react on the whole Colony. Kakamega would become a small edition of Johannesburg, and its inhabitants would need to be fed; thus export of dairy produce and other foodstuffs would become unnecessary, for a ready market would be found nearer at hand and farmers would begin to have a much easier time. We begin to look forward to this already, but whether it will happen during my lifetime it is at present very hard to say; but the rising generation have every prospect of becoming wealthy citizens.[1]

Kakamega was a very hot and unhealthy district, and we were rather glad to get out of it, especially as we had taken no precautions against malaria and just trusted to luck. From there we drove on to Kitale, where we were entertained for two days by the District Commissioner and his wife. At the end of our visit we drove still further afield into the Soux and Turkana country, which was very sparsely populated by a primitive people who walked about stark naked.

Kapenguria, where Mr Champion the Provincial Commissioner lived, was very nearly at the end of all things. The *boma* was on the top of a hill looking down on indescribably wild and beautiful country. We drove for five miles winding up the side of a hill along a hair-raising road with a sheer precipice of thousands of feet all the way on our left which dropped down onto the tops of trees so far below us that they resembled a dark green meadow. When we reached the top, the world was before us. Never have I seen such a panorama of magnificence. Range upon range of hills indescribable in beauty and brilliance of colour. Away and away our eyes travelled over the deeply serrated tops of mountains to a gap in the last range of all through which we glimpsed the desert, still visible as the setting sun sank to rest behind us, throwing its golden afterglow over such a view as I shall never in my life gaze upon again.

Thank God my sister has a head like a stone. I do not know anyone else whom I would have trusted to drive me down that narrow hillside road, where one mistake or slip would have sent us, car and all, hurtling down through space to perdition. But it was worth it every time to have looked for a moment on such a supremacy of splendour.

The next day we drove through Eldoret over the Uasin Gishu

---

[1] Unfortunately the gold never came to very much. When we lived in Kakamega from 1946 to 1950, there was an operating mine known as Rostermans but it did not thrive. Eds.

plateau through Timboroa – where it rained like the very mischief and we nearly stuck in many a mud hole – to Rongai, where we spent the night with a friend, and then on to Nakuru. From there we took the new road up the Escarpment, over which I had ridden my black horse so many years ago. We drove through tangled bamboo forest and out on to the top of the world again, looking back across the sweeping world below us to the vivid blue lakes of Nakuru and Elmenteita. After a long run down to the Dundori ridges we came home to my farm, where we found all well and nothing particularly dead.

* * *

I do not remember who it was that first succeeded in driving from Nairobi to Mombasa by car but not so long afterwards my sister and I drove our two cars from Nairobi through Mombasa to Kilifi and on to Malindi, making the return journey by Moshi and through the great game reserve[2] home.

It was seldom that we ever took a holiday, and still more seldom we had had the opportunity to enjoy a spell off work together.

I drove down from Gilgil, arriving at Kabete by midday, and I spent the afternoon helping Olive to pack chop-boxes, camp-beds, and cooking pots. The latter took up so much room that we reduced the amount to one kettle and a frying-pan. Tents are a bore and we had no intention of taking any, both of us much preferring to sleep in the open. I purposely left my guns at home, being sure that Olive would pack hers; the outcome of this was that at our first stop for the night we discovered the unpleasant fact that we were quite unarmed.

One of the pleasures I derive from travelling about the country casually with Olive is that she never worries at all over anything. She will happily eat with relish any odd stuff one fries, even if it gets covered

---

[2] Now known as Serengeti.

with ashes or dust. Now, finding ourselves in the wilds with no guns, it did not affect her outlook in the least. We had been stupid enough to forget them and that was that. I cannot say I felt quite the same way about it myself, for at times I have found a gun to be quite useful!

As my sister was a shocking bad starter, we did not get away from Nairobi until 11.30 a.m., meaning to arrive in Makindu that night and sleep at the station. But little did we guess what the so-called road was like or how slowly we would have to drive. In the middle of vast plains near Machakos I had a puncture and found a tin-tack in my tyre.

Having got twenty-five miles south of Sultan Hamud, and still eleven miles before us to reach Makindu, we had to stop as it was nearly dark and the track was difficult to follow by car lights over open country. We hunted about for a while with lanterns and we discovered a pool of water which had been made into mud paste by multitudes of zebra. Our tea was toughly flavoured, but it was a matter of Hobson's choice, so we put out our camp-beds, made a fire of what little fuel we could cut and turned in, only to be kept awake nearly all night by yapping zebra and howling hyenas. The zebra were racing about so crazily they must have been stampeded by lion and as our beds were out in the open, I quite thought we might have the whole herd on top of us.

The next morning we got going in fairly good time, and it was just as well we did, for Olive ran her Chev. into an appalling hole at the Kiboko Swamp and the car had to be unloaded before we could jack up the wheel and get it out. A beautiful waterbuck came and looked at us; something we might otherwise have missed, and near the river-bed we found a bush of mauve hibiscus which I had not seen before.

At Makindu we filled up with petrol, bought bananas and journeyed on to Tsavo. The road was terrible, and watercourses so deep and narrow that the hind wheels of the car were not fully at the bottom of one bank before the front ones were climbing up the other side. I wonder the cars did not break their backs. All through the 'dead' forest we crawled along at ten miles an hour, heat like the inside of an oven, and nothing to be seen but the hanging nests of weaver birds, giant red castles of mud built by white ants, and one long snake that flashed across the track in front of my car.

This section was waterless, dreary, dead forest for mile upon mile, through which forty years ago the first pioneers and missionaries had to march and cut their way, often watched and followed by armed and hostile inhabitants. Our minds were full of the books we had read about this trek by Thomson[3] and other explorers who had more than once safaried through this waterless tract of country. And horse lovers though we were, our hearts rejoiced that our day had come later, when the same journey, so bravely faced by those first European people, could now be accomplished with comparative ease in mechanical conveyances.

Between Makindu and the Tsavo River we struck no water at all, and it was a relief to our dust-filled eyes when, rounding a bend, we came upon a beautiful green oasis. It was really a lovely corner, the wide shallow river rippling in crystal wavelets over a stony bed; great boulders of coloured rock twisting and turning the channels of water into curves of beauty, the banks a verdant green of long lush grass out of which rose the pinky-grey stems of flat-topped acacias.

After what we had just driven through this was much too good to pass with only a fleeting glance. We stopped and brewed some tea, paddled about in the cool stream and talked of the days when the man-eaters of the Tsavo raided the gangers on the railway line every night, actually pushing open doors of railway carriages, and pulling men from their blankets as they lay asleep on the seats.

---

[3] Joseph Thomson came from Dumfriesshire, Scotland. He described this area as a 'skeleton forest. Weird and ghastly is the aspect of the greyish-coloured trees and bushes…The wind…raised only a mournful whistling or dreary croaking, 'eerie' and full of sadness, as if it said, 'Here is all death and desolation!'…The porter, wearied already with a long march, and parched for want of water, presses on panting and perspiring under a broiling sun, made worse by the glaring red soil which reflects the rays as though they came from the mouth of a furnace.' [*The Lunatic Express*' by Charles Miller]

Filling up tins and bottles in case of a further dearth of water, we drove on towards Voi, stopping four miles short of the station at an inviting-looking camping ground amongst some shady trees which provided us with plenty of ready-cut fuel. Here I cooked a most delectable meal in the frying-pan, of chicken, potatoes and cabbage, all mixed up together, which not only smelt good but positively tickled the palate. And here we spent a most peaceful night, with no wild beasts to annoy us.

The following morning, for a change, we made a really early beginning. Not stopping at Voi, we went right through to Samburu, where we nearly ran out of petrol, having done fifty miles without a check on a fairly good road. We filled up our tanks at the Indian *duka* (small shop) and we pushed on at once for Mombasa, this lap of the road was excellent except for the many Irish bridges which we took at racing speed but were apt to break springs. From Mariakani the broad winding road descending to the coast is extremely pretty, the hills being covered with many kinds of refreshingly green tropical growth. As we got nearer to sea level the atmosphere gradually changed from dry heat to tropical hot-house heat. We drove over a new bridge which was horribly narrow and arrived on Mombasa island. Here we again took on plenty of petrol and then crossed on the ferry-boat to the mainland where my servant, who had not before been further than Nairobi, became greatly alarmed.

He had, of course, never seen the sea and he could not imagine what we were up to when we drove both cars on to a small raft with the deep blue water all around it. As the ferry pushed off, he took a firm grip round my waist, determined that if he was going to be drowned, I most certainly should drown as well. The blue water puzzled him very much. He had only seen blue water when we put 'paint' in it to wash clothes.[4] He wondered how so much water was made blue. Then giving up the

---

[4] This used to be known as 'booloo.' It helped to keep white clothes white, rather than red from the dust.

riddle he murmured that it was *shauri ya Mungu* (God's affair) and didn't bother any more about it.

It was 4.30 p.m. before we crossed the first ferry and got on to the road to Kilifi, which was very narrow, but not too bad. We had to cross inlets of the sea by two more ferries, but it was the mile of narrow cement causeway, built about twenty feet above the water, that took at least ten years off my life. There was not more than a foot to spare on either side of the wheels and no sort of guard-rail or even cement ledges to stop one slipping splosh into the water. Olive was leading at this point and I was on the thing before I realized how fearsome it was. I kept my eyes fixed on her rear light and dared not glance at the water or I should have driven straight over the edge for a certainty. I have no head for heights and cannot walk across a plank even three feet above the water. I thanked my stars when that part of the journey was over and I vowed I would never cross the place again.

We reached the Kilifi *Boma* (District Commissioner's house and police lines) at 7.00 p.m. and it was now quite dark. We could not find the road through the forest which would take us to the *banda*[5] on the shore for which we were making. We drove down one newly-cut track full of tree stumps which ended in nothing and here Olive said we would stay for the night, as we were both too tired to go on; but remembering in time that the forest was full of elephant and that we had no guns, she thought better of it and decided to have one more try to find the road. This time we struck the right turning and drove in pitch darkness through trees until we came out on a sandy shore, the sea in front of us, and on our right was the wooden shanty where a friend of ours was living. We had long since been given up as lost or strayed, but our welcome was none the less warm. We had driven one hundred and sixty miles that day, crossed three ferries, come safely over the causeway, and were still alive to tell the tale.

---

5 *Banda* is a word used in Africa to describe a simple house generally for guests.

GEDI

We spent a week at Kilifi doing nothing, which I did not enjoy. The *banda* was dirty and uncomfortable, and there was no fresh water to be had unless we fetched it in tins from a tap four miles away. I dislike bathing in the sea unless I can have a freshwater tub after it, and for a week I never saw a bath at all. We had one lovely day, when Olive and I drove to Malindi and back.

Malindi is another small coast town, entirely Arab in its architecture and inhabitants. The road to it from Kilifi runs all the way through virgin forest, which is most entrancing, and we stopped to visit the 'Hidden City of Gedi', a half-buried ruin of great antiquity and interest. Very little excavating had been done, for it lay in the middle of dense forest, and the cost of clearing it would be considerable. The few archways and walls that had been cleared were in good preservation and they looked as though some kind of cement had been used in the building of them. The stone was of a grey-blue colour and very pretty, so also is the formation of the arches and windows. There are many niches to be seen, which must have at one time been the resting-places for small statuettes.

The place was entirely ghostly and haunted with evil. I sat in what may have been a chapel and made a sketch, while Olive lost herself in the undergrowth and shouted for directions back. I could not have gone alone to that spot; it was too eerie, and alive with invisible beings who gave me no peace in which to work. We were both quite glad to get away from those ruins and continued the drive into Malindi, where a fish auction was taking place in the market by the sea. Both large and small shark realised top prices.

We slightly varied our return journey back to Kilifi by bearing to the right and going through the native village of Ganda, built in the centre of a coconut plantation which in flickering sunlight looked to me like fairyland.

8.30 a.m. on August 16th saw us packed and again in our cars bound for Voi via Mariakani. The first part of the journey took us through large coconut plantations and one or two sisal farms. At Mariakani we joined the main Mombasa-Nairobi road, returning on our old tracks as far as Voi, where we swung left-handed for Taveta and Moshi. Getting to Voi at about 4.30 p.m., we had tea at the station, and here we met Mr Denys Finch Hatton[6], who was taking out a small safari to his permanent camp in the game reserve. Hearing that we intended to return to Nairobi through the reserve without even a revolver between us, he evidently thought there were no fools like old fools and that we had been long enough in the country to know better.[7] After tea we drove six miles along the Moshi road and pitched camp at the side of the Voi river, where we washed off the sticky salt and grubbiness of Kilifi from our bodies.

Taveta was of interest to both of us, as it had been my brother's first home in Kenya when he came out as an Assistant District Commissioner[8]. Also much fighting had taken place hereabouts during the war. From Taveta we crossed the border into Tanganyika to Moshi. The road was excellent, having been made by the Germans when Kilimanjaro belonged to the Kaiser[9]. This great snow-topped mountain now

---

[6] Son of the Earl of Winchilsea, Finch Hatton has latterly become known as Karen von Blixen's lover, but at the time he was renowned as a 'superb organiser of safaris'. He organised a successful safari for the Prince of Wales in 1930.

[7] Kenya was a peaceful country at that time and the firearms they should have had with them would only have been used to protect the two 'old fools' from wild animals or to shoot for the pot.

[8] See Appendix II

[9] After WWI, not just Mount Kilimanjaro but Tanganyika Territory itself was administered by the British under the auspices of the League of Nations.

loomed on our right, but a mist-covered cap shrouded the peaks and cast a deep blue gloom over its rugged sides.

What we saw of the town of Moshi with its enormous Market Square and small market rather impressed us; but the heat was colossal, and the paving burnt our feet as we walked about buying a few stores. We were glad to get into our cars and drive at a leisurely pace until we found a pretty camp in which to stay the night. The splendour of the roads and bridges was an eye-opener after those we suffered from in Kenya, and we gave credit to the Germans as being the better colonists and vastly superior to us in engineering work. The bridges were solid constructions of cement and iron, not cedar logs thrown across from bank to bank with a little earth dusted over them, such as were scattered about Kenya. The Tanganyika roads were wide, well made and properly cambered, the principal throughfares being surfaces with either murram or well-pounded stone. It is a thousand pities that our district councils do not learn the art of road-making from our late enemies, for there is much they could be taught in this line of work.

Fifteen miles out of Moshi we found what we were looking for, a Masai *boma* on a well-watered plain below the foot hills of the mountain. Here Olive was really happy for the first time since leaving Kabete, for there were cows in hundreds and plenty of fresh milk to be had for the asking. Much as my sister loves a cup of tea, she cannot touch it when laced with tinned milk. Cows were not known at Kilifi, for they died of (tsetse) 'fly', so for over a week the poor dear had drunk her tea, uncomplainingly, neat.

It was advisable when getting milk from the Masai to send your own jug and your own servant to milk the cow; for they prefer to wash all their dairying utensils in the urine from the cows, and if you object to this idea never take milk from one of their gourds. The name of this wild flower garden in which we now found ourselves was '*Boma ya Ngombi*', the cattle-yard or literally the yard of the cattle.

When we awakened early next morning a Scottish mist was falling on our faces and blankets; but a little later the sun broke through, and we saw the towering snow-peaks in all their glory with a glittering white canopy faintly washed with the pink of dawn. Wild flowers in quantities were all around us, and masses of the sweet-scented white delphinium filled the air with their delicious fragrance. Flowering shrubs of many varieties were also in bloom, which made us long to stay and forage for treasures. But time was passing, so we could do no more than dig up a few roots of the scented beauty for our gardens and hurry on.

Our next stop was Mwanga, the gate leading into our great game reserve, only instead of being a gate it was a small tin shanty, where I believe we could have got petrol at enormous cost had we happened to want any. Down a steep bank we went to a ford then up the bank on the other side, and here we made our last camp before going home. The small river was so lovely and clear we had a bathe (with soap) and washed the sea water out of our hair. We were supremely happy; but it was not the place to sleep out in the open without guns and I would not risk it again on any account. I was not nervous about lion and leopard, but I was afraid that rhino might come along and smash our cars to pieces as a practical joke, for it is a way they have at times when the spirit moves them. Being very short-sighted, they get wind of something strange, and not waiting to find out what it is, they charge the offensive smell; which is unfortunate if it happens to be petrol that is annoying them, for your car will be matchwood before they recover their temper. We took the precaution of building bonfires and hanging lanterns on the cars, and as it happened we were left in peace, only being disturbed at intervals by distant rumblings and gruntings in the forest behind us.

Wishing to see the great zoo at dawning, we had tea before it was light and set off immediately afterwards. Herds of game of all descriptions were having breakfast. Five silver jackal were taking a dust-bath on the sandy road and we had to slacken speed to allow them time to

A VASE OF KENYA FLOWERS BY MARGARET COLLYER

Our thanks to Mrs Anna McWilliam whose mother was given this painting by another of Margaret's sisters, Mrs Violet Bousanquet

walk out of our way, which they did slowly, standing at the side to watch us pass.

Crossing over a wide dry river-bed well sheltered by trees we came into the middle of a mob of impala, who were also quite fearless and just carried on with what they were doing. A rhino was sighted in the distance, but too far away for us to get a good view of him. After passing Longido we now were in the country beloved of giraffe and there were hundreds of them in every direction, many standing close to the road and idly watching us as we drove slowly along. Even when once or twice we stopped the cars to look at them they never moved. It was an astonishing sight, for in the reserve the animals are never shot at, so own no fear of man nor cars at all. We were unlucky in not sighting elephant as we neared Kajiado, but we had seen enough to keep us marvelling for many moons.

After passing Kajiado the track became so impossible that it was all we could do to bring the cars through in safety; but we managed to reach Kabete and home at 7.00 p.m., having driven just over 1,000 miles since our departure a fortnight before.

It had been a most successful holiday. We had carried no spares for the cars, and had only had one puncture and broken a leaf in one spring.

OLIVE COLLYER BY THE BIRD BATH THAT MARGARET
COLLYER DESIGNED AND BUILT UNDER WHICH SHE
WISHED TO BE BURIED. ALAS THIS DID NOT HAPPEN

Afterglow

Chapter XVII

Step by step my life in Kenya became more ordered and even civilised. By this year of 1934 I was no longer living in cold and untidy discomfort. My old hut had gone up in flames in 1927 and I had been forced to build again; a house which this time is airy, comfortable and pretty.

When, in December 1927, my original hut was burnt to the ground all my manuscripts, hunting trophies and diaries were destroyed, as well as my personal possessions. The weather had been very hot and I had been sitting out of doors for the last two evenings, no fire having been lit on the hearth. At around midnight I awoke to find the whole of the grass roof blazing over my head. The light from the fire must have roused me, and it was very lucky that it did, for in another few minutes I would have been burnt in my bed; already red hot ash was falling in chunks about the room. There was no time to put on clothes and after unchaining two dogs I ran out to call the men on the off-chance of salvaging something. I had gone about fifty yards when I remembered an airedale bitch I had shut up in the bedroom at the opposite end of the hut to my own sleeping apartment, so I had to turn back to set her free. Every moment the old dry thatch was flaming higher and higher.

On starting off again towards the boys' houses I met a bunch of them tearing down to my assistance with Kago in the lead. They were wonderful in the way they braved the fire and succeeded in rescuing a box of clothes as well as my bed and blankets. The heat and flames were terrible as I made a dive into the furnace to try to reach my papers and farm books; but Kago caught my arm and pulled me back. A second afterwards the whole roof fell in. Half a gale was blowing and at any minute this might have shifted, taking sparks across to kitchen and stables. The house being done for, we turned our attention to saving these, by letting the horses out and throwing what water we had, which was not much, onto the thatch of the stables.

The sudden outbreak of the fire, when I least expected anything of the sort, was such a shock to me that I really felt nothing at all, not even the red hot cinder that had stuck in the flesh and was burning deeply into my instep. Kago noticed it, but I did not. The first house I had ever even tried to build, and had put up under the greatest difficulties, with no proper materials, no nails, and with few implements; the house which had been my only home for ten years was now but a heap of smouldering ashes at my feet, and one of those was burnt! I had no feeling but I can remember thinking what a pity it was that a passion fruit creeper had been done to death.

The dogs and horses were safe. Still in pyjamas I caught the latter, put them back to bed and gave them an extra feed of corn to console them for being so rudely disturbed. Kago had taken my bed and box into the dairy hut so I lay down until daylight and then sent a note over to Captain C's[1] house, asking him to come to me as soon as possible. I need hardly say that he arrived quickly in his car and offered all the sympathy and consolation possible; but this could not amount to much under such trying circumstances and he took me back with him for breakfast, which gave me time to collect my scattered wits.

As news of disaster flies on the wings of the wind in Africa, I began

---

[1] Mrs Tobina Cole was a child when Margaret lived on her farm and they knew each other. She tells us that 'Captain C' was Captain Dickie Crofton MC and Bar. His farm on the Thomsons Falls road was too small to be a paying concern and so he became a successful white hunter.

to fear that my sister might get some garbled tale in which I would be represented as next door to a cinder; so I decided to drive down to Kabete and let her hear the catastrophe from my own lips. It was as well to be doing something active instead of sitting by my dead home.

On my return, a day or two later, Captain C. lent me his tent to live in and I was once more under canvas for four months, moving into my new and present house on April 21st 1928. The rains broke that very night.

On January the 7th 1928, while I was living in my borrowed tent, some people walked over to see me from a neighbouring farm. We had tea in the tent and they stayed chatting until nearly sundown, when I drove them home in the car. On the return journey I was so struck by the strangeness of the sky that I stopped the car to watch it for a few minutes. I had never seen anything like it before. It was flaring angry red, with blue black lumps of cloud rising behind the mountains. I could only think that an awful storm would shortly break so I hurried home to find Kago who was very alarmed and standing outside my tent. I did not need to enquire why he had run to be near me, for under the earth there was a noise like a smothered hell let loose. Grumblings, groanings, and a roar such as an underground torrent might have made. Neither of us had any idea what it was or what it meant, and I now saw all the men flocking towards me wanting to know what I was going to do about it.

It really was the most astounding phenomenon and to tell the truth I did not know what I could do about it. My people being all huddled together like a flock of frightened sheep, I told them to wait until I had had my bath and I called my servant to bring it. The tent was so small that I had to sit on the bed while the bath was being prepared and as he poured the water into the tub the boy fell head first after it! For an instant I thought he was drunk; then the whole earth appeared to rise up in waves under my feet, the guy ropes of the tent snapping like string.

Clinging onto the pole I stared out aghast, for all the trees rose, fell and swayed, while the ground was moving like waves of the sea. Never have I seen a more horrible sight. My people were now terrified and the women screaming at the pitch of their lungs. It seemed an eternity before the dream vanished and all inanimate objects once more resumed their natural places.

I do not suppose the worst part of the earthquake lasted more than sixty seconds but it was enough to frighten one into the grave. During the whole of the rest of the night there were continual tremors going on and underground rumblings at intervals: a night never to be forgotten.

The severity of this earthquake varied much in different parts of the country. It was violent enough here, but in some places, the earth opened, forming wide and deep fissures, altering the formation of the landscape. Native huts were reported to have been buried and stone houses suffered considerably, some falling completely down. Houses built of wood and iron stood the shock much better; being pliable they rocked, but did not fall or break. Curiously enough, it did not affect the animals at all. The dogs were worried about the noise but took little notice of the movement; neither did the horses, to whom I ran at once, thinking they would suffer much from fear. I found them snorting a little and that was all.

I had now been through flood, fire and earthquake and I wondered what the last grand finale would be like!

To build my new house I cut four hundred young cedar trees and used the round trunks for the outside walls which are ten feet high. All this outside work I did with the aid of a friend and my own labour. This good woman and I put in over four hundred piles for the floor and levelled every one ourselves. We only had one Seychelles carpenter who did the iron roof extremely well, laid the floorboards and built part of the stone chimney. The inside of the house I lined with celotex and Kavirondo mats, panelling walls and ceiling with narrow strips of cedar wood. The doors were made of cedar and I have proper windows with glass. Both bedroom and sitting room are spacious and the rough stone fireplace across one corner is safe while lovely big wood fires can be made in it.

In fact, I am now the proud possessor of quite a nice mansion and have designed and made an extremely attractive garden, even with a stone birdbath raised on two steps, which looks exactly like a font, under which my sister has orders to bury me. I hope she will re-erect it straight, for, being diamond shaped it was troublesome to build and took me quite a while to accomplish.

So I suppose that the fire in 1927 was indeed an ill wind that blows no one any good.

At the beginning of 1930 I began to get together a picked herd of

'QUITE A NICE MANSION'.
The second house that Miss Collyer built

345

dairy cows. Having tried everything else we could think of on the farm without much success, we decided to return to our original idea of keeping it solely as a stock farm. We gave up trying to grow cereals for doubtful profit and only sowed feed to sustain the cows during the dry seasons. I drove about the country a good deal, picking a few animals here and a few there until I succeeded in collecting quite a nice little bunch of high class beasts. What with breeding and adding to this lot from time to time when I had the ready money, I now possess a valuable little mob of milkers, eighty-six in number, headed by a handsome red shorthorn bull. At that moment I considered myself a dairy farmer and if we could manage to carry over for the next two years I believed this farm would make a good living and be a paying proposition.

I look after the stock myself, helping with the milking and I hand feed the calves to allow more whole milk to go through the separator. The milk is recorded, and services noted, so if the herd is ever sold, people will know exactly what they are buying. We have just suffered two years of bad drought, which has not helped us on our way; but I managed to get the animals safely through this without losing any. As I write, all the cows are calving down, and I have my nurseries full of small children, the care of which takes me all my time. Calves are exceedingly difficult to rear in Africa and require all the attention it is possible to give them.

To keep a herd of high-class dairy cows with any success, personal supervision is essential. This entails being up early every morning and working late in the evening after milking time. I know every cow on the place by name and can give her history without any reference to the stock book. Also I know all the calves and how they are bred. Taking so much interest in the cattle makes the men keen on their work and proud of the animals under their charge. A word of praise goes a long way and my cowman is delighted if my occasional visitors admire the condition of the stock. I always make a point of repeating to him any compliments I receive. Working with Africans it is much better to speak of 'our' cows and not 'my' cows; it gives them a partnership in one's property that

LORD DELAMERE
With thanks to Muthaiga Club and Nigel Pavitt

they very much like to possess, and encourages them to do their best in helping to preserve the animals from disease and accidents.

Ever since we came here together I have always shared everything with Kago and I should have felt selfish had I not done so. He now takes almost entire charge of the cultivation, measures out his 'akkers' as he calls acres, weighs his seed and puts in so many pounds to the seventy square yards. He can weigh sacks of corn and knows how many should go to a ton. I taught him to write figures and he notes down the weight of each sack, many perhaps being as much as two hundred pounds. After writing this amount a few times he gets tired of making so many noughts and writes 20 instead, or sometimes only two; but so long as I understand it, it is all right. His sevens are often upside down and nines turned round the wrong way, but I have no trouble in understanding his weights although they might trouble other people less brilliant than myself! He also paints my initial 'C' on the backs of the bacon pigs when they are sent to the factory. His description of the letter 'C' is good. 'An 'O' not quite finished!' Having had much practice he makes 'C's' quite well.

When HRH The Prince of Wales visited Kenya he arranged to meet all the settlers of this District at the GilGil Club. Lord Delamere sent a summons up to me, and I took Kago down to see the Prince. I told Lord Delamere, who knew all about him, that I was anxious for him to see his future King and I suppose this was repeated to the Prince. On leaving the building HRH sent for me into the garden and asked me to call Kago, as he would like to shake hands with him. Kago saluted very nicely when he shook hands with the Prince – and his grip is something to be remembered, especially if one wears a ring on one's finger.

Kago's only remark on the way home was that 'The son of the English King was rather small for a great Chief.' The next day he asked for a fortnight's leave to go round his tribe telling everyone that the child of the King of England had shaken his hand.

My tale is fast drawing to a close. The much needed rain is now pattering on my roof and I can hear the pleasant sound of water running into almost empty tanks. The whole country, including my beloved plains, is green once more. Newly sown crops of oats and barley are forcing their delicate shoots through the now saturated soil; the dam is full to the brim and the wild duck at long last have returned to their bullrushy home. The cattle, their recent hunger appeased, are resting contentedly in the paddocks where no longer the roar of lions disturbs their dreams.

All is at peace on my African farm, excepting the dogs who are asking me to take them to bed.

TEA IN THE GARDEN, FROM LEFT TO RIGHT –
OLIVE COLLYER, NANCY SOUTHERN AND MARGARET COLLYER

GLORIOSA LILY PAINTED FOR *GARDENING IN EAST AFRICA*
COMPILED BY DR AND LADY MURIEL JEX-BLAKE

With thanks to Barry Cameron of 'Roses Galore'

Epilogue

Margaret Collyer died in Mombasa in 1945, ten years after publishing this book. Mrs Tobina Cole, who was married to Arthur, the son of Galbraith Cole (see Chapter II) liked her very much. As a child Tobina led rather a lonely life on her mother's farm, but she enjoyed riding over to stay with Margaret who taught her how to make *potpourri*. She tells us that Miss Collyer was well liked in Kenya which was, anyway, 'a friendly place.'

Both Margaret and Olive Collyer were sensible with their assets and careful farmers. They were not given to wild parties – indeed there was no hint of a liaison or romance attached to either of them – nor did they indulge in such extravagances as big game hunting safaris. Consequently when Kenya became independent in 1963, the two farms of Chatu and Ndumbwini which they had created with such courage and care, were passed on by their heirs to African ownership in healthy working order.

The national flower of Kenya, the Gloriosa – or Tiger – Lily was included in what is now a rare edition of *'Gardening in East Africa'* edited by a friend of Margaret and Olive Collyer, Dr A. J. Jex-Blake M.A., M.D. (Oxon.), F.R.C.P. (Lond.). Later editions were without the coloured plates *'having been destroyed by enemy action'*.

She published a book entitled *'Our Dogs*: *Most Prevalent Diseases and Treatment'* and she wrote a regular column called *'Kennel Notes'* in *'The East African Standard.'*

Susan Duke and Veronica Bellers

Appendix I

MISS OLIVE ELEANOR COLLYER
1876–1949

'She spent her whole life for others, without thought for herself.'

Olive Collyer was the youngest girl of six siblings: Helen (Mrs Lindsay Smith), Margaret, Violet (Mrs Bousanquet), Olive, Charles and Arthur. They were the children of William James Collyer and his wife, Eveleen née Clarke. The fearless horsemanship and love of hunting enjoyed by Olive and Margaret probably came from their maternal grandfather, Rev. Charles Clarke. It seems that his church duties may have somewhat competed with hunting and it is thought that the following lines written by his friend and a well-known sporting poet, Whyte Melville, were based on Clarke:

> *Next comes the parson,*
> *The parson, the parson,*
> *Next comes the parson,*
> *The shortest way to seek.*
> *And like a phantom lost to view,*
> *From point to point the parson flew,*
> *The parish, at a pinch can do*
> *Without him for a week.*

Rev. Charles Clarke wrote ten books that were popular in their time about hunting, racing and murder, and they had such enticing titles as *'Charlie Thornhill or The Dunce of the Family'* and *'The Flying Scud'*. (A letter survives from Whyte Melville encouraging Charles Clarke to write his first novel.)

Although these snippets of information fill in some of the gaps, we

353

'EDITH'S DANGER'
From Charlie Thornhill
by The Rev. Charles Clarke

know very little of Olive's early life. Family lore has it that someone fell in love with her and, on being turned down, he committed suicide. We do know that it was Olive who cared for her elderly parents, William and Eveleen Collyer, when they moved across the Channel to Bruges, until they died.

In 1908 she sailed for British East Africa – later to be known as Kenya – to join her brother Arthur. She lived with him at Rumuruti, north of the Rift Valley, where he was District Commissioner, administering the five northern sections of the Masai tribe.

She was a talented horticulturalist and made a beautiful garden around the house out of hostile, dry terrain, which, we were told many years later, was a joy to succeeding DCs and their wives. We like to think that those brief years between 1908 and 1911 were especially enjoyable. She went on safari with Arthur as he went about his duties as the administrator of the Northern clans of the Masai tribe, and it appears that at times they may have also been accompanied by their relative by marriage, Lt. Col. Algernon Fox Eric Smith. Lt. Col. Smith was considered by others outside the family to be a curmudgeonly fellow but we believe that we have him to thank for the photographs we have of that brief and happy period.

In 1911 Arthur was suddenly transferred to Nyeri. This struck a dark note in their lives because he was bitter about the reasons behind his transfer. It seems then that his health deteriorated sharply (he had tuberculosis) and she found herself increasingly taking on his duties as District Commissioner. The letters of condolence to Olive after her

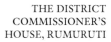

brother's death in 1912 indicate that his end was unexpected even though it was known that he was ill. She was away tax-collecting when he died and it must have been a painful shock on her return to find she had not been with him during his final hours.

Her English friends and relations expected her to return to England but instead she bought a small property at Kabete, nine miles outside Nairobi. It had a house on it built by one of East Africa's pioneer adventurers and she set about earning her living by growing vegetables and flowers which she sent into Nairobi by bullock cart. Later she bought more land where she cultivated coffee, bred horses and had a small herd of cows.

These lines from a poem written by Helene Boedecker in 1919 about Ndumbwini probably best describes something of the delightful haven that Olive created:

OLIVE AND MASAI
WARRIORS

To N'Dombuini's velvet lawns,

In flowery shrubs and rosy dawns

I now must say farewell!

Eight peaceful, dreamy days I've spent

With Hostess hospitality bent on weaving some weird spell

To make her guests forget their pain,

To better them both with flower linked chain

Of purples, pinks and blues,

While sunbirds flutt'ring in the trees

And soothing hum of drowsy bees

And cats; pathetic mious,

Combine to bring forgetfulness

Of all that breathes of strain or stress,

Beyond its gay-clad borders.

The juicy lemon and the lime, the orange with its golden rind

Fall straight from nature's larders.

And as at dawn our Hostess cuts the flowers for Town,

The spaniels' yells announce their joyful waking.
As supportively they lend a hand
In fastening some dear cherished strand:
Alas! It ends in breaking.

THE EARLIEST
PICTURE OF OLIVE'S
HOUSE AT KABETE,
KNOWN AS
NDUMBWINI

Amongst her neighbours and friends were Charles and Kit Taylor. Their daughter, Kathini, remembers Olive as a good looking woman who wore long divided skirts and long-sleeved coats made in a faded khaki. Her only concession to femininity was a pretty scarf. She was described by another neighbour, the missionary Canon Harry Leakey, as 'a real lady'.

The little church of St Mary's, Kabete was 'particularly her own' and she was not afraid to speak out. She would not allow stained glass windows. One Sunday when the Parson announced 'Let us pray for rain', 'Hear, hear' resonated Olive's response.

She had a formidable manner and even though we were rather wild children, we held her in considerable awe. Nonetheless she had great kindness. Kit Taylor told us of how, when bread was rationed during

A PARTY IN THE
GARDEN AT
NDUMBWINI

wartime, Olive gave her entire ration to the African children and she thought nothing of sitting up all night in the hut of a sick child. Mrs Victoria Kabetu remembers Olive driving round the roads in the area and collecting her and the other Kikuyu children to take them to her house for a party. Mrs Kabetu's father, Stefano, who was the first African train driver in the Colony, had Olive to thank for his education and his entry onto the drivers' course.

One afternoon in the very early days of the Kabete community, Canon Leakey gave a large tea party for some visitors to his mission. His wife was in England at the time and the preparations were all down to him. His letter to her describes how nerve-wracking he had found those preparations but, after rushing hither and thither, all was finally ready.

The whole community turned out and the tea party seemed to be going well when, suddenly, he caught sight of Olive galloping down the drive with a bundle of sticks under her arm. To his horror he found he had forgotten to boil the water.

OLIVE COLLYER

358

Miss Collyer never missed Christmas dinner with the Taylors and every year she was seated on Charles's right until Kit decided, one year, to rearrange the seating plan because, she said, she wanted to stop Charles and Olive passing the whole evening discussing manure. That year, the servants, who knew perfectly well that the lady on the right of the host should be served first, ignored the convention and firmly served Olive first. She was much admired by the Kikuyu and was known as '*Nya Weru*' – the woman who works hard.

And work hard she did. She '*entered whole-heartedly into all those interests and activities which come the way of a Kenya settler. Her coffee shamba alone might reasonably have been a whole-time job; but she found time for so much else – horses, dogs, flowers…*' She was a founding member of the Horticultural Society and she was an active visitor to Mathari Mental Hospital. She was a fearless, highly knowledgeable horsewoman and bred some good horses which she raced at the racecourse at Ngong.

OLIVE COLLYER
WITH HER NIECE
JOY WILLIAMS
(NEE COLLYER)

We have a newspaper clipping entitled '*An Appreciation – OLIVE COLLYER*' which describes her last hours in 1949.[1]

'*The end came as she doubtless would have wished. Having gone up to the farm at Ol'Kalou after Christmas she made her last journey back to her home on the third day of the New Year. On the next day she rode round her coffee shamba, as usual, and with that last job done she admitted reluctantly to friends who were staying with her that she was feeling ill. She died that same night, three hours after she had been taken to hospital.*'

Our mother – her niece, Joy Williams – told us that the church of St Mary's was full and many people had to remain outside in the churchyard. The mourners were from all the communities. '*The large number of Africans who thronged to her funeral was a sign of the deep respect and affection of her African neighbours, who she had always helped with such unselfish care. It is the simple truth to say that Olive Collyer spent her whole life for others, without thought for herself.*'

Susan Duke and Veronica Bellers

---

[1] With grateful thanks to Mrs Geraldine Macoun and Mrs Jenny Falkiner.

Appendix II

ARTHUR JOHN MORICE COLLYER
1880–1912

'A GOOD ENGLISHMAN'
ARTHUR JOHN MORICE COLLYER 1880–1912

Arthur Collyer was one of two sons in a family of six siblings, two of whom were Margaret and Olive Collyer. The only other son was Charles Collyer (our grandfather) and they were known in the family as Cain (Arthur) and Abel. Arthur was educated at King William's College, Isle of Man and Lincoln College, Oxford.

He went out to what was then British East Africa some time between 1900 and 1902 as an official of the British East Africa Company. When Meinertzagen met him in 1904, he noted in his 'Kenya Diary', *'The poor fellow is suffering from consumption and I fear has not long to live.'* Nonetheless during that encounter he and Meinertzagen together walked to the flats east of Lake Naivasha where they observed the unusual and poignant sight of a herd of wildebeeste attacking a stalking cheetah and killing her cub.

Later that same year in Nyeri, on a punitive expedition against the Kikuyu who had murdered some Indian traders, Meinertzagen watched Collyer – who had been sent out to shoot meat for the camp – stalking a rhino. He was unaware that another rhino was hidden in a fold in the ground between him and his quarry. Meinertzagen described how the hidden rhino and Collyer met at the top of a rise. Collyer fired, missed, and the rhino charged: so did Collyer. As he was no mean exponent of rugby football, weighing some 15 stone and endowed with great physical strength, he was more bruised than injured but, getting back to camp, he vowed he would never again attempt a rough and tumble with a rhinoceros.

Meinertzagen also recounted Collyer's medical skills at Taveta when a woman was *'brought in who had just been bitten by a snake. She was on the point of collapse, so we poured whisky down her throat, lanced the wound and poured ammonia into the fang marks. Meanwhile we set two sturdy policemen to keep her on the move at a brisk trot. She pulled round in about an hour and was then conducted to her hut, roaring drunk but out of danger.'*

It is comforting to imagine that Arthur must have enjoyed such moments as these because thereafter his short life was blighted with torn loyalties and disillusion as well as the knowledge that his inexorable disease would lead to an untimely death.

In 1906 he was posted to Rumuruti as District Commissioner, where in 1908, he was joined by his sister, Olive.

The Colonial Administration's prime responsibility was to the native peoples whose welfare was paramount. Collyer meticulously carried out that obligation and spoke Masai. His DC's duties to that intelligent and fiercely independent tribe could have been interesting but uneventful were it not for the fact that he found himself embroiled in one of the less savoury episodes of the colonial administration.

A FAMILY REUNION.
LT. COL. SMITH,
OLIVE AND ARTHUR
COLLYER
Taken at Rumuruti
between 1908 and 1911

The British Government was earnestly trying to effect a move of the five northern sections of the Masai tribe out of the Rumuruti area (also known as Laikipia) to join the four sections that grazed their flocks and herds south of the Ngong Hills to the border of what is now Kenya and Tanzania. The Government proposed to accommodate them on an extended, less watered grazing area alongside these existing southern Masai lands.

Collyer was ordered to walk the proposed extended area. He stoically walked for days and days with the elders of the northern clans, discussing with them the availability of water and grazing, and trying to reach a consensus as to whether or not they believed they should move south.

As if that was not difficult enough he was under great pressure from his superiors in Nairobi to persuade the tribe to agree to move, attending meetings between the Masai and the Government, as interpreter,

ARTHUR COLLYER
AND MASAI ELDERS

minute-taker and persuader. He was torn between loyalty to his superiors and distaste for what he was being asked to do.

Although Collyer believed that the tribe should be together in one tribal area, he felt that the Governor, Sir Percy Girouard, was taking away Masai grazing areas simply in order to accommodate British settlers who had cast longing eyes on the wonderful Laikipia grazing. He also believed that the Governor's guile bordered on the dishonourable and that lands allocated to Africans by treaty should be as sacrosanct as free-hold land in Britain.

In 1910 he wrote a 'Report on the Masai Question'.[1] This was not forwarded to London for eighteen months and in the meantime he was 'sacked' as DC Rumuruti and posted to Nyeri.

In 1911 the highly respected Laibon of the southern Masai, Lenana, died, expressing as his final wish that his people should always obey the Government, especially by leaving Laikipia. It was a highly controversial decision but it was also supported by the elders of the northern sections at a meeting with Sir Percy in 1910, the Minutes of which were taken by Collyer and which, in addition to the Masai, was attended by such people as Lord Delamere and members of the Administration.

---

[1] 'The Moving of the Maasai: A Colonial Misadventure' by Lotte Hughes.

Legolishu made certain requests regarding details which H.E. assured him would be attended to by the Officers arranging the move.

After this the Laikipia Chiefs with Crew and Lenana requested H.E. to send Sendeyo back to German territory as he (Sendeyo) was an enemy and had bewitched him (Lenana).

H.E. suggested that he should send Sendeyo to the North .? toward the Rendile Country, pointing out that if Sendeyo was in British territory he could be watched but this was not possible in German territory —

Lenana was pleased with the idea and Mr Collyer was instructed to make Enquiries about a suitable locality in the vicinity of Meru + inform McClure. The Meeting then broke up.

Kiserian.   A. M. Collyer.
24 Feb 1910.   R.C. Laikipia.

LAST PAGE OF NOTES ON A MEETING WITH THE MASAI LEADERS, LENANA – PARAMOUNT CHIEF OF THE MASAI, MASIKONDI AND LEGOLISHU – CHIEFS OF THE NORTHERN MASAI RESERVE, AND SABURI – LENANA'S CHIEF ELDER, AGALI – HALF BROTHER OF LENANA AND OLE YELI, THE GOVERNOR, SIR PERCY GIROUARD AND LORD DELAMERE. IT WAS HELD ON 24TH FEBRUARY 1910 NEAR NGONG.

MASIKONDE –
Leader of the northern
Masai Clans

The Masai move to the enlarged southern grazing areas took place in 1912. It was an awful move, over the high Mau hills south of the Rift in cold, wet weather and both humans and animals suffered badly.

Arthur's condition deteriorated in Nyeri and Olive took over his duties. Margaret said later that he worshipped the ground Olive trod on but he died alone at the age of 32 in 1912, because she was away standing in for him on safari. He was described by Margaret as *'a fine character [who] faced his broken life with the utmost courage and patience. Had he been strong … he would have gone far.'*

The letters of condolence received by Olive are touching. As well as expressing great concern for her and offering help and accommodation, the consensus seems to have been that Arthur was a gentle and a very nice man. A Mr Adams wrote: *'You know that I have always looked upon him as my best friend in East Africa, and I made my start in this country under his eye, and with his absolute straightness and conscientiousness in his work as a guide to me.'*

The wife of Dr Norman Leys[2], Janey, wrote, *'I feel that Mr Collyer*

---

[2]   Norman Leys, M.B., D.P.H. wrote *'Kenya'* first published in 1924. Professor Gilbert Murray, who wrote the introduction to the second edition said that Leys 'spent some twenty years in the medical service in different parts of Africa, both Portuguese and British. He felt deeply the complexities and the horrors which still seem inseparable from the contact of white and black…' Trying to find a way through those complexities, Leys doughtily opposed the authorities if he felt an injustice had been done to the African people but he also believed that 'the rule of black by white' was a necessity because if Africa was abandoned 'it would fall into the hands of adventurers and speculators.' Arthur Collyer was certainly among the majority who believed the same thing, but believing in justice, he joined Leys in speaking out in defence of the Masai.

has fought a good fight and is now resting after his labours; he never allowed his illness to interfere with his work and he will be buried here in Africa where he has been of so much use to his fellow-creatures.'

We are told that the Masai and Samburu people still use the name Colyon or Kolian. In 2006 the Editor of *Old Africa* Magazine told us that a Samburu friend of his called Kolian told him that he was named 'after a good Englishman.'

'One forgets the endless scroll of past failure on which the names of men of every race are written, and the miseries they have inflicted on this continent of suffering, and remembers only those who with patient fidelity gave their lives to bring nearer in Africa the long-delayed victory of justice. To one of these men A.J.M. Collyer, whose grave lies among the people he served, these words are fittingly addressed':

> *'Content thee, howsoe'er, whose days are done;*
> *There lies not any troublous thing before,*
> *Nor sight nor sound to war against thee more,*
> *For whom all winds are quiet as the sun*
> *All waters as the shore.'*

Dr Norman Leys M.B., D.P.H in dedication to A.J.M. Collyer

Susan Duke and Veronica Bellers

ARTHUR AND
FRIEZE ON
SAFARI